THE ENCYCLOPAEDIA

The **AC/DC** Encyclopaedia
by Malcolm Dome and Jerry Ewing

A CHROME DREAMS PUBLICATION
First Edition 2008

Published by Chrome Dreams
PO BOX 230, New Malden, Surrey,
KT3 6YY, UK
books@chromedreams.co.uk
WWW.CHROMEDREAMS.CO.UK

ISBN 9781842404362
Copyright © 2008 by Chrome Dreams

Edited by   Cathy Johnstone
Cover Design   Sylwia Grzeszczuk
Layout Design   Marek Niedziewicz

Printed in the UK by CPI William Clowes Beccles NR34 7TL

AC/DC

THE ENCYCLOPAEDIA

Malcolm Dome and Jerry Ewing

INTRO

There's a famous Angus Young quote which goes along the lines of,

"A writer once accused us of making the same album 11 times. In fact, we've made 12 albums that sound exactly the same."

Not many AC/DC fans will agree with the accusation, but they'll enjoy the tongue-in-cheek sentiment which shows that, despite being one of the more insular heavy rock acts the world has ever seen, a sense of humour is not something that ever passed AC/DC by. In fact, it is that sense of humour, allied to a roguish charm and the relentless pursuit of the riff that makes AC/DC such an attractive proposition to rock fans. And just to prove the band's unique appeal, they are almost always the token rock band enjoyed by those whose tastes don't normally stretch to the loud and the heavy.

There has long been something that sets AC/DC apart from the rest of the rock pack. In a story coloured by both triumph and tragedy, the band's never ending drive onwards, often seeming oblivious to what was going on around them, is one that many fans applaud. In a manner similar to those equally loved heavy metal titans Iron Maiden, AC/DC don't take the eye off their own particular ball. They don't chase trends, they just get down to their own business. And for the past 35 years it's been some seriously good business.

There is a school of thought that AC/DC's unique sound is a pretty simple one. True, it might be based around the simplest of rock 'n' roll techniques handed down from the likes of Chuck Berry and Little Richard to the Rolling Stones and then on to a bunch of snot-nosed Antipodeans like AC/DC, but most musicians you talk to will be more than happy to tell you it is a sound which is actually pretty difficult to replicate. It's not simply a matter of attaining Angus Young's unique but instantly identifiable guitar tone, or replicating the rock hard but steady beat laid down by Phil Rudd and Cliff Williams. But dig deeper and you'll find behind Malcolm Young's tenacious riffing a series of sturdy, memorable rock songs built to last; and the man's now in his fourth decade of delivering over and over again. Marry that to having had two of the best-loved frontmen in rock, namely the late Bon Scott and now the ever-affable Brian Johnson, and you start to see the formula that many bands have attempted to copy, but that none have ever managed.

"All the songs we do are basically about one of three things," Bon Scott once said. *"Booze, sex or rock 'n' roll."*

Those songs still are, And those three traits which make up the staple diet of most rock fans, let's not deny it. And that's because AC/DC are fans themselves. Angus' school boy regalia aside, the rest of the band look pretty much just like you and us. And it's this almost simplistic, no frills attitude to life and their craft that's helped AC/DC forge a relationship with their fans that most bands could never hope to equal. Watching them on stage allows those in the audience to dream about the fact that, "It could be me up there", just as much as they get off on the groove being laid down. And with tales of AC/DC being denied access to their own stage because they don't look like rock stars being the stuff of legend, theirs is a state of being that you can't copy. It comes from within. It's what makes them tick.

The chances are strong that if you're reading this, you're an AC/DC fan. In fact, it would be a bit odd if you weren't! And maybe you don't need any of this told to you, because in your heart you know it all anyway.

Because that's what being an AC/DC fan is all about. Like belonging to one of the biggest clubs in the world. Never exclusive – AC/DC just don't operate that way – but comprised of like-minded people who just get it. We've been getting it for 35 years now, and as long as AC/DC want to keep rolling out the songs and the classic live shows, we'll all be there, rocking 'til the very end.

"People can go out and hear R.E.M. if they want to hear deep lyrics," Malcolm Young once said. *"But at the end of the night they just wanna go home and get fucked. That's where AC/DC comes into it."*

We couldn't have put it better ourselves.

Malcolm Done
and Jerry Ewing

London, July 2008

THE AUTHORS WOULD LIKE TO THANK...

...the following people for their support and assistance:

All at Chrome Dreams

Roxy and Adair.

All at *Total Rock*:
Tony Wilson, Talita, Holly,
The Bat, Thekkles, Tina,
PMQ, Zed, TP, Pixie, Chloe,
Emma 'SF' Bellamy, Werthers,
Cam, Ratchetto, Catbird.

Everyone at
The Crobar/Evensong:
Rich, Steve, Johanna, Benjy,
Mitch, Joey, Nicole, Olivia,
The Rector, Sir Barrence,
Dave Everley, The Unique
One, The Crazy Bitch, Steve
Hammonds, The Scamp, Sir
Hugebert, Kurt, Harjaholic, Jonty,
Jacques, Anna Maria,
Janet Abrooooooooo, Matron,
Jo Dear, The Lonely Doctor,
Orange Goblin, Dozzer

The *Metal Hammer* mob:
Chris Ingham, Alex Milas,
Caren Gibson, Gill, Jonathan
Selzer, Jamez Isaacs, Hards,
Kimberley Tarry,
Bezer the Geezer

The *Classic Rock* crew:
Scott Rowley, Sian Llewellyn,
Geoff Barton, Paul Henderson,
Ian Fortnam, Alex Burrows,
Dave Ling is still gay

SOURCES FROM WHICH QUOTES HAVE BEEN TAKEN

Classic Rock magazine

Metal Hammer magazine

Sounds magazine

Shock To The System
by Mark Putterford

The World's Heaviest Rock
by Martin Huxley

www.ac-dc.net

www.bonscott.com.au

www.buoy.com/
~bonfire/interviews

www.crabsodyinblue.com

www.acdc.com

www.ac-dc.cc

www.acdcpower.net

www.acdcnews.com

www.gregjames.com

www.kolumbus.fi/
nononsense/index.htm

en.wikipedia.org

MALCOLM/DOME

Malcolm Dome first spotted AC/DC in a pub – which, if you knew Bon Scott at all, would come as no surprise. It was actually the band's first ever UK show, at the Red Cow in Hammersmith, West London.

Dome started writing for *Record Mirror* – the now defunct weekly UK music paper – in 1979. His first feature was on Samson (featuring vocalist Bruce Dickinson!) His first live review was Iron Maiden at The Marquee in London, his first album review was Samson's debut, and his first interview was with Hawkwind.

Since then, he's worked for a number of magazines – *Kerrang!, Metal Mania, RAW, Metal Hammer, Classic Rock, Metal Forces* and *Rocks* to name but a small selection. He has waffled inanely on numerous TV, film and DVD documentaries about the glories of metal music and he is the author of *Encyclopaedia Metallica* (with Jerry Ewing), *Bon Jovi – Faith and Glory; The Official Biography* and is the editor of *AC/DC - The Kerrang Files*

He continues to write regularly for *Metal Hammer* and *Classic Rock*, and is heavily involved with the respected radio station TotalRock (www.totalrock.com).

Malcolm's favourite AC/DC albums? Well, anything from the Bon Scott era, although he readily admits there have been some mighty records subsequently - he even confesses to a sneaking admiration for *Fly On The Wall*, which sends co-author Jerry Ewing into uncontrollable guffaws.

JERRY EWING

When Jerry Ewing grew up in North Sydney in the 1970s you either loved AC/DC or their arch rivals Skyhooks. Seeing as he not only wanted his cake but frequently ate it too, he loved both, but probably liked AC/DC a bit more - which is just as well, because otherwise you might be holding a book about Australia's forgotten glam rock heroes instead.

Moving to England wasn't anywhere near as much fun, but at least AC/DC had managed to find their way over here too. He was lucky enough to find himself working on the groundbreaking and respected UK metal mag *Metal Forces* in 1989, where only his hair was bigger than his ego. Since then he's been found within the pages of *Metal Hammer, Terror Magazine, Vox, Cutting Edge, Maxim, Stuff, Bizarre* and *Rocks.*

In 1998 Ewing devised and set up *Classic Rock Magazine* for Dennis Publishing, something of which he is immensely proud, and he continues to write for the journal to this day. He also hosts several shows on Total Rock Radio and is regularly featured on television and DVD with his views on metal and rock acts.

His favourite AC/DC albums are *Powerage* and *Back In Black* and he confesses to never listening to *Fly On The Wall.*

He is still adamant that one day he will own a club called 'The Shaking Hand' (in honour of Bon Scott), hopefully in Sydney. And when he does, if you turn up with a copy of this book, you'll get a free drink. He promises.

ACDC LANE
(Melbourne)

This is a short lane in the central business area of the city from which AC/DC hail. It was originally called Corporation Lane, but was renamed on October 1, 2004 after a unanimous decision by the local council. Incidentally, the trademark lightning flash was omitted, as it contravened the naming policy of the Office Of The Registrar Of Geographic Names. Appropriately, a rock bar called Cherry's is in the Lane.

AC/DC: AND THEN THERE WAS ROCK
(DVD)

Released in 2005, this DVD chronicles the band's early years, revolving inevitably around Bon Scott. It includes rare footage of the late singer in his pre-AC/DC bands, plus interviews with Dave Evans and Colin Burgess, both early members of 'DC.

AC/DC: MUSIC IN REVIEW
(DVD)

This two-disc DVD set was released in 2005 by Classic Rock Legends. It concentrates solely on the Bon Scott era, with analysis and interviews featuring both musicians and critics. The two authors of this book are included. There's

also an accompanying booklet detailing every track released by AC/DC from 1975-2000.

AC/DC ROCK N ROLL COMIC

Published by Revolutionary Comics in 1991, this was the 22nd edition in a series which show-cased one band per issue. Each comic told the story of the act in question, in comic book settings.

There are a couple of interesting points here. Firstly, it's claimed here that Phil Rudd quit AC/DC because he thought they were get-ting stale – he was actually fired. Secondly, it has a short story at the end depicting Malcolm Young as a drunkard being helped by... the ghost of Bon Scott. This was pub-lished just a couple of years after

Young had been forced to leave the band temporarily as he dealt with an alcohol problem.

Others represented in the series are Guns n' Roses, Metallica, Bon Jovi, Motley Crue, Def Lep-pard, the Rolling Stones, The Who, Kiss, Whitesnake, Warrant, Aerosmith, Led Zeppelin, Poison, Sex Pistols, Van Halen and Alice Cooper.

AC/DC ROCKS
(Official website)

The address for this one is www.acdcrocks.com. After a period of inactivity, the site – run by Sony BMG Records – has now been re-activated with the news of the band's forthcoming new album.

AC/DC: THE DEFINITIVE HISTORY (KERRANG! FILES)

The first and, so far, only book in the Kerrang! Files series. This was put together by Malcolm Dome from articles, reviews and news stories that originally appeared in UK weekly music magazine *Sounds* and also in *Kerrang!* The latest edition was published by Virgin Books in 2001.

Razors Edge, Live, Ballbreaker, Bonfire and *Stiff Upper Lip.*

However, the best value for money has to be this 800 page offering that features the music for no less than 85 AC/DC tracks, from early demo versions like 'Dirty Eyes' – which would later evolve into 'Whole Lotta Rosie' – all the way through to the likes of 'Satellite Blues' from *Stiff Upper Lip.*

Published by Amsco in March 2003, the book is still available and a must for any would be Angus or Malcolm.

AC/DC: THE DEFINITIVE SONGBOOK

Song and guitar tablature books exist for the following AC/DC albums: *High Voltage, Let There Be Rock, Powerage, Back In Black, For Those About To Rock (We Salute You), Who Made Who, The*

AC/DC: THUNDER ROCK INTERVIEWS
(DVD)

Originally released in 1999, this DVD features a series of previously televised interviews largely with Angus Young.

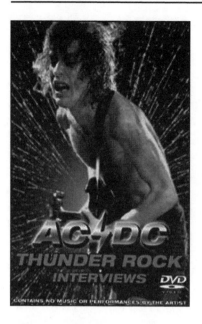

AC/DC: TWO SIDES TO EVERY GLORY
(Paul Stenning)

Published by Chrome Dreams in 2005, this comprehensive book covers the whole of the band's

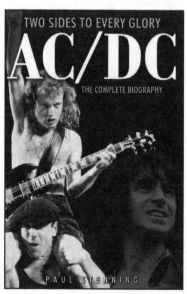

history, and is incredibly detailed and well researched. Stenning has also written books on Guns n' Roses, My Chemical Romance, Iron Maiden and Slash.

AC/DC
(VHS)

For a long time this VHS only release, which saw the light of day in Australia alone in 1987, was the only chance AC/DC fans had to view any of the band's earliest promotional clips and rare live footage of Bon Scott era songs, before the timely release of both *Family Jewels* and *PlugMe In*.

Collating the very first promo films that AC/DC recorded in Australia for their record label Alberts, from a 1975 version of 'High Voltage' to an incredibly rare (until it surfaced on *Family Jewels*) promo video for 'If You Want Blood (You Got It)', as well as a couple of live tracks filmed at Glasgow Apollo in 1978, this is a fantastic collection which was, as has so often been the case with AC/DC, denied greater viewing by only being released in Australia.

Given the dearth of AC/DC material that actually ever gets shown on either terrestrial or satellite television (even given the latter's increased access to music related material) anywhere around the world, this makes the decision to restrict this release to Australia only even more astonishing, not least given that the immense sub-sequent success of *Family Jewels* and *Plug Me In* further down the line, made it patently clear that AC/DC fans had long clamoured for such archive fare.

Still, Alberts released this in 1987 (it was only ever available in the UK as an import, and given this was the pre-Amazon and Ebay era, was never that easy to track down), and somewhat typically there was a track listing discrepancy. Original versions of the VHS featured the record company promotional film of 'Jailbreak' and a live perform-ance of 'Dog Eat Dog' that was recorded in London in 1977 on the *Let There Be Rock* tour, and origi-nally shown on the Australian TV show *Countdown*. However, when the VHS was re-issued in 1989, the 'Jailbreak' promotional film had been exchanged for one of the band performing the song on Countdown in 1976, whilst the live version of 'Dog Eat Dog' was now taken from the same Glas-gow Apollo show as the other live material.

Needless to say, finding a copy of the original 1987 VHS version would be somewhat lucrative.

Full track listing: *High Voltage* (1975 promo film)/*Jailbreak* (1976 Countdown clip)/*Let There Be Roc/k* (1977 promo film)/*Riff Raff* (live from Glasgow Apollo, 1978)/*Dog Eat Dog* (live from Glasgow Apollo, 1978)/*Highway To Hell*

(1979 promo film)/*Shot Down In Flames* (1979 promo film)/ *Touch Too Much* (1979 promo film)/*If You Want Blood (You've Got It)* (1979 promo film).

AIN'T NO FUN (WAITING ROUND TO BE A MILLIONAIRE)

Song from 1976's *Dirty Deeds Done Dirt Cheap* album, this was written by the Young broth-ers and Bon Scott. It's AC/DC's longest studio recording at seven minutes and 29 seconds, although an edited version also exists at six minutes and 58 seconds, and also includes a rare example of the band swearing, when Bon Scott comes out with the immortal line, 'Get your fucking jumbo jet out of my airport'. The song is semi-autobiographical, with lyrics penned by Scott at a time when the band was struggling to make their mark. While still believing in their ambitions, he was becoming impatient for success. The track was covered by another Aussie band, The Screaming Jets. It appears on their 1992 EP *Living In England.*

AIR SUPPLY

These soft rockers won the American Music Award for Best Rock Band in 1982, despite AC/DC being nominated. The result not only surprised many, who didn't actually believe Air Supply could rock, but showed how loose the definition of rock was in America. This was the first time that 'DC had ever been nominated for such an award in the States.

ALBERT PRODUCTIONS

The label/publishing company who've been constantly involved with the band since their ear-liest days. The Sydney-based concern was started in 1964 by Ted Albert, as an offshoot of the considerably more venerable J. Albert & Son publishers; Ted was the great-grandson of the original firm's founder. Billy Thorpe & The Aztecs were the first act snapped up by the new label, with The Easybeats, featuring Harry Vanda and George Young, being the second. Vanda & Young would be highly involved in AC/DC's career, and also became the in-house producers for the label, amassing a huge roster of hits. Other notable acts on the label have included John Paul Young, The Angels and more recently Irish rockers, The Answer and Breed 77.

ALL SCREWED UP

Song from the 2000 album *Stiff Upper Lip*, co-written by Angus and Malcolm Young, as were all the tracks on that record. It really deals with life not quite being the way the protagonist sees it: 'Things go tough/And you strut your stuff/And I want your thing/Then you're out of luck'.

ALRIGHT TONIGHT

A song recorded during the sessions for *Blow Up Your Video.* Written by Brian Johnson, Angus

Young and Malcolm Young, the track exists only in demo form, although it has appeared as a b-side to a bootleg single of 'That's The Way I Wanna Rock'N'Roll'.

With lyrics like: 'Do you wanna boogie/Do you wanna blow/She said I do, I do, I do' it's not difficult to see what was on the band's mind when it came to writing the lyrics.

ANTIPODEAN PUNK EXTRAVAGANZA

The rather grand title given to a free show in London, at the Nashville Rooms, on May 24, 1976 and headlined by AC/DC. Now while they were not a punk band, nonetheless this was proof that here was one group that could cross barriers and genres. They could appeal to a cross-section of fans, all of whom enjoyed the 'DC brand of high energy rock.

APLAUSO

A Spanish TV show on which Bon Scott made his final public appearance, ten days prior to his death. The band flew into Madrid and filmed three songs for the show: 'Beating Around The Bush', 'Girls Got Rhythm' and 'Highway To Hell'.

It's also worth noting that on February 10, the group did a press conference, during which Malcolm Young had something to say about certain bands:

"What do you think of the Ramones?"
"Ramones..? Yuck."
"What do you think of Led Zeppelin?"
"Oh! Good long ago but... now are too old to play."
"And Foreigner?"
"They aren't original, play same as us."

ARE YOU READY

A song from the band's 1990 album *The Razors Edge*, written by Angus and Malcolm Young. The video features a prisoner having his head shaved, leaving only the AC/DC logo and was directed by David Mallet. A still from the video features on the cover of the 1991 VHS/DVD *Clipped*. Lyrically... well, this says it all: 'Sweet apple pie/Standing in the street/Hands outta

17

line/Looking for some meat'. No, we're not talking about something culinary!

ASHFIELD BOYS HIGH SCHOOL

Sydney

A public school for boys, located in Ashfield, an inner Western suburb of Sydney. Angus Young's original schoolboy uniform onstage was that of this school – he went to Ashfield, and myth has it that he used to rehearse in his uniform, as he didn't have time to change prior to band practice. It was his sister Margaret who suggested Angus wear this uniform onstage, as each member of 'DC was asked to come up with a gimmick. Another famous former pupil of the school is Australian cricketer Dirk Wellham, who played six Tests in the 1980s for his country.

ATLANTIC RECORDS

The label that signed AC/DC in December 1975. The deal originated in London, with executive Phil Carson putting them under contract. Atlantic Records was founded in 1947 by Ahmet Ertegun and Herb Abramson, and over the years worked with some of the biggest names in rock and metal, from Led Zeppelin to Emerson, Lake & Palmer and Genesis to the Rolling Stones. AC/DC's first release under this contract was

High Voltage in May 1976 – this was actually a compilation of tracks from their first two Aussie records: *High Voltage* and *T.N.T.* Their last record for Atlantic was *Ballbreaker* in 1995.

ATLANTIC STUDIOS

The New York studio where AC/DC recorded their celebrated *Live From The Atlantic Studios* album on December 7, 1977, in front of a select audience. At the time, 'DC were touring the US with Kiss and Rush, and had just played in New York. This was a performance specifically set up for radio broadcast purposes. Limited edition promotional copies were sent out to DJs across the US, the aim being to get the band a higher profile, and these have become highly-valued collector's items. Although only officially made commercially available as part of the *Bonfire* box set in 1997, it has been released in bootleg form on more than one occasion.

AUSTRALIAN RECORDING INDUSTRY HALL OF FAME

The Hall Of Fame has been part of the annual ARIA Awards since1988. AC/DC were among the first into this select company in '88. They were inducted alongside Vanda & Young (their longtime producers), Dame Joan Sutherland, Johnny O'Keefe, Slim Dusty and Cole Joye.

BABY, PLEASE DON'T GO

This song dates back to 1935, when it was first recorded by blues artist Big Joe Williams and is a plea from a man for his wife/girlfriend to come back home. Since then, it's been covered by a number of top names, perhaps the best known version being by Them (featuring Van Morrison) but also by Aerosmith and the Amboy Dukes with Ted Nugent.

AC/DC first recorded the track with original singer Dave Evans and they visited it again with Bon Scott during the sessions for debut album *High Voltage* in 1975. However, this version wasn't released until 1984, as part of the *'74 Jailbreak* album. A clip of the band performing it on Australian TV show Countdown is included on the DVD *Family Jewels*. Here, Scott is seen singing it over a backing track – while dressed in drag!

The track was released as a rare single in a long deleted French box set that coupled together the international releases *High Voltage*, *Dirty Deeds Done Dirt Cheap* and *Powerage*.

BACK IN BLACK

The statistics surrounding this album are remarkable indeed. To date, it has sold over 42 million copies globally, making it the second biggest selling original studio record of all time, only beaten by Michael Jackson's Thriller. It's also the fifth biggest selling album of any type in America, and the biggest selling album by any Australian artist.

Yet, its background was distinctly unpromising. The death of Bon Scott in February 1980 had left many believing that the band had no future. After all, how do you replace a character like Scott? As was to become the norm with the band in subsequent years, they set about the task methodically and away from the public glare. Bringing in Brian Johnson as the new singer, after extensive auditions, expansive rumours and an exhaustive search, 'DC went to Compass Point Studios in Nassau, with producer 'Mutt' Lange during April 1980, spending two months working on what was to be the most important and significant record of their career.

The result was released in July of that year, and took everyone by surprise. While many expected something that was a pale shadow of what had gone before, especially *Highway To Hell*, the new-look band took everything to fresher heights. Focused and determined, the band's sound had a thicker, sharper and perhaps darker edge than ever. This was still clearly the style and sound the band had made their own over the previous seven years, but now it had a revitalised vigour. The fact that every song on the album was to become something of a classic clearly helped the cause, but there was a lot more to the record that anything superficial. Dressed in a black sleeve, and with that title, many felt the band were paying their own tribute to a lost colleague, bandmate and pal. However, they were making their own statement of intent, heading for the future at the start of a new decade.

From the opening, ominous bell tollings of 'Hells Bells' to the last strains of closer 'Rock 'N' Roll Ain't Noise Pollution', every note, each chord seems to have a real significance – it's as if the band had perfectly captured the zeitgeist. Lyrically, they also hit their straps in a remarkable way, with the Young brothers and Johnson combining impressively. There has been some controversy in recent years, with claims that the band might have incorporated lines written by Scott just before he died into certain songs. These allegations have been strenuously denied by the band and while they remain hovering, nobody has ever

suggested anything other than that one or two Scott ideas were used – the majority of the lyrics are unquestionably the work of those so credited.

The album reached number one in the UK and Australia, and number four in the US. Interestingly, it was included in the 1997 *Bonfire* box set, which was released as a tribute to Bon Scott – exactly why the band chose to put in a record with which the late singer had officially no connection remains a mystery to this day.

As well as in the UK and Australia the album reached the number one spot almost all over the world upon its release, aside from America, where its number four slot made it the band's highest US chart position at that point.

The full track listing is: *Hells Bells/Shoot To Thrill/What Do You Do For Money Honey/ Given The Dog A Bone/Let Me Put My Love Into You/Back In Black/You Shook me All Night Long/Have A Drink On Me/Shake A Leg/Rock And Roll Ain't Noise Pollution.*

BACK IN BLACK
(Song)

The title track of the band's biggest selling album, this song has one of the most distinctive riffs in the group's history. Ostensibly it's a tribute to Bon Scott, although

Audrey Hepburn

the lyrics do seem to have little direct connection with the band's late singer. Subsequently, it's been covered or sampled by the likes of Beastie Boys, Kid Rock, Refused, Living Colour, Shakira and Six Feet Under. And the original has had more than a million downloads as a ringtone.

In a rare move, during 2006 AC/DC allowed the song to be used in a TV ad campaign for Gap. The commercial featured the late Audrey Hepburn as she appeared in the film *Funny Face*, seemingly dancing to 'Back In Black'. The campaign was used to relaunch Gap's skinny black pants, and includes the tagline, "It's Back – The Skinny Black Pant." This marked the first time in over 12 years that a film clip of Hepburn had been authorized for use in endorsing a commercial product in North America. "We wanted to do something really special to relaunch our skinny black pants and thought who better to showcase them than actress Audrey Hepburn – an iconic woman famous for dressing with sophistication and classic style," said Trey Laird, creative director of the company. The 30- and 60-second spots aired in October 2006, and the symbiosis of Hepburn and 'DC worked brilliantly,

BACK IN BLACK: A CLASSIC ALBUM UNDER REVIEW *(DVD)*

Released on the Sexy Intellectual label, this DVD takes a look at the story behind the album, featuring contributions from a

A Classic Album Under Review
BACK IN BLACK

number of associates, journalists and experts as well as some fascinating insight from the album's engineer, Tony Platt.

BACK IN BUSINESS

Track from the band's ninth studio album, *Fly On The Wall*, which was released in 1985. It was written by the tried and trusted combination of Angus and Malcolm Young and Brian Johnson.

Lyrically, it's typical 1980s 'DC fodder, with much talk about being a wrecking ball, stinging knife, and also about being the king of vice. It's a real statement of intent at a time when there were many trying to challenge the band's pre-eminence in the world of hard rock.

BACK SEAT CONFIDENTIAL

Part of the *Volts* CD in the *Bonfire* box set, this song was an early version of what was to become 'Beating Around The Bush' on the *Highway To Hell* album. Lyrically, there's a huge difference between the two versions. While 'Back Street Confidential' was salacious and thrusting, 'Beating Around The Bush' is a lot more to do with a direct relationship. However, the former does contain some priceless Scott lines, like: 'Said to buy my rubber at the cigarette stand/Dying to get it off so I can get it in'.

BAD BOY BOOGIE

Track four from the band's 1977 album *Let There Be Rock*. The song became infamous to some extent, because Angus would often strip off (from the waist upwards) while it was performed live, the routine often culminating in the diminutive guitarist dropping his trousers to moon at the audience following an extended guitar solo section.

Lyrically, it's typical of Bon Scott's approach to life, always being the one standing on the outside, being contrary and individual. Talk about being the seventh son of a seventh son, of dirty women, of being born to love… it was Scott revelling in his reputation and delighting in the shock value of his lifestyle.

BADLANDS

The penultimate track from the 1983 album *Flick Of The Switch*, this one was written by the Young brothers and Brian Johnson, and uses outlaw and gun-toting imagery to reflect rock 'n' roll's lifestyle – riding into town, enjoying the women and the notoriety and riding back out again.

BAILEY/ROB

Bassist with AC/DC from April 1974 until January 1975, Bailey was actually in the band during

the recording of the *High Voltage* album, although he did very little on the record, with most of the studio work being handled by producer George Young. However, he is seen in what's regarded as the earliest video clip of the group yet unearthed, performing 'Can I Sit Next To You Girl?' during a gig at The Last Picture Show Theater in Cronulla. Now retired from the music industry, Bailey was last heard of helping to run a hotel in Australia.

BALLBREAKER

Released in 1995, this was the band's first album since 1990's *The Razors Edge*, and also marked the return of drummer Phil Rudd, whom many regard as the ultimate AC/DC skinsman, but who had left the band in 1983. It also marked the arrival of producer Rick Rubin, a self-confessed fan

of the band who had waited a long time to work with them.

In many ways, Rubin encouraged AC/DC to return to their roots, at least in terms of the sound they got on the album. As a devotee of the band's career to date, Rubin was able to approach things from a different perspective, and to some extent this worked, giving the record a retro dimension that nonetheless managed to sound fresh, even if the overall quality was a little below par, especially when it came to the songwriting. Only 'Hard As A Rock', 'Hail Caesar' and 'Ballbreaker' (the first pair released as singles, of which only the former cracked the Top 40 in the UK, the last AC/DC single to date to do so) reached the sort of level one usually

took for granted with the group. Too many others seemed content to tread water, with the Young brothers' liberal use of double entendres in their lyrics all too often sounding a bit tired and dated.

Although the album did well on its release, making it to number six in America, number four in the UK and actually topping the Australian charts, this is not regarded as a classic 'DC release.

The full track listing is: *Hard As A Rock/Cover You In Oil/The Furor/Boogie Man/The Honey Roll/Burnin' Alive/Hail Caesar/ Love Bomb/Caught With Your Pants Down/Whiskey On The Rocks/Ballbreaker*

BALLBREAKER
(Song)

The title track of their 1995 album, this is one of the best songs recorded by the band during the 1990s. It opened their live show for a time, characterised by Brian Johnson sitting on top of a wrecking ball that had swung into action at the start of the show. Lyrically, it uses sexual innuendo in a manner that was the norm for the band during much of this period.

BANDIT

A mid-1970s UK band that featured AC/DC bassist Cliff Williams. Formed in 1974, they released one self-titled album in 1977 on Arista, before Williams joined 'DC, replacing Mark Evans. Bandit also included drummer Graham Broad, who has become a renowned session man, working for the likes of Roger Waters and vocalist Jim Diamond, who has enjoyed major solo success, especially in the 1980s.

BBC TRANSCRIPTION SERVICES

In 1976 the BBC released a rare and now much sought after promo album with AC/DC's legendary July 1976 Marquee show on side one (aside from, for some inexplicable reason, 'Baby Please Don't Go'). The other side features Australian rock and rollers Maxx Merritt And The Meteors. Now incredibly rare, collectors should be aware that the original BBC releases came in a plain yellow sleeve with a green and white label. A bogus copy of this surfaced in the '80s but features Def Leppard on the other side.

AC/DC track listing: *Live Wire/ It's A Long Way To The Top (If You Wanna Rock 'N' Roll)/Soul Stripper/High Voltage*

Two further BBC discs exist. One features a 1977 show from Hammersmith Odeon on the *Let There Be Rock* tour (a one sided disc) whilst the other, a whole album, carries a 1979 Hammersmith Odeon show from the *Highway To Hell* tour.

All three originals are very rare and some exist in bootleg form.

BEATING AROUND THE BUSH

Track from the *Highway To Hell* album, this actually started out as 'Back Seat Confidential', which, if anything, was a lot more risqué than the final version. In fact, 'Beating Around The Bush' is more a song about someone suspicious of what his girl's been up to behind his back, with Scott railing about the way he's been treated, and how his woman's been cheating on him. He even says at one juncture: 'I'm gonna give you just a one more chance/ Try to save our romance'. It shows Scott's ability not only to use wink-wink, nudge-nudge tactics, but to be vulnerable as well. Many AC/DC fans have noted the similarity between 'Beating Around The Bush' and Fleetwood Mac's early blues rocker 'Oh Well'.

BEAVIS & BUTT-HEAD

The celebrated 1990s cartoon characters that came to represent metal and hard rock to the masses, as much taking the piss out of the various genres as delighting in their clichés. Perennial losers who actually won out, they were forever dreaming of getting laid and being rock heroes. The truth was that they were inevitably doomed to be outcasts.

Created by Mike Judge, Beavis & Butt-Head had their own MTV series from 1993-1997, and even did a movie in 1996, titled *Beavis & Butt-Head Do America,* which features the AC/DC song 'Gone

Shootin' on its soundtrack. Their AC/DC connection was sealed in 1996, when a short film with the pair was screened as an intro. In it, B&B attempt to score with girls going backstage at a 'DC show. Eventually a cartoon Angus Young gets the 'Ballbreaker' woman to chase them off.

BEDLAM IN BELGIUM

Track eight from the 1983 album *Flick Of The Switch* and based on an actual encounter with the police in Belgium, during which a gun was pulled on Angus Young. The line 'There was a cop with a gun, who was runnin' around insane' was more than mere dramatic input!

BEDLAM IN BELGIUM
(Website)

This is at www.ac-dc.cc. Started in 1995, it hasn't actually been updated since 2006. You can access this in English, French or Spanish.

BEEN UP IN THE HILLS TOO LONG

A song written by Bon Scott during his time with Fraternity, but never recorded. Very much a rarity, in fact, the only known recording was made by country group, The Stetsons.

BIG BALLS

A song from the *Dirty Deeds Done Dirt Cheap* album, this is most celebrated for the cunning way that Bon Scott uses his mastery of the double entendre, masquerading sexual prowess within lyrics about social balls. It brings a smile – or more than a smile – to the face as Scott leers his way through lines like 'Some balls are held for charity/And some for fancy dress/But when they're held for pleasure/They're the balls that I like best'. Wrestler Balls Mahoney has used both the original song and also a new version as his intro for ECW bouts.

BIG GUN

Single released in 1993, backed by a live version of Back In Black. It reached number 23 in the UK charts, and number 65 in America, although it did top the main-

stream rock chart in the States. The song features in the movie *Last Action Hero*, starring Arnold Schwarzenneger, who also played a major role in the video, directed by David Mallet. This starts with Schwarzenegger kicking down the door to an AC/DC concert and walking through the crowd, before morphing into Angus, complete with school uniform, Gibson SG and trademark moves. The video is also significant for an appearance from one Shavo Odadjian, who would become bassist with System Of A Down.

Written by the Young brothers, lyrically it's something of a shoot up as the band claim, 'There's a bad man cruising around/In a big black limousine/Don't let it be wrong/Don't let it be right'.

BLACK ICE

AC/DC's first new studio album since 2000's *Stiff Upper Lip*, released worldwide on October 20 2008, this was the year's most hotly anticipated new rock record.. The 15 tracks were recorded with producer Brendan O'Brien and engineer Mike Fraser at Warehouse Studios in Vancouver.

In an unusual move, the band's label Columbia decided to sell this record in America exclusively through Wal-Mart and Sam's Club retail locations, at a special price. Online, though, the

CD was available with free shipping and handling via the oficcial website, www.acdc.com.

Rolling Stone magazine described the album thus:

> "Sweet vindication! Last year in this column, AC/DC singer Brian Johnson promised that they'd tour in 2008. Well, he wasn't kidding. Soon they'll begin rehearsals in a secret location, before hitting US arenas in late fall. We heard this news at the Sony HQ on New York's Madison Avenue, before hearing all 15 tracks of Black Ice. Brian wails about skies on fire, blood in his eyes, storms raging, lightning flashes, hard rain and pretty women. Angus Young shreds throughout (we dig his slide work on "Decibel"), and the rhythm cats — Malcom Young, Cliff Williams and Phil Rudd — are solid as a rock. The first single is 'Rock 'N' Roll Train', 'She Likes Rock' N' Roll' will be a stripper anthem and 'War Machine' (our favourite) will tear you to pieces."

As this book went to press, the band were about to start what was due to be an 18-month world tour. The full track listing for the album is: *Rock 'N' Roll Train/Skies On Fire/Big Jack/*

Anything Goes/War Machine/ Smash 'N Grab/Spoilin' For A Fight/Wheels/Decibel/Stormy May Day/She Likes Rock 'N' Roll /Money Made /Rock 'N' Roll Dream/Rocking All The Way/Black Ice.

BLACKFEATHER

Aussie group from the early 1970s, their debut album, *At The Mountains Of Madness*, features Bon Scott on recorder, timbales and tambourine; he played the recorder on a track called 'Seasons Of Change', which was actually written for Fraternity.

Recorded in late 1970, a few months after the band's formation, and released by Infinity Records early the next year, the record reached number seven on the Australian charts. It was re-issued by Festival Records in the 1990s. Scott was never a member of Blackfeather, but guested on the album.

Guitarist and mainman John Robinson describes the band's sound: "To me now, the influences are very apparent on the record. Zeppelin, Hendrix, Clapton, Free, Chicago Blues, Kettleby, Greensleeves, Morricone, Ravel, Arabic motives. Everyone else involved was blissfully unaware of them. Maybe that was a good thing, as they put their hearts into their parts, and made it what it is."

BLACK SABBATH

In April 1977, AC/DC got the chance of playing 11 dates in Europe opening for Black Sabbath – a major opportunity and taking in shows across France, Germany, Switzerland, Belgium, Holland and Sweden. And it was in Sweden – on April 29 – that things went wrong. An argument between Sabbath bassist Geezer Butler (below) and 'DC took a nasty turn when the former pulled a knife on Malcolm Young. What happened next is that Young is said to have punched out the bassist. Result? AC/DC were thrown off the Sabbath tour.

BLOW UP YOUR VIDEO

The band's 1988 album, recorded with returning co-producers Harry Vanda and George Young in Miravel Studios, France, in August and September 1987. There are several noteables here, apart from the return of the Vanda & Young production team. Firstly, it marked the last time Brian Johnson wrote most of the lyrics for an AC/DC album – after this, Angus and Malcolm Young took over that task. It was also the band's final album with drummer Simon Wright. Moreover, it was their biggest success since *For Those About To Rock*, reaching number two in the UK and number 12 in America. A number of the songs from this record are regarded as being among the best the band released during this era, including 'Heatseeker' and 'That's The Way I Wanna Rock 'N' Roll', both of which were released as singles and charted in the UK. It was during the subsequent tour that Malcolm Young took a break from the band to deal with his alcohol problems. His cousin, Steve Young, temporarily took over.

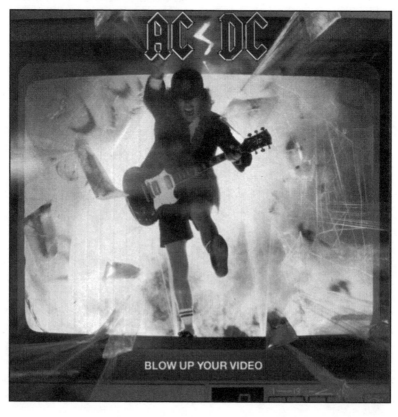

BLOW UP YOUR VIDEO

BONDI LIFESAVERS
Sydney

On March 27, 1976, AC/DC played their last show in Australia before heading over to England, and becoming global stars. Angus says farewell by mooning everyone, an event which would eventually become a regular occurrence during AC/DC's live shows. In July 1977, the band played two secret shows at the club, to introduce new bassist Cliff Williams. For these gigs, 'DC are billed The Seedies and also Dirty Deeds.

BONFIRE

This five-disc box set was released in 1997 as a tribute to the late Bon Scott – hence the title – and has each CD in its own jewel case, plus a booklet, poster, backstage pass and a key ring. The first CD, featuring *Live From The Atlantic Studios*, recorded during a session in New York on December 7, 1977, was given out as a promotional album to radio stations at the time and had been widely bootlegged prior to becoming officially availably through *Bonfire*.

The soundtrack to *Let There Be Rock: The Movie* is sprawled across two CDs and had been recorded at the Pavillon de Paris on December 9, 1979. The show was filmed and enjoyed a theatrical release as well as coming out on video. There are differences between the movie and the soundtrack though: while the latter features TNT, missing from the film, the former has band interviews, omitted from the CDs.

The fourth disc is titled *Volts*. This is the one of especial interest to fans as it features alternative versions of known songs from the *Let There Be Rock* and *Highway To Hell* albums, plus previously unreleased tracks. For instance, 'Dirty Eyes' here became 'Whole Lotta Rosie', 'Back Seat Confidential' developed into 'Beating Around The Bush'.

The final CD is a re-mastered version of 'Back In Black'.

Critics of the box set point out that it was meant as a tribute to Scott, but includes 'Back In Black' with Brian Johnson. The band have never answered such criticisms satisfactorily, but some have wondered whether this was 'DC's way of acknowledging Scott's influence on the album.

BOOGIE MAN

Song from the band's 1995 album *Ballbreaker*. Lyrically, it's dark and sleazy, and might be construed as dealing with a pimp or drug dealer – one of the seedy people who inhabit the shadows of normal life.

BOOM BOX

The title of a box set released in Australia only in December 1991, and containing every AC/DC album up until that point.

BORROWED TIME

The B-side to the single 'That's The Way I Wanna Rock 'N' Roll', which was released in 1988, and credited to the writing combination of Young, Young & Johnson. In a way, this is real party-themed song, about going out and never worrying about tomorrow. Cos 'if the mule don't kick you, know the mule don't ride'. A rarity in as much as AC/DC have rarely released tracks not from any album when it comes to B-sides.

BOX SETS

Aside from *Bonfire* that the band released in 2003, there have also been several box sets collating a variety of AC/DC's albums over the years.

In October 2003, Sony released in America *The AC/DC Vinyl Reissues – Limited Edition Collectors Box*. Pressed on 180 gsm vinyl, this features all 15 of the re-mastered reissue albums from *'74 Jailbreak* to *Stiff Upper Lip*, presented in a heavy duty leatherette box with the band's trademark logo stamped in silver on the front.

The Festival Mushroom label in Australia released an Australian only box set featuring 17 AC/DC albums, from the Australian version of *High Voltage* all the way through to *Stiff Upper Lip*.

In 1987 Atlantic put out a set comprising the albums *High Voltage*, *T.N.T.*, *Dirty Deeds Done Dirt Cheap*, *Let There Be Rock*, *Powerage* and *Highway To Hell*, as well as a 12" single featuring the track 'Cold Hearted Man' and a sticker. Originally available on vinyl, it was later released on CD as well.

Atlantic swiftly followed this up with a second set featuring *Back In Black*, *For Those About To Rock (We Salute You)*, *Flick Of The Switch*, *Fly On The Wall* and *Who Made Who*, as well as a poster and another sticker.

In France, Atlantic released a three album set in 1980 consisting of the *High Voltage*, *Dirty Deeds Done Dirt Cheap* and *Powerage* as well as a seven inch single of 'Baby Please Don't Go' backed with 'Jailbreak' and 'Soul Stripper' and a poster.

The Australian and New Zealand only *Boom Box* offers every AC/DC album from *High Voltage* to *The Razors Edge* in 1991, and was re-issued in 1995 with the addition of the special collector's edition of *Live*.

In 2000, the band's German label Elektra released the *AC/DC In The 20th Century* box set of 17 CD's, as vinyl replicas, from *High Voltage* through to *Ballbreaker*, and also included the *Live At Atlantic Studios* release.

Most of these sets are all still available.

BRAIN SHAKE

The final song from the *Flick Of The Switch* album, this is about taking everything to the point of excess, when your brain's in a spin and you're really not quite sure what happens next. But the insanity is worth all the pain.

BREAKING THE RULES

The eighth track from the album *For Those About To Rock (We Salute You)*. In a way, this is an anthem to individuality. Don't follow the crowd for its own sake, be a 'society rash, ready to brain, ready to gash'.

BRIGHTON LE SANDS MASONIC HALL
Sydney

It was here in September 1974 that AC/DC made their live debut with Bon Scott. Little did this venue know what a part it would play in the history of this illustrious band.

BROWNING, MICHAEL

The brother and sister team (Browning worked with sister Coral, who had little or no involvement with AC/DC) who managed the group in their early days. Michael Browning was manager of the Hard Rock Café in Melbourne when he saw them playing at a gay night. By November of that year, the band had fired manager Dennis Laughlin, formerly the singer with Aussie group Sherbet, and Browning took over.

By this time, Browning had already made a name for himself as a success in the business. He'd been involved in one of the country's first discos, Sebastian's Penthouse, which opened in the 1960s. He also founded Consolidated Rock, Australia's first ever national music booking agency, and launched The Daily Planet, a music magazine he hoped would rival Rolling Stone (it didn't).

Working with Albert Productions, Browning helped to establish AC/DC as a major Aussie force, and then guided them to international fame, securing their deal with Atlantic Records. In

1979, however, he lost the band to the powerful Leber-Krebs organisation. Subsequently, he spent much of the 1980s in Los Angeles, managing Warrior among others, before returning to Australia to look after Noiseworks. These days, he runs 301 Records.

BURGESS/COLIN

AC/DC's original drummer, Burgess started out with cult Aussies The Masters Apprentices, with whom he played for four years from 1968. He joined 'DC on their formation at the end of 1973, but left in February 1974. According to most reports, he was fired for being drunk onstage at Chequers during the first of two sets the band were due to play at the club, although he insisted his drink had been spiked; George Young took over on drums for the second set. There are stories that he co-founded the band with Malcolm Young, and quit when Angus was brought in, believing it wasn't a serious band. Inducted into the ARIA Hall Of Fame (Australia's official music industry body), he now tours with his brother Denny in the The Burgess Brothers Band.

BURNIN' ALIVE

Track from the 1995 album *Ballbreaker*. Is there a slightly social commentary here? About society running out of control? That seems to be the way, although little hope is offered at the end.

BURSTEIN/CLIFF

Regarded as one of the shrewdest managers in rock music, Cliff Burnstein's long-standing business partnership with Peter Mensch has seen them represent Def Leppard, Metallica, the Rolling Stones and Madonna during their career. He started out as an A&R man for the Mercury label, before teaming up with Mensch in what has become Q. Prime Inc. Mensch had represented the band while they were under the auspices of the Leber-Krebs management company, for whom Mensch worked at the time. When he and Burnstein began their own company, 'DC were among their first clients. However, the relationship was brief.

BUSTER BROWN

1970s band featuring AC/DC drummer Phil Rudd and future Rose Tattoo singer Angry Anderson. Originally known as the Colored Balls, they released two singles under that name before the name change. However, by early 1975 Rudd had left to join 'DC.

whose character is one of the most important in the game. The singer said that he drew on the experiences of his father, a sergeant-major during the Second World War, for inspiration for the role. The game is available for PS2, Xbox and GameCube platforms.

CAN I SIT NEXT TO YOU GIRL

There are two version of this song. The first features the line-up of Dave Evans (vocals), Angus Young (lead guitar), Malcolm Young (rhythm guitar), Rob Bailey (bass) and Peter Clack (drums). It was released as a single in Australia and New Zealand only during 1974, and is the only record from this line-up, or indeed to boast Evans on vocals. The B-side is 'Rockin' In The Parlour'. Copies of the New Zealand version, on the Polydor label, are said to be worth $700.

After bringing in Bon Scott for Evans (as well as Mark Evans and Phil Rudd for Bailey and Clack, respectively), the band slightly revamped the song for inclusion on their 1975 album *T.N.T.*, which was only put out in Australia. It is, however, included on the international edition of *High Voltage*, released in 1976.

The lyrical difference between the two versions is minimal and both are credited solely to Angus and Malcolm Young. In the Evans' recording the lyrics include: 'At intermission we were

CALLE DE AC/DC
(Leganes, Spain)

A street named after the band in Leganes, Spain. The idea for this came from the mayor, Jose Perez Rais. The naming happened on March 22, 2000, with Angus and Malcolm Young in attendance. Incidentally, Leganes is just outside of Madrid.

CALL OF DUTY
Finest Hour

An Activision war game featuring the voice of Brian Johnson, doing alright/Until this guy came up and stood by her side/Then he took ME by surprise/ When HE threw her one of my lines'. With Scott, this became: 'At intermission we were doing alright/Til this guy came up and stood by her side/I took him by surprise/When I gave her one of my lines'.

CAN'T STAND STILL

Track six from the 2000 album *Stiff Upper Lip*. This was Brian Johnson's choice as a single, but he was overruled, and *Satellite Blues* was the generally preferred option. Written by Angus and Malcolm Young, the lyrics are libido-fuelled, in the manner the band have made their own since their inception.

CAN'T STOP ROCK 'N' ROLL

Track seven from the band's 2000 album *Stiff Upper Lip*. A statement of intent written by the Young brothers, it still manages the occasional innuendo. 'Too much clap make you blind' is one line that stands out.

CARLOTTA

Transvestite performer, whom AC/DC supported during a six-week residency at Perth's

Beethoven Disco in August 1974. This is noteworthy partly because singer Dave Evans doesn't do all the shows. He is occasionally replaced by the band's manager Dennis Laughlin, who was previously the frontman for successful Aussie band Sherbet.

CARPENTER/RON

AC/DC's second drummer. He replaced Colin Burgess, but only lasted a matter of weeks.

CARRY ME HOME

A track AC/DC recorded at Vineyard Studios in London in 1976 and was originally used as the b-side to the Australian version of the 'Dog Eat Dog' single. It wasn't a major success and failed to chart, which means this song has become a major rarity for AC/DC collectors, although it did begin appearing on a variety of bootlegs throughout the '90s.

The tracks 'Love At First Feel', 'Dirty Eyes' (an early version of 'Whole Lotta Rosie') and 'Cold Hearted Man' were also recorded at the same sessions, which were the only recording sessions outside of Australia to feature bassist Mark Evans.

Written by Angus Young, Malcolm Young and Bon Scott, the lyrics tell the tale of a man who goes out drinking with a woman, gets drunk and is astonished at his female drinking partner's ability to hold her liquor, ending with the somewhat prophetic line: 'I'm dead drunk and heave'n, hanging upside down/And you're getting up and leaving, you think I'm going to drown'. Quite possibly written from Scott's own personal experiences.

CARSON, PHIL

The man who signed AC/DC to Atlantic Records in December 1975, and consequently played a major role in taking them forward on a global scale. Carson started his music-associated career working for legendary Led Zeppelin manager Peter Grant, and developed it from there. While employed by Atlantic Records, he also signed Twisted Sister and gained the reputation of being a man who understood rock bands and how to work them. He remains a music business executive, having started his own label,

Victory, and has also experienced life as a manager.

CAUGHT WITH YOUR PANTS DOWN

The ninth track from the 1995 album *Ballbreaker*. Written by the Young brothers, inevitably it has more to do with sexual activities than being embarrassed in public.

CAVANAUGH, PETER C.

American radio mogul and promoter in Michigan, it was his station – AM 600 WTAC – who gave the band their first vital exposure in the US. Cavanaugh subsequently booked the group to play at the Capitol Theater in Flint, Michigan, supported by none other than local heroes MC5.

CELEBS IN AC/DC SHIRTS

Lots of celebrities have been filmed or photographed in AC/DC T-shirts, among the more notable being Drew Barrymore in the movie *Charlie's Angels*, supermodel Gisele Bundchen (above), actress Drea DeMatteo of *The Sopranos* fame, Spice Girl Geri Halliwell and *Friends* star Matt LeBlanc. England international footballer David Bentley recently confirmed that AC/DC are, in fact, his favourite band, and the same can be said of horror author Stephen King.

CHASE THE ACE

Instrumental track from the 1986 album *Who Made Who*. Given the nature of the song, it doesn't involve Brian Johnson in any way, shape or form. The song features in the movie *Maximum Overdrive*.

CHEQUERS CLUB

Although AC/DC made a number of appearances at this Sydney venue, it's most renowned for being the location for original drummer Colin Burgess' last appearance with the band. The official version says that Burgess passed out after the first of the two sets the band were due to play, because he was drunk. Incapable of carrying on, Burgess was replaced by George Young, elder brother of Angus and Malcolm, for the second set, and was subsequently fired. The drummer insists his drinks were spiked.

CLACK/PETER

Early drummer with AC/DC, Clack was with the band from April 1974 to January 1975. Although he was in the line-up when their Australian debut album *High Voltage* was recorded, he apparently played no part in the recording sessions.

CLASSIC ROCK CARES

A tour set up in 2007 to raise money for the John Entwistle Foundation, which aims to provide free music education and instruments for children in need. The tour featured both Brian Johnson and Cliff Williams, as well as Grand Funk Railroad leader Mark Farner, former Rainbow/Deep Purple singer Joe Lynn Turner, guitarist Mark Hitt and one-time John Entwistle Band drummer Steve Luongo.

The ensemble played 15 shows in July '07. Turner did a series of Rainbow and Purple hits and Farner would then take the microphone for some Grand Funk classics, before Johnson, Williams, Hitt and Luongo ran through some of AC/DC's biggest songs.

CLIPPED
(DVD)

Originally released as a long-form video in 1991, this was finally issued on DVD in 2002. It features three clips from the album *The Razors Edge* ('Thunderstruck', 'Money Talks' and 'Are You Ready') and two from *Blow Up Your Video* ('Heatseaker' and 'That's The Way I Wanna Rock N Roll'). The DVD also boasts promo videos for 'Big Gun' and 'Hard As A Rock'.

COCK CROWS, THE

Recorded by the band during the sessions for the *Stiff Upper Lip* album and written by Angus and Malcolm Young, this song has never seen the light of day.

C.O.D.

Track seven from the album *For Those About To Rock (We Salute You)*. Written by the Young Brothers and Brian Johnson, exactly what 'C.O.D.' stands for remains a mystery. During the song, such phrases as 'Call Of a Dog', 'Cry Of The Doctor', 'Care Of the Devil' and 'Cash On Demand' are all mentioned.

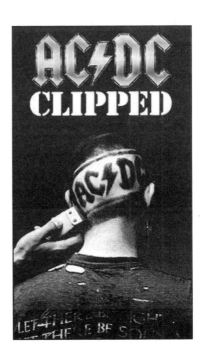

COLD HEARTED MAN

A song that still remains somewhat rare, and originally appeared on the European only version of the *Powerage* album in 1978. It only got an Australian release in '87, as part of a box set of Bon Scott era vinyl albums, being included as a 12 inch single. Written by Bon Scott and the Young brothers, the lyrics tell the story of one Leroy Kincade, a formidable character.

COLEMAN, RUSSELL

One of several drummers to work with AC/DC in their early days, Coleman was in the band for a very brief period in February 1974, replacing Ron Carpenter, before making way for Noel Taylor.

COMPASS POINT STUDIOS

Famed recording studio in Nassau, Bahamas, built in 1977 by Chris Blackwell, who founded Island Records. AC/DC first went there with producer 'Mutt' Lange for the 1980 album *Back In Black*. Subsequently, they returned in 1983 for *Flick Of The Switch* and three years later for *Who Made Who*.

COUNTDOWN

Celebrated Australian TV show, wherein AC/DC made a number of appearances in their early days, the first being in March 1975. Three of these are featured in the *Family Jewels* DVD collection: 'Baby, Please Don't Go' from 1975, 'Jailbreak' (1976) and 'Dog Eat Dog' (1977). Countdown is regarded as the most successful music show in the history of Australian TV, running from 1974-1987.

COVER YOU IN OIL

Second track from the 1995 album *Ballbreaker*, this was released as a single in 1996, backed by 'Ballbreaker' and 'Love Bomb'. The lyrics, written by the Young Brothers, left little to the imagination, talking about giving 'good lip service' and 'Comin' in honey, we're heading to the top'.

CRABSODY IN BLUE

Track six from the Australian only version of the 1977 album *Let There Be Rock*, the title is a play on the George Gershwin standard 'Rhapsody In Blue', and the lyrics caused a bit of consternation in America, where it was removed from the international edition of the album, to be replaced by a shortened version of 'Problem

Child'. Dealing as it did with the results of a sexually transmitted disease was obviously one step too far for some!

CRABSODY IN BLUE
(Website)

One of the most respected AC/DC fan-run websites, you can find this at www.crabsodyinblue.com. Unlike some, it is regularly updated.

CRAWLER

Originally called Back Street Crawler, this was the band AC/DC were due to support when they first moved to the UK..

The band were put together under the Back Street Crawler moniker in 1975 by guitarist Paul Kossoff, who'd previously made his name with Free; BSB took their name from the title of Kossoff's 1973 debut solo album. They were quickly signed up by Atlantic Records and, according to legend, they celebrated getting this deal by spelling out the name 'Back Street Crawler' in cocaine on a glass table, and then snorting the lot. It was Kossoff's own growing and unabated drug problems that eventually held the group back. He would often use any excuse to get out of playing live and became notoriously unreliable. On more than one occasion he mimicked collapsing

onstage, much to the irritation of the crowds.

By the end of 1975, Back Street Crawler had released their debut album The Band Plays On, but Kossoff's ill health was becoming a major cause for concern. A stomach ulcer forced them to cancel a string of dates, and when they did play, all too often BSC were a shambles. In 1976, they went to America to work on new record Second Street, but by now a session guitarist had to be brought in to do much of the studio work and to fill in for Kossoff on certain live dates.

On March 19th 1976, Paul Kossoff died from a drugs overdose on a flight between Los Angeles and New York. Subsequently, the band shortened their name to Crawler, and brought in Geoff Whitehorn on guitar to replace their former leader. But Kossoff's death was essentially the start of the end for the band, even though Crawler eventually fulfilled some of their live commitments in the UK with 'DC. But it was obvious that the new look, post-Kossoff outfit had little or nothing to offer.

One renowned gig played by the two bands took place at the Marquee Club in London on May 11th 1976, the first of two successive nights at the club for Crawler and 'DC. The hot young Aussies, already gaining a reputation around town for being a livewire band to watch, were in tremendous form, and it was clear from the huge response, courtesy of a sweaty, packed crowd, that the support act were drawing in more punters than the headliners. AC/DC made it impossible for Crawler, who, by comparison, seemed middle-aged, stale and totally out of touch with what was going on musically at the time – punk was about to explode.

Crawler never fully recovered from this dose of harsh reality. They carried on into the 1980s, but it was all rather worthless and depressing. Eventually, White-horn would team up with former Free vocalist Paul Rodgers, while frontman Terry Wilson-Slesser would be among the rumoured names in the frame to replace Bon Scott following his tragic death in 1980.

CREMORNE STRATA INN

The location in Sydney of the band's last ever gig in Australia with Bon Scott. Not an official show, it was an impromptu performance in front of about 100 people. Scott was said to be standing on a table swigging scotch, while singing. Aussie photographer Philip Morris, who shot the band a number of times in their early days, caught the occasion on camera.

CRITERIA STUDIOS
Miami

One of the most renowned studios in America, opened in 1958. Since then, some of the biggest names in music have recorded there, including AC/DC for the *Highway To Hell* album.

CURRENTI, TONY

One of the numerous drummers to play with AC/DC prior to Phil Rudd's joining and providing some stability, Currenti is credited with playing drums on the Australian version of the *High Voltage* album. As a session drummer, whether he was ever a full-time member of the band remains open to doubt.

CYBERSPACE

Track recorded during the sessions for 2000's *Stiff Upper Lip* album, but left out of the final running order. It eventually surfaced as the B-side to the single 'Safe In New York City'.

DAMNED

Track nine from the band's 2000 album *Stiff Upper Lip*. Written by Angus and Malcolm Young, it has a surprisingly political content, being an attack on the way individual liberties are being eroded in America: 'No jokes, no rights, sit tight, don't fool around/You are a guest of Uncle Sam!'

DANGER

Fourth song form the 1985 album *Fly On The Wall,* 'Danger' was also the first single from the album in the UK. It didn't fare too well however, only reaching number 48 in July 1985, highlighting the band's dip in popularity around that time. Written by Brian Johnson and the Young brothers, it has a similar theme to Dio's song 'Don't Talk To Strangers', warning of how you can get yourself in trouble just by having a good time: 'Gotta hit the bottle/ But my head hit the floor'.

DAY ON THE GREEN

A series of huge outdoor events held at the Oakland Coliseum in Oakland, California and launched

in 1973, continuing through to 1992. AC/DC made their first appearance on the bill in 1978. The date was July 23, the third of the four Days On The Green shows held that year. They opened for a line-up that was headlined by Aerosmith, and also featured Foreigner, Pat Travers and Van Halen.

The band returned one year later on July 21 (previous page), again playing the third leg of the Day On The Green shows. This time they were right in the middle of the bill with Ted Nugent the main attraction and Aerosmith second, in front of 'DC, while Frank Marino & Mahogany Rush and St. Paradise were the openers.

This was the last time the band played the event.

DEEP IN THE HOLE

Track seven from 1983's *Flick Of The Switch* album. Dare one suggest that Young, Young and Johnson were being rather salacious with lines like being 'Deep in, deep in, deep in the hole'?

DEEP PURPLE

The famed British hard rockers, among the pioneers of the genre, didn't exactly get on well with AC/DC when they appeared on a bill with them in Melbourne in 1975. It was the Sunbury festival, with Purple headlining (below). But the band refused to allow AC/DC to follow them, as had apparently been agreed in advance. Result? A huge fight between the Purple people and 'DC plus George Young – in front of 20,000. Yes, this all happened in public. As a result AC/DC, by then superstars in Melbourne, never got to play. Several years later, things had clearly calmed down when 'DC headlined the second Monsters

Of Rock Festival at Donington in 1981. Second on the bill? Whitesnake, featuring David Coverdale, Jon Lord and Ian Paice – all of whom were members of Purple on that day six years earlier.

DEFRIN/BOB

Art director at Atlantic Records in the 1970s, Defrin is the man who came up with the now famous AC/DC logo, which was first used on 1977's *Let There Be Rock* album. During his 19 years at the label, Defrin also worked on releases from Foreigner, Motley Crue, Eric Clapton, Count Basie and Bette Midler.

DIAMOND AWARD

While some awards really are all about prestige and status, others represent something more

substantial, and reflect a band's commercial worth, as assessed by the RIAA (Record Industry Association of America), the body that regulates and collates official sales figures.

Now, usually awards are given for gold albums (sales of 500,000), platinum albums (sales of one million) or multi-platinum (incremental sales in millions), but there is one rare award handed out, and that's the Diamond. This is given for album sales that make it to the ten million unit mark. On March 16, 1999, AC/DC officially reached that figure for *Back In Black*. A ceremony was held at the Roseland Ballroom in New York, which was attended by Brian Johnson and Cliff Williams.

Now, something needs to be explained here. *Back In Black* has sold considerably more copies in the US than that. The thing is, Diamond Awards only take into account sales up to ten million, so its presentation didn't suggest that the album had ONLY done this many copies, more that it had exceeded that mark. And *Back In Black* was only awarded it in 1999 because that was the date when the Diamond was introduced.

DIRTY DEEDS DONE DIRT CHEAP

The third album from 'DC, this was released in September 1976 in Australia and in December internationally, and once again features production from Harry Vanda and George Young. The title itself was a homage to cartoon series *Beany And Cecil*, which Angus had watched as a kid. One of the characters, Dishonest John, carried a card which read 'Dirty deeds done dirt cheap. Holidays, Sundays and special rates'.

In many respects this album saw the band making a giant leap forward. The songs seemed more confident and strident than ever before and it appeared that, having felt their way forward on the two previous Aussie-only albums, now they had a more edgy take on what they needed to do to achieve big-time success.

Two tracks stand out as almost definitive Scott lyricism, showcasing the different sides of his personality. 'Problem Child' sees him revelling in being the bad boy, the lone gun, the one who'd set the fire ablaze. Although on stage he'd often introduce this song as being about Angus, the anti-social tendencies were definitively autobiographical.

'Ride On', on the other hand, is surprisingly mournful and introspective, telling of a life full of regrets, with solace in the bottle and through the company of women who lasted one night or less. Both of these songs relate the

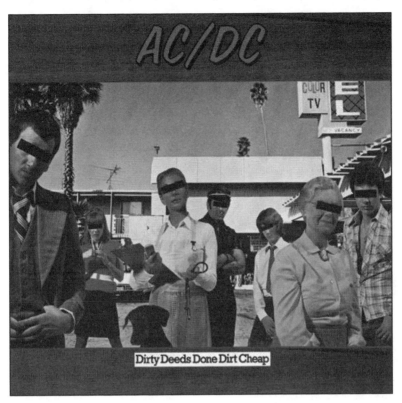

Dirty Deeds Done Dirt Cheap

life of a loner, and, despite being the bon viveur and a lover of life and excess, Scott was to some extent a lone gunman. There were occasions when he could seem alone in a crowded room, while still holding court. These songs readily capture that spirit of the man – something he never attempted to do again. 'Ride On' is also one of the slowest songs in the AC/DC canon, featuring some surprisingly effective blues guitar soloing from Angus Young.

Elsewhere, 'Jailbreak' deals with a man who escapes from jail after being sentenced for murdering his girlfriend's lover, but is shot in the back. We're never told

whether he survived, but the song is said to be based on the story of a friend of Scott's. 'Ain't No Fun (Waitin' Round To Be A Millionaire)' is about someone dreaming of rock 'n' roll success, and features the glorious line 'Get your fucking jumbo jet off my airport'. And the title track has a real glint in its eye.

Interestingly, the Australian version of the album is different to the international one, with the cover being changed, plus both 'Jailbreak' and 'R.I.P. (Rock In Peace)' being removed in favour of 'Rocker' (from the T.N.T. album) and 'Love At First Feel', which was only ever released as

a single in Australia. Even odder, the US release didn't happen until 1981, when it reached number three in the charts. 'Jailbreak' eventually turned up on the 1984 release *'74 Jailbreak,* but 'R.I.P.' remains unreleased outside of Australia.

The full track listing is*: Dirty Deeds Done Dirt Cheap/Love At First Feel/Big Balls/Rocker/ Problem Child/There's Gonna Be Some Rockin'/Ain't No Fun (Waitin' Round To Be A Millionaire)/Ride On/Squealer'*

DIRTY DEEDS DONE DIRT CHEAP
(Song)

The title track of the band's third album… well, their second international release. It was written by Young, Young and Scott, and includes Malcolm Young intoning the title on the chorus – the first time he'd been heard 'singing' on a 'DC track. There are also some strange heavy breathing noises throughout, adding to the atmosphere. During the song the phone number 362 436, which is actually the perfect female measurement of 36-24-36, is mentioned, and became the subject of a court case from Illinois couple Norman and Marilyn White, whose telephone number was similar to the aforementioned 362 436, although not identical. The couple filed a $250,000 invasion of privacy suit against the band.

The song deals with the various services offered by the narrator which include 'High Voltage' and 'T.N.T.', both of which are 'DC album titles, of course! Shame they never did records called Cyanide or Concrete Shoes.

DIRTY EYES

The original title for 'Whole Lotta Rosie', and included on the *Volts* CD from the *Bonfire* box set. While the song is musically similar to its more celebrated successor, lyrically it's radically different. None of the references to the larger woman made in 'Whole Lotta Rosie' are present here at all.

DOG EAT DOG

Track two from the 1977 album *Let There Be Rock*, it was released as a single with 'Carry Me Home' on the B-side. Written by Young, Young and Scott, it's not a lurid tale of Sapphic love but rather a story of greed, with everyone snapping at everyone else ('Business man when

you make a deal/Do you know who you can trust?'), but ultimately it's a reminder that every dog has its day.

DONINGTON MONSTERS OF ROCK

AC/DC have headlined this legendary festival on a record-breaking three separate occasions. They first appeared in 1981 and, in fact, one could say they were headlining the first annual Monsters Of Rock, as the previous year – with Rainbow – had been a one-off. The support bill featured Whitesnake, Blue Oyster Cult (who were so poor on the day that mainman Eric Bloom famously jumped up and down on his commemorative mirror backstage in frustration), Slade, Blackfoot and More.

The band were back in 1984, joined by Van Halen (who tried – and failed – to upstage 'DC with backstage antics), Ozzy Osbourne, Gary Moore, Y&T, Accept and Motley Crue.

Finally, they returned in 1991, with Metallica, Motley Crue, Queensryche and the Black Crowes. Their set that day was recorded for the 1992 *Live* album.

DOWN ON THE BORDERLINE

A song recorded during sessions for *Blow Up Your Video* at Miraval Studios in La Val, France in 1987. The track, written by Brian Johnson, Angus Young and Malcolm Young, eventually surfaced as the b-side to the Australian version of the 'Moneytalks' single in 1990.

With lyrics like: 'She can spread them around and she shows them off/With a neon sign saying don't you touch' it deals with being at the mercy of a female temptress.

The song has also appeared on various AC/DC bootlegs and is readily available to be heard via the website www.youtube.com.

DOWN PAYMENT BLUES

Track from the 1978 album *Powerage*. Lyrically, it deals with a man who gets himself into terrible debt to impress a girl. ('I'm living in a nightmare/She's look-

ing like a wet dream). This may be based on a real event, but is another example of Scott's amazing ability to tap into the seamier side of life, but to do so with sympathy and understanding, without being judgemental. For trivia freaks, please note the US version is 13 seconds longer than the European one.

D.T.

Track from the 1986 album *Who Made Who*. This is one of two instrumentals on the record – the other being *Chase The Ace* – and doesn't feature Brian Johnson. On this track Cliff Williams drops his tuning, for the only time. What does 'DT' stand for? Usually it would be Delirium Tremens, a possible side effect of an addict giving up alcohol. But that's not guaranteed in this case.

DYE/CRISPIN

A former Alberts executive, he was the man appointed as the band's new manager early in 1984. They'd been working with Ian Jeffrey, their sometime tour manager, in this capacity since firing Peter Mensch in 1982. Now they went for someone with more business experience.

EASYBEATS, THE

The 1960s Aussie rockers with whom both George Young and Harry Vanda cut their teeth in the music business. They started out in 1964, split five years later and are generally regarded as the first Australian rock band to have an international hit, with 'Friday On My Mind' in 1966. The Seekers and Frank Ifield had both beaten The Easybeats to such global acclaim, but, of course, neither fits into this category.

Vanda and Young wrote 'Friday On My Mind' (later covered to some acclaim by Gary Moore), however Young also co-wrote several hits with band singer Stevie Wright, including the Aussie chart toppers 'She's So Fine', 'Woman (Make You Feel Alright)', 'Come And See Her' and 'I'll Make You Happy'.

The Easybeats re-located to London towards the end of their career, and once the band had split up, Vanda and Young remained in the city, writing and recording in various guises, including Paint-box and Band Of Hope. They returned to Australia in 1973 and became the house producers for Albert Productions, work-ing with the likes of Rose Tattoo, Stevie Wright and The Angels. They also had several hits in the late '70s and early '80s under the name of Flash & The Pan.

However, they are most closely associated with AC/DC, Mal-colm and Angus being George's younger siblings. Vanda & Young produced everything the band released from debut single 'Can I Sit Next To You Girl' up to the live album *If You Want Blood... You've Got It*. They returned for *Blow Up Your Video* in 1988, and Young on his own did the *Stiff Upper Lip* record.

So, just how big were the Easybeats? Rock historian Glenn A. Baker once stated: "It is not naive to say that no incident of Beatlemania or Rolling Stone fever anywhere in the world sur-passed the absolute peak of Easy-fever. Airports, TV stations, thea-tres and hire cars were reduced to rubble, fans were hospitalised and general mayhem reigned wher-ever they turned up."

ELECTRIC SHOCK

This is another of the impres-sive AC/DC websites, and can be found at www.ac-dc.net. In recent years, this one almost became the semi-official website for the band, although never publicly endorsed by them.

EMI RECORDS

The major label became involved with AC/DC when they released the *Stiff Upper Lip* album in 2000. This was a one-off deal for the UK and Europe, which hasn't been extended. EMI felt at the time that, unless they had the band on a worldwide deal, it wouldn't prove to be financially viable in the long term.

EMIR & FROZEN CAMELS

Band started by Sarajevo born Emir Bukovica in 1994, shortly after he emigrated to the States. AC/DC bassist Cliff Williams worked with the band on their 2002 debut album *San*. Williams also played with them when they toured Europe in November of the same year.

EPIC RECORDS

The label where you'll now find the AC/DC catalogue, which over the past several years has been gradually reissued with extensive re-packaging. The band has signed to the label for new product as well, including their forthcoming 15th international studio album.

EVANS/DAVE

The band's original singer. Born on July 20, 1953 in Wales, he emigrated with his family to Australia in 1956. He was one of the founding members of the band, alongside Malcolm and Angus Young, Colin Burgess (drums) and Larry Van Kriedt (bass). As is often documented, the group's early days were punctuated by regular changes to the rhythm section, but Evans lasted long enough to record one single, 'Can I Sit Next

Emir & Frozen Camels with Cliff Williams

To You, Girl', backed by 'Rockin' In The Parlour'. The former song was eventually re-vamped by the band with Bon Scott, and re-recorded for debut their album *High Voltage*.

Evans was ousted after he fell out with the Youngs. Subsequently, they've tried to suggest that the singer was attempting to steer the band in a more glam direction, something he refutes. In fact, the reality might well be that this was no more than an excuse, as both Young brothers were fond of wearing costumes onstage; in the case of Angus this was the birth of that school uniform.

During the time that Dave Evans was in the group the set list regularly included songs which would be revamped later, or end up on the scrapheap. Among these were 'Old Bay Road' (a Malcolm Young composition which quickly disappeared) ,'Sunset Strip' (which later became 'Show Business'), Fell In Love (which would become 'Love Song') and 'Midnight Rock', which again seems to have just floated away into the ether. None of these were ever recorded with Evans.

Evans himself remembers those songs he enjoyed performing with the band:

"Apart from 'Can I Sit Next To You Girl' and 'Rockin' In The Parlour' (both of the aforementioned single), I recorded 'Rock 'N' Roll Singer' and 'Soul Stripper', which were re-recorded by Bon for the first AC/DC album

(High Voltage). I also enjoyed performing 'Baby, Please Don't Go', plus several Chuck Berry numbers – that's who Angus took the duck walk from – plus a great heavy version of Elvis' 'Heartbreak Hotel', which we performed at the Sydney Opera House and received a great review."

After being fired from AC/DC, Evans joined another Aussie band, Rabbit, enjoying modest success over two albums. Since then he's released two solo records, the first being *Hell Of A Night*, showcasing a live performance paying tribute to Bon Scott (an ironic twist), that came out in 2001. *Sinner*, a studio based effort, appeared in 2006.

Says Evans of his time with 'DC:

"We were all young guys and full of testosterone and things just didn't work out personality-wise as does happen with most bands in the very beginning. A lot happened and quickly in those early days. I guess that I was out of my depth, too, with being so abruptly thrust into the very top in the music scene. I did not have the support of family as some other members had nor the counsel that Malcolm and Angus Young had from their older brother George. I was having a great time, but I probably was not as astute as I should have been either with dealing with the situation around me. Also having

a severe falling out with our manager didn't help.

"By the time I split with the band, we were onto our third bass player and drummer, and third manager and I wasn't talking to the other band members or the current manager. I wasn't happy that things had deteriorated between me and the other personnel. At the time of the split, we were riding high with our single 'Can I Sit Next To You, Girl'.

"People also ask me about the so called 'glam' period of AC/DC and we were originally a jeans and t-shirt band, until Malcolm Young told us at a rehearsal, just before our single was to be released, that Angus was going to wear a schoolboy uniform and that he was going to wear a silk jumpsuit like an airman. He wanted the rest of us to think of something just as distinctive to make us look different to all the other Australian bands."

In recent times, the Young brothers have been particularly dismissive of Evans' contribution to the band in the early days, but he holds no grudges: "I've seen what they said about me, and it is a little hurtful. But I still respect them, and what they've achieved over the years. It has been amazing. And how can anyone knock Bon? He was a great choice to replace me. I feel privileged to have got to know him."

"In the last few years I've done a couple of Bon Scott tribute concerts, which is a little weird, singing the songs of the man who took over from you in a band. But it's been great fun as well, and I've got to meet lots of amazing people. Right now, I want to concentrate on my future, rather than always looking back."

Now living in Texas, Evans would like nothing better than to get the chance to play shows in the UK, where his name is barely known. "It would be some dream come true for me to get the opportunity to come home and play dates again. But I have no complaints about my life at all. I get to do live gigs, to record and sing… that can't be a bad thing."

Away from music, Evans has also been turning up in movies, playing various roles in the likes of *Coming Of Age, Leonora* and *Come And Get It.*

"I love playing the bad guys. Walking down the street, shooting people. That's just marvellous. I could do that sort of thing all day!"

He has also been working in the theatre, expanding his horizons as a thespian.

"Do I wonder what life might have been like if I'd stayed with AC/DC? No, never. What's the point? Who knows, maybe you'd never have heard of the band."

EVANS/MARK

Evans was the bassist with AC/DC for just over two years, from 1975-1977, during which time he appeared on the albums *T.N.T.,*

High Voltage, Dirty Deeds Done Dirt Cheap and *Let There Be Rock*.

Born on March 2, 1956, Evans met AC/DC in March 1975, when they played a show at the Station Hotel in Melbourne. The night before this fateful meeting, Evans and some of his pals had been thrown out of the venue for being too rowdy and fighting. Although now barred, Evans sneaked back in, only to be thrown out again by the bouncers when he was recognised. However, Bon Scott and 'DC roadie Steve McGrath successfully intervened on his behalf and he was allowed back in.

Well, that's the way the story goes. But this is what Evans says:

"That story is not quite true. It was Station Hotel in suburban Melbourne, where I lived. And I did meet the guys when they were playing in that hotel. But the thing about fighting, that was not quite right. That was our manager's idea. But I met the guys in the Station Hotel. The link between me and the band basically was a good friend

of mine, who was roadie for them – a guy called Steve McGrath – and he mentioned that they needed a guitar player. As Malcolm was playing the bass at that stage and the band was just a four-piece. But when I got in Malcolm said that he wanted to play guitar, so I became bassist overnight. We did one audition, which was on the Sunday afternoon. Then we played next Tuesday night at the same hotel again. We

Hall's dirty deeds rock AC/DC man

By PETER HOLMES
MUSIC WRITER

A MUSICIAN who played on some of supergroup AC/DC's biggest hits has been left shattered by a snub from the US Rock'n'Roll Hall of Fame.

Bass guitarist Mark Evans learnt last November he and fellow AC/DC band members Angus Young, Malcolm Young, Brian Johnson, Cliff Williams, Phil Rudd and the late Bon Scott were to be inducted into the Hall of Fame at a March ceremony in New York's Waldorf Astoria hotel.

Rudd, the band's drummer, and Evans were believed to be the first Australian-born musicians invited to enter the hall, joining icons such as Elvis Presley, Bob Dylan and the Beatles.

"When I was told I was to be inducted I thought it was fantastic," Evans said. "I was really chuffed for the band, but also that Bon and myself were to be recognised for our contribution towards [AC/DC]. I've got to tell you, it's a big deal because a lot of the people in the hall of fame are my heroes."

Evans's name was posted on the official hall of fame website (www.rockhall.com) in November and subsequently published in news reports around the world.

His joy was brief. In mid-December his manager Roly McAdam wrote to the Hall of Fame Foundation - a private company steered by American lawyer Suzan Evans and *Rolling Stone* magazine founder Jann Wenner - seeking ticketing and travelling advice. Within days, McAdam claimed, he received a phone call from a Hall of Fame executive stating Evans's inclusion had been a mistake. His name was quietly removed from the website without explanation and no correction was sent to media.

Mr McAdam again wrote to the Hall of Fame seeking clarification. Suzan Evans wrote back: "In the case of AC/DC, we have followed our normal procedures to determine which members are appropriate for induction based on all available information, which was carefully reviewed by our historians, who have determined Mark Evans does not meet our criteria."

as an inductee, and that we are trying to lobby to have him included."

A vintage guitar salesman by day who plays in a blues duo with Dave Tice by night, Evans joined AC/DC in 1975 as a 19-year-old. He played bass on three albums and was sacked in 1977, shortly after AC/DC had been thrown off a tour with Ozzy Osbourne's Black Sabbath. *Rock Australia* magazine reported: "Mark Evans, the quiet, well-behaved member of AC/DC, has left the group." Evans settled a financial claim with AC/DC in the 1980s.

"My beef, and my only beef, is with the Hall of Fame," he said.

In an emailed response to *The Sun-Herald*, Suzan Evans said: "Please be advised that our November announcement was made for the purpose of announcing that the band AC/DC was being inducted. We subsequently determined which members of the band to include during our customary review process. Our committee determined that Mark Evans was not appropriate for induction based on our criteria."

Singers and musicians are eligible for induction into the US Rock'n'Roll Hall of Fame 25 years after their first recording. Other 2003 inductees include the Clash, the Police, Elvis

AC/DC CLASSICS

■ These are some of the hit songs on which Mark Evans played:

Dirty Deeds Done Dirt Cheap, Let There Be Rock, Jailbreak, High Voltage, Whole Lotta Rosie, Can I Sit Next To You Girl, T.N.T, It's A Long Way To The Top (If You Wanna Rock'n'Roll).

ROCK AND ROLL DAMNATION: Mark Evans on bass guitar with Bon Scott during left, at his Lilyfield home last week.

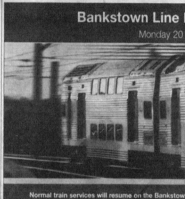

Bankstown Line
Monday 20

Normal train services will resume on the Bankstow
20 January. CityRail would like to thank our custom
community for your cooperation during this major

---

never used to rehearse a much. The audition I did, that was the only rehearsal. That was about it, we started gigging around Melbourne."

Two weeks later, Evans was in the band, playing one of his shows at… yep, the Station Hotel.

Evans' tenure in the group came to juddering halt after the recording of *Let There Be Rock* in 1977.

By this time, he had apparently fallen out with Angus Young, and was fired. Here's his memory of the event:

"It was in Germany, we were going to Helsinki. And we were

planning to fly to America after Helsinki. There was a problem with record company in America at that stage, they had chosen not to release Dirty Deeds Done Dirt Cheap. Americans knocked us back as we were really eager to go over and promote the album. So, the US tour at that stage was cancelled. We were in Germany with Black Sabbath. We went back to London and we had a month off before Helsinki. That's when the whole scenario happened, when I split from the band. I think the main reservation the Americans had was something to do with Bon. I didn't get the full picture because the band was Malcolm's and not much info came to me. I think that the Americans wanted to change the singer, which seems unbelievable now."

Wasting little time, he formed Contraband with drummer Peter McFarlane and vocalist Owen Orford, releasing three albums. In 1983 he joined an Aussie band called Heaven, with strong AC/DC connections. Not only were they managed by Michael Browning, with whom he'd worked during his time in 'DC, but their singer was Allan Fryer, briefly considered as a replacement for Bon Scott when he died in 1980. Evans played rhythm guitar for Heaven replacing Mick Cocks.

If Evans thought that the passage of time had smoothed out his relationship with the Youngs

he was rudely awakened to reality in 2003. That year AC/DC were inducted into the Rock 'N' Roll Hall Of Fame, and Evans, together with Bon Scott, were the only two former members of the band on the list of inductees, along with the current incarnation. However, without any explanation Evans had his invitation rescinded. It was a massive, humiliating slap in the face for him.

Talking at the time about the situation, the bassist told Australia's Undercover News:

"I am absolutely thrilled for the band to finally make it into the Hall of Fame. It is something the band really deserves. I was really quite chuffed when I heard.

"I knew from about the middle of last year that this was coming, and I was assuming that it would be the current line-up and Bon. Then word started coming back to me that I was going to be nominated also. I thought that was good and I'd wait and see how it all comes out.

"I was really, really happy about the whole thing. To having that turn around has become a bigger surprise than making it in. I was very disappointed about it. I went through a situation where people would come up and congratulate me and I had to bite my tongue, because at that stage I knew the whole thing had been retracted. As much as I am fairly immune

to embarrassment, I have been put in a very uncomfortable situation.

"When you consider the last 20 years, what immediately comes to mind... 'Thunderstruck' maybe? 'Who Made Who'? At the end of the day, had they come around and said the current line-up of the band as well as Bon would be inducted, I would have just gone, 'Oh well, missed out'. I would have taken it on the chin. That's just part of life. But to be told you are inducted and have it splashed all over the world and then have it retracted, that to me is unacceptable.

"I don't have any real regrets. What I am now with my family, and what I am doing musically since I left the band, I have had a very good and full life. I think if I was one of those unfortunate beings who didn't want to get on with things and

kept on looking back I think I'd have a problem. I am very, very satisfied with what I am doing and who I am. My regrets are probably not being able to play with the band. I loved playing with that band and I do regret losing a couple of friendships out of it. Bon is exclusive of this because that was out of anyone's control. I had a very good friendship with both Phil Rudd and Malcolm Young, and unfortunately those friendships have gone by the board now. We had a lot of great times, did some great things, but I had a couple of great friendships there. My one regret is losing those friendships."

Today, Evans works with one Dave Tice, formerly the singer with a band called Buffalo, in The Dave Tice Band, and also with The Party Boys.

EVIL WALKS

The sixth track from the band's 1981 album *For Those About To Rock (We Salute You)*. This was written by Young, Young and Johnson. The song can be interpreted in a supernatural way, or else as a warning concerning the negative forces in the world. However, lines like 'There's bad poison runnin' thru your veins' suggest it might be about addictions.

FAIRBAIRN/BRUCE

Canadian producer who worked with AC/DC on their 1990 album *The Razors Edge* and 1991's *Live*. Fairbairn first made his name by working with fellow Maple Leafers Prism and Loverboy, leading both to major success. In 1980 he won a prestigious Juno award (the Canadian equivalent of the Grammy and the Brits) for the Prism album *Young & Restless*. The same year, Loverboy's self-titled debut went multi-platinum in Canada and, at the age of 30, Fairbairn stared to get noticed on the international stage.

It was 1983's *The Revolution By Night* album for Blue Oyster Cult and *The Blitz* recorded with Krokus the next year that gave him a real taste of major action, something that was to become even more accentuated when he worked with Bon Jovi on the landmark *Slippery When Wet* record in 1987, and then with Aerosmith's *Permanent Vacation* the same year. Following this double with further success on *New Jersey* (Bon Jovi – 1988) and *Pump* (Aerosmith – 1989),

Fairbairn then took on the task of working with AC/DC.

Over the next several years, he produced INXS, Aerosmith (for a third time, on *Get A Grip*), Scorpions and Van Halen. However, on May 17, 1999, he was found dead by Yes singer Jon Anderson at his house in Vancouver; Fairbairn was working on the band's new album, *The Ladder* at the time.

Apart from his own production triumphs, Fairbairn nurtured protégé Bob Rock, and also founded Little Mountain Studios in Vancouver. Unlike many celebrity producers of the time, he was low-key and preferred to enhance what a band already had, rather than change them to suit his own character.

Recalling their relationship with Fairbairn, Malcolm Young said:

"When we first walked into that studio, he said, 'I am glad to have the REAL band here because we have tried for so many times with many other bands to get your sound. It has been fucking hard!' He was just so amazed at the way we worked and how we

just plugged in and played. The reason why I think it worked for us and Bruce was that he was a fan. He really liked the band and wanted the chance to work with us, and watch the magic happen in the studio."

In 2000, Fairbairn was inducted into the Canadian Music Hall Of Fame. The Toronto Sun newspaper summed up his career thus, in a piece run prior to the awards:

"Over his 20-year-plus career, Vancouver producer Bruce Fairbairn worked with some of the biggest bands in rock: Aerosmith, Bon Jovi, AC/DC, INXS, KISS, Van Halen, The Cranberries and Yes, along with Canadian acts Loverboy, Prism and Honeymoon Suite.

"That musical legacy has led to Fairbairn's posthumous induction into the Canadian Music Hall Of Fame.

"Fairbairn, who learned to play the trumpet at age five and began his producing duties with '70s band Prism, died suddenly in his sleep last May, at the age of 49 while producing the latest Yes album, *The Ladder.*

"'It's very unusual that we could rally round after that event and say, let's get this album finished and dedicate it to Bruce, because he'd given us so much, you know?' said Yes singer Jon Anderson.

"'He was such a beautiful guy,' continued Anderson, who actually discovered Fairbairn's body

The Canadian Music
Hall of Fame

Bruce Fairbairn never liked to blow his own horn, even when he was blowing his own horn.

A classically trained trumpet Player who loved the late '60s brassy pop of Blood, Sweat & Tears and Chicago, the Vancouver native rarely turned down the invitation to jam. But it was his sort-spoken, polite and unobtrusive mannerisms in the studio that brought Bruce Fairbairn fame, fortune and respect, producing blockbuster albums for Loverboy, Aerosmith, Bon Jovi, and Cranberries that literally rocketed their careers to new stratospheres. Unlike some overseers who trumpet their contributions, Fairbairn instead let his reputation speak volumes: Bon Jovi's Slippery When Wet, 20 million copies sold; the Aerosmith trilogy of Permanent Vacation, Pump and Get A Grip, along with the greatest hits compilation Big Ones, 30 million sold; the library of Loverboy, Get Lucky, Keep It Up, Lovin' Every Minute Of It, and Wildside, 15 million sold.

at the latter's Vancouver home. 'It's hard to explain how we felt about him. We had great respect for him.'

"The Hall Of Fame award will actually be presented to Fairbairn's wife, Julie Glover, and their three sons, Scott, 21, Kevin, 18, and Brent, 14, by the members of Loverboy about halfway through the two-hour Juno broadcast.

"The presentation will be preceded by a three-minute taped tribute to Fairbairn, which will include appearances by Aerosmith's Steven Tyler and Jon Bon Jovi.

"Coincidentally, members of AC/DC – lead and rhythm guitarists Angus and Malcolm Young, along with drummer Phil Rudd – arrive in Toronto over the weekend to promote their latest album, *Stiff Upper Lip.*

"'People don't know the names of producers,' says Michelle Parise, the associate producer of the Hall Of Fame tribute. 'And Bruce Fairbairn's responsible for (Bon Jovi's) *Slippery When Wet,* which sold 13 million copies worldwide. It was the biggest selling album of 1986, so he had a pretty big impact.'

"He was also responsible for Aerosmith's comeback album, 1987's *Permanent Vacation,* which produced their first hit in a decade, *Angel.*

"Other notable albums were 1997's *Elegantly Wasted,* the last album by INXS before singer Michael Hutchence committed suicide, and 1998's *Psycho Circus* from KISS.

"'He used to come and see Yes play because he did like the band, which helps a heck of a lot,' said Anderson. 'The guy who's going to produce you understands who you are and what you're trying to achieve musically.'"

FAMILY JEWELS

This double DVD was released in 2005. One disc showcases film from the Bon Scott era, while the other features Brian Johnson. The rarely seen Scott clips include TV appearances on Australian programme *Countdown* and *The Midnight Special,* live footage from the Glasgow Apollo (1978), film of the band in action during the BBC TV show *Rock Goes To College* (1978) and an appearance on Spain's TVE1 programme *Aplauso* on February 9, 1980, Scott's final television performance.

Johnson's disc features a combination of promo clips and live footage spanning his entire time with the band, to that point.

It's an impressive collection and was deservedly voted the DVD Of The Year Award by UK magazine *Classic Rock* in 2005.

The full track listing is:
Disc One – *Baby Please Don't Go* (live, April 1975)/*Show Business* (live, June 1975)/*High Voltage* (promo clip, June 1975)/*It's A Long Way To The Top (If You Wanna Rock 'N' Roll)* (promo clip, February 1976)/*TNT* (live, 1976)/*Jailbreak* (promo clip, 1976)/*Dirty Deeds Done Dirt Cheap* (live, December 1976)/*Dog Eat Dog* (promo clip, 1977)/*Let There Be Rock* (promo clip, 1977)/*Rock N Roll Damnation* (promo clip, 1978)/*Sin City* (from The

Midnight Special, September 1978)/*Riff Raff* (live from Glasgow, April 1978)/*Fling Thing/Rocker* (live from Glasgow, April 1978)/*Whole Lotta Rosie* (Live from BBC show Rock Goes To College, October 1978)/ *Shot Down In Flames* (promo clip, July 1979)/*Walk All Over You* (promo clip, July 1979)/*Touch Too Much* (promo clip July 1979)/*If You Want Blood* (promo clip, July 1979)/ *Girls Got Rhythm* (live from Aplauso TV Show, February 1980)/*Highway To Hell* (live from Aplauso TV Show, February 1980)

Disc Two - *Hells Bells* (promo clip, 1980)/*Back In Black*(promo clip, 1980)/*What Do You Do For Money Honey* (promo clip, 1980)/*Rock And Roll Ain't Noise Pollution* (promo clip, 1980)/ *Let's Get it Up* (live promo clip, 1981)/*For Those About To Rock* (live promo clip, 1983)/*Flick Of The Switch* (promo clip, 1984)/ *Nervous Shakedown* (promo clip, 1984)/*Fly On The Wall* (promo clip, 1985)/*Danger* (promo clip, 1985)/*Sink The Pink* (promo clip, 1985)/*Stand Up* (promo clip, 1985)/*Shake Your Foundations* (promo clip, 1985)/*Who Made Who* (promo clip, 1986)/*You Shook Me All Night Long* (promo clip, 1985)/*Heatseeker* (promo clip, 1988)/*That's The Way I Wanna Rock & Roll* (promo clip, 1988)/ *Thunderstruck* (promo clip, 1990)/*Moneytalks* (promo clip, 1990)/*Are You Ready* (promo clip, 1991)

FANG

The name of one of Bon Scott's pre-AC/DC bands who he joined in 1970, when they were called Fraternity. The Adelaide rockers released two albums under this name – *Livestock* and *Flaming Galah* – before becoming Fang in 1971. Over the next two years, they toured in Australia, getting big breaks supporting both Status Quo and Geordie – the latter fronted by none other than Brian Johnson. In 1973, the band went on hiatus, at which point Scott left, to join the Mount Lofty Rangers, who also included other former members of Fraternity.

FELL IN LOVE

A song written by AC/DC rhythm guitarist Malcolm Young and original singer Dave Evans that was never recorded by the band, but eventually evolved into 'Love Song', with lyrics added by Bon Scott, and which features on the Australian version of *High Voltage*.

FIRE YOUR GUNS

The short, snappy second track from the 1990 album *The Razors*

Edge. Written by the Young brothers, the sexual connotations are obvious in lyrics like: 'Fire, when she's going down/ fire, then she make you drown/Fire, then she blow you round'.

FIRST BLOOD

Track three from 1985's *Fly On The Wall* album. This was written by the Young brothers with Brian Johnson. It does contain some distinctly unwieldy lines such as 'Some like it hot/Some like it quite not so hot'. But then, this band has never been that bothered by the notion of etymological correctness.

FLAKE

Sydney band, who featured bassist Rob Bailey and drummer Peter Clack, both of whom were briefly with AC/DC in their formative stages. Flake's biggest hit was a cover of Bob Dylan's 'This Wheel's On Fire'.

Flake

FLASH AND THE PAN

Flash And The Pan were a new-wave style band formed by AC/DC producers George Young and Harry Vanda (above) in 1976. The pair had been guitarists and main songwriters for Australia's best-known '60s band The Easybeats, as well as in-house producers for Albert Productions, and Flash And The Pan was merely a studio project for the pair.

Three years after the band formed, their debut single, 'Hey St. Peter' was something of a novelty hit for the pair, reaching number 76 in the US charts. The duo's second single 'And The Band Played On (Down Among The Dead Men)' fared even better scoring at home in Australia and reaching number 54 in the UK charts. Both tracks can be found on the band's 1979 debut album *Flash And The Pan*, released by Epic Records.

The major highlight in Flash And The Pan's career, however, was the hit 'Waiting For A Train' which reached number seven in the UK in 1983 and can be found on their *Headlines* record, also on Epic.

An album entitled *Burning Up The Night* appeared in 1993, but since then there has been no new material from the group. AC/DC fans should be warned that Flash And The Pan's music, although quirky and original, sounds nothing at all like AC/DC in any way, and only the most open minded should, if they feel so inclined, investigate.

FLICK OF THE SWITCH

Album released in 1983 by AC/DC, this marked a departure from producer 'Mutt' Lange after three successive records. The band had, of course, by now acquired a decade of studio experience. However, the decision not to work with Lange again seems to have been forced on them, because of his unavailability.

Amusingly, American magazines ran a story at the time that Lange was still being consulted. According to these reports, every night 'DC would courier tapes to the producer, who would then listen to them and make comments and suggestions, which would then be followed. This was, naturally, utter tosh. The band were producing themselves, and never even thought about working with Lange in such a way.

It's also hard to know exactly where their erstwhile producer would have been able to exert any influence. AC/DC had always been self-sufficient, and once

they had decided it was time to go it alone, it's doubtful that anyone could have had a big impact from the outside.

There have been those who criticised *Flick Of The Switch* for lacking the strength in depth song-wise of its three predecessors. And, while it may be true that Lange could have finessed certain elements of the songs, nonetheless there's sufficient good material here to offset any negatives.

Listen to the title track, or 'Bedlam In Belgium'. Or 'Nervous Shakedown'. Or 'This House Is On Fire'. Or 'Rising Power'. These are impressive, and wouldn't have been out of place on what had gone before. Here were AC/DC, or particularly the combination of Angus and Malcolm Young plus Brian Johnson, still able to write strong songs, proving once more that, while it may seem like the easiest thing in the world to mimic the band, nobody did this stuff as well as the originals.

In many ways, the production was a return to the basics of the 1970s and the Vanda/Young era. Left to their own devices, the band didn't embrace technology, but were determined to get an energetic live sound – it worked.

Halfway through the recording process for the album, Phil Rudd left to be replaced by Simon Wright, who'd featured in NWOBHM act AIIZ. But as Rudd had already laid down all his parts, Wright doesn't appear

on the record at all, although he features in the videos for 'Flick Of The Switch', 'Nervous Shakedown' and 'Guns For Hire'.

Prior to Wright's arrival, B.J. Wilson, the original drummer with Procol Harum, had been drafted in to help the band out, although none of the material Wilson actually drummed on made it onto the final album.

Interestingly, this was the first record in the Johnson era to feature a member of the band on the front cover. A drawing of Angus reaching for a giant switch almost seems a little ghostly, being drawn in a basic pencil format. But it added to the feel of the band returning to their roots.

Released in August 1983, the record was something of a commercial disappointment at the time, only reaching number four in the UK charts and number 15 in America. However, time has suggested this is a better album than it was deemed on its release.

The full track listing is: *Rising Power/This House Is On Fire/ Flick Of The Switch/Nervous Shakedown/Landslide/Guns For Hire/Deep In The Hole/ Bedlam In Belgium/Badlands/ Brain Shake*

FLICK OF THE SWITCH (Song)

Title track of the band's 1983 album and was written by Young, Young & Johnson. It was released as a single in Australia and America, and the video for it features footage of Simon Wright on drums, even though it was his predecessor, Phil Rudd, who's on the actual track. As per usual, there's a connection between sexual highs and sheer, undiluted power in the lyrics: 'With a flick of the switch she'll blow you sky high'.

FLINC THINC

Based on the traditional Scottish song 'The Bonnie Banks O' Loch Lomond', this is one of those rare 'DC tracks that only turned up as the B-aide to *Jailbreak*, when this was released as a single. It was recorded during the sessions for the album *Dirty Deeds Done Dirt Cheap.*

Two interesting points: it was part of the band's set in 1978, when they played the Glasgow Apollo, and the *If You Want Blood...You've Got It* live album was recorded, but the song was omitted from the final running order. And, after Scott's death, the track was re-titled *Bonny* in his honour.

FLY ON THE WALL

The band's 1985 album, following on from *Flick Of The Switch*, although the *'74 Jailbreak* record did come out between these two.

Again, as on *Flick...*, the group decided to produce themselves, although with less convincing results than was the case in 1983.

Many regard this album, recorded at Mountain Studios in Montreux, as the band's nadir, a true low-point in their career – possibly the lowest. And while it is fair to admit that *Fly On The Wall* pales in comparison with much that had gone before, nonetheless for a minority it does possess a certain ham-fisted charm. But 'Shake Your Foundations', 'Sink The Pink', 'Danger' and 'Playing With Girls' have an adolescent awkwardness which is quite surprising given the expertise the band had acquired at innuendo and double entendres. Exactly why they decided to be more overt in their lyrical approach this time is a little difficult to explain.

The very cartoonish album cover perhaps gives away the fact that the group were in something of a creative dip. While the energy is still present, what they don't have is that cutting edge which had made them so successful in the first place. There is little doubt that 'DC desperately needed to find a fresh spirit to drive themselves forward. They seemed so determined to remain basic and straightforward that the Young brothers especially might have lost sight of the band's positives.

Still, 'Sink The Pink' and 'Shake Your Foundations' were both included on the soundtrack for the movie *Maximum Overdrive*,

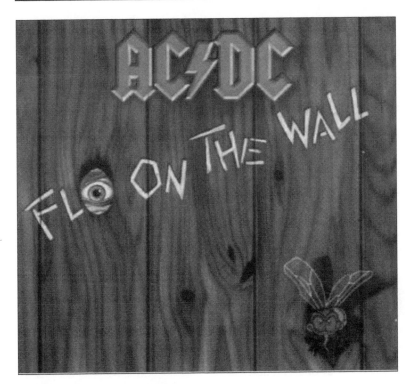

while a live video was released later that year, showcasing five songs performed at a small New York location. These were 'Fly On The Wall', 'Shake Your Foundations', 'Sink The Pink', 'Stand Up' and 'Danger'.

Just how far the band had slipped may be gauged by the fact that the album, put out in June 1985, only reached number 32 in America and number seven in the UK – disappointing indeed.

The full track listing is: *Fly On The Wall/Shake Your Foundations/First Blood/Danger/Sink The Pink/Playing With Girls/Stand Up/Hell Or High Water/Back In Business/Send For The Man*

FLY ON THE WALL
(Song)

The title track of the band's 1985 album. Written by Angus Young, Malcolm Young and Brian Johnson, it's regarded as one of the few high spots on what was dismissed by most AC/DC fans as a massively disappointing record. It has an ominous, quite heavy timbre that's almost dark in atmosphere.

FLY ON THE WALL
(Video)

Released in 1985, this is a conceptual video featuring the band playing five songs from the album of the same title – 'Fly On The Wall', 'Danger', 'Sink The Pink', 'Stand Up' and 'Shake Your Foundations' – in a Brooklyn Bar named The Crystal Ballroom, while various shady and odd characters interact with an animated fly that's reminiscent of the creature on the record sleeve. The list of characters in question includes photographer Super Snoop, the MC Decadent Dan, a mystery woman in pink, playing pool, and an unimpressed barman.

The video climaxes with the bar collapsing leaving 'DC to perform 'Shake Your Foundations' against a backdrop of the World Trade Center, before the song 'Playing With Girls' is played out over the final credits. The video was directed by long-time AC/DC associate David Mallet, but it must be said, much like the album it's named after, the inherent humour and approach on offer tends to miss the point.

The video in its entirety turned up on the 2005 double disc DVD *Plug Me In.*

FOREIGNER US AC/DC
DJ Copy

A promotional album given away by Atlantic Records in Japan to radio DJs for AC/DC's second Japanese tour in 1982. Side one features the AOR band Foreigner whilst AC/DC occupy the other. The disc has a colour cover with pictures of AC/DC and their album sleeves. Very rare.

AC/DC tracklisting: *Back In Black* (live)/*Let's Get It Up*/*For Those About To Rock (We Salute You)*/*Hells Bells*/*Inject The Venom*/*Whole Lotta Rosie* (live)

FOREST NATIONAL

If anyone ever asks you to name the only time that the band have ever allowed a musician who wasn't a member to get up and jam with them, then this is the answer. It happened at the above venue on January 25, 1981, on the last night of their *Back In Black* European tour. It was in Brussels and the musician so honoured was... Phil Carson, an executive at their label, Atlantic. The song he performed with them was 'Lucille', the Little Richard classic.

AC/DC have never been know for opening themselves up to play with others, so this was a rare moment. In fact, unique.

FOR THOSE ABOUT TO ROCK (WE SALUTE YOU)

How do you follow the biggest album of your career, a record so successful it eclipses almost everything you've previously done? That was the challenge facing AC/DC after *Back In Black*. Typically, they didn't even try. What had been achieved on *Back In Black*, with its vast sales, was not allowed to put pressure on the band. Sure, they elected once again to work with producer 'Mutt' Lange, for the third time in a row, but on this occasion they recorded in France (at a rehearsal space in Paris).

What strikes immediately about *For Those About To Rock* is that it doesn't have the darkness and intensity of its predecessor. Deliberately, the band chose to go for a slightly lighter groove, albeit one in keeping with the style they'd landed before. Johnson had slotted right in, and it was as if he'd been the band's vocalist for a lot longer than a year.

Lange again kept the perfect union of technology and feel, never allowing his own studio mastery to offset the band's natural rhythms, but enhancing what was clearly there. Unlike most bands he's worked with, the producer has no overt influence on the songwriting. Whatever influence he exerted was kept very much behind the proverbial closed doors.

Perhaps it's only fair to point out that *For Those About To Rock* doesn't have quite the same astonishing consistency of *Back In Black*. At its best, however, as on the title track, 'Evil Walks', 'Let's Get It Up' and 'Night Of The Long Knives', this is as good as any-

thing 'DC have done since Back In Black – probably better. But there are also some dips. 'Snowballed' and 'Breaking The Rules' are not triumphs. However, the overall feel and style of the album is one that never tried to be *Back In Black 2*, but set out to explore the limits of the band's philosophy, musically and lyrically. A pattern and purpose was established here that one could say marks out what would happen next.

If *Back In Black* is a one-off, then *For Those About To Rock* is really the beginning of a new era. The album is still their only number one record in America, and is credited with opening the doors for so many other hard rock acts to get their chance in the States. Incidentally, one interesting aside is that early copies of the Spanish pressings of the album saw the colours of the sleeve reversed, with a gold cannon and a black background.

The full track listing is: *For Those About To Rock (We Salute You)/Put The Finger On You/Let's Get It Up/Inject The Venom/Snowballed/Evil Walks/ C.O.D./Breaking The Rules/ Night Of The Long Knives/ Spellbound*

FOR THOSE ABOUT TO ROCK (WE SALUTE YOU)
(Song)

The title track of the band's 1981 album, and one of their classic moments. Written by the Young brothers and Brian Johnson, it has become a highlight of the band's live performance, accompanied by cannon fire onstage at the end of their set. The title was inspired by a book Angus came across called *For Those About To Die, We Salute You*, which deals with Roman gladiators, who, before going into the arena, would hail Caesar with the words 'We who are about to die, salute you'.

The song is very much a rallying cry to fans and bands alike, united by the love of rock.

This is also the title of a video (*For Those About To Rock: Monsters In Moscow*), filmed during an open air show in Moscow in September 1991. It features performances from AC/DC, Metallica, Pantera and the Black Crowes, in front of 500,000 fans.

FRASER, MIKE

A Canadian producer/engineer, Fraser worked on the first AC/DC album since 2000's Stiff Upper Lip, which was released in 2008. He began his career working with Bruce Fairbairn at Little Mountain Studios in Vancouver, and had previously worked on no less than three 'DC albums, namely *The Razors Edge, Ballbreaker* and *Stiff Upper Lip.* Away from this band, Fraser has also collaborated either as producer or

engineer with a whole host of top names, including Metallica, Aerosmith, Guns n' Roses, Led Zeppelin, Loverboy and Dio.

FRATERNITY

One of the groups with whom Bon Scott performed prior to joining AC/DC. He hooked up with the Adelaide band in 1970, becoming their first vocalist. With Scott they released the albums *Livestock* (1971) and *Flaming Galah* (1972). However, after a failed attempt to make it in the UK, Fraternity changed their name to Fang, with little impact. The band underwent something of a hiatus in 1973, at which point Scott got the call from 'DC. When they re-grouped in 1974, they hired one Jimmy Barnes as their new singer. He would go on to find fame with Cold Chisel.

Talking of the mad early days in the band, keyboard player John Bisset has related: "Initially in Sydney, Bruce (How, bassist), Mick (Jurd, guitarist), Tony (Buetell, drummer) and Bon lived a short distance from my flat, which was across the road from Centennial Park. They rented a two-storey terraced house in Jersey Road. There was a lot of booze, marijuana and acid and a lot of socialising with other musicians. In Sydney, John Robinson (Black Feather guitarist) was a regular visitor and other characters like Leo De Castro

(New Zealand vocalist). Bon was a great one for dispelling myths about acid culture, like the vegetarianism that many hippies embraced. I remember him wandering around gleefully chomping on a large leg of roast beef at one very acid-soaked party in Jersey Road.

"I was primarily a boozer and womaniser and had a torrid relationship with my wife. My wife Cheryl and I were both incredibly suspicious and jealous of each other (with good reason) so our son grew up in a war zone. Bon was one of the few people who brought cheer into our lives and was totally non-judgmental of our lack of maturity. He always owned a motorbike and used to visit and take our son for rides. He would also spend time with our son and entertain him with somersaults and other athletic feats on the back lawn.

"Adelaide millionaire Hamish Henry took over management of Fraternity soon after Bon joined. We moved to Adelaide and most of the band took up residence in a large property in the Adelaide Hills. Hamish let Cheryl and I rent a beautiful flat above his art gallery in North Adelaide. By this time John Freeman from Adelaide had taken over on drums and John Eyers had joined on harmonica. Sam See was the last to join on guitar and keyboards – sometime after we won the Australian 'Battle of the Sounds' in 1971.

"New Fraternity members from Bon onwards were basically musicians with personalities that made them naturals for the Fraternity culture. They were like family. We just liked them and got on really well with them. They also shared our taste for booze, marijuana and acid. There was an amazingly tolerant spirit in the band. I was easily the most erratic personality, prone to severe mood swings and extreme, blackout drunkenness. Yet I was never once lectured or censured by the band. That was just 'JB' (as I was called). Bon used to drink as much or more than me but he didn't undergo the extreme personality change that I did. I was a Jekyll and Hyde but Bon was always Bon – straight Bon, stoned Bon, tripping Bon, legless drunk Bon.

"Later on (towards the end of 1971, early 1972) Bruce and Bon moved into a large house in a more working class suburb of Adelaide with me and Cheryl and my son Brent (and Clutch the dog, of course – he had the honour of getting his photo on the back cover of the Flaming Galah album). Bon was really good with Brent and continued to take him for rides on his trail bike and put up with Brent (who was four at the time) playing pranks on him. Brent's favourite prank was to adjust the temperature of the water when Bon was in the shower, by turning the taps in the laundry off and on.

"We did an amazing tour of the smaller towns around South Australia. On arriving in a new town we would descend upon the local pub. The locals would initially make fun of our appearance with comments like 'long-haired poofters (queers)' or 'drug-crazed hippies', but as the alcohol flowed and we proved our skill on the pool table, they would befriend us.

On our German tour we had to add table football to our skills but otherwise things were pretty similar to Australia."

FREMANTLE CEMETERY

South of Perth, this is where Bon Scott's ashes are interred. Apparently the most visited gravesite in Australia, it was deemed important enough to be declared a classified heritage spot by the National Trust of Australia. Fans come from all over the world, on pilgrimages to "Have a beer with Bon". The position, in the lower left hand corner of the cemetery, is marked by a commemorative stone bench from Bon's parents, Isa and Chick. A new plaque was erected, but this was stolen on July 9, 2006, which would have been the singer's 60th birthday.

More recently, the actor Heath Ledger was buried here.

FREMANTLE SCOTS PIPE BAND

Bon Scott briefly joined this band as a youngster, and it was during his tenure with the Pipe Band that he learned to play drums.

FRYER/ALLAN

Aussie singer with 1980s band Heaven, Fryer was rumoured to be

on the short list to replace Bon Scott in 1980. A few years later, the man himself confirmed this, stating:

"Yes, I was put forward for the job, and it might have been Heaven's manager, Michael Browning, who suggested me. He had managed AC/DC and had an in with them. Anyway, I gather I was considered, but rejected, because I was too much like Bon, as a singer and personality-wise."

Fryer has made little impact in subsequent years, and now lives in America, where various incarnations of Heaven have been formed and failed. Some still believe he was Scott's natural successor in 'DC.

FUROR, THE

The third track from the 1995 album *Ballbreaker*. Written by the Young brothers, the lyrics have the feel of the open road, the freedom of the outlaw and the outcast: 'Find a mine/Gonna build me a new place/No knockin' door to door'.

GEORDIE

Brian Johnson's band prior to joining AC/DC, and something of a success in their own right. A glam-style band from, with the exception of Johnson, Newcastle – hence the name – they also included Vic Malcolm (guitar/ vocals), Tom Hill (bass) and Brian Gibson (drums).

The group actually started out in 1971 under the name of USA, before the name change to the more geographically appropriate Geordie a year later. The glam, stomp-a-long style fitted the times perfectly, and they quickly built up a loyal live following. Debut single 'Don't Do That'

was released in 1972, and got to Number 32 in the charts, leading to a deal with EMI.

Their first album, *Hope You Like It*, was released in 1973 – the same year that 'DC were formed and gave them the massive hit 'All Because Of You', which got to number six. In Europe, the band also enjoyed success with 'Ain't It Just like a Woman'.

Later in the same year, the singles 'Can You Do It' and 'Electric Lady' kept the momentum going. In 1974, Geordie issued the album 'Don't Be Fooled By The Name', followed two years later by 'Save The World'. However, the rise of punk hit the foursome hard, and although they still attracted good live crowds, they were now struggling to make ends meets. So much so that Johnson was forced to do voiceovers for a vacuum cleaner TV commercial! A couple of solo albums kept the singer's name in the frame, but he seemed to be drifting – until the call came from 'DC.

Not too surprisingly, in the wake of *Back In Black*'s mega success, Geordie re-formed without Johnson, but with little impact. The Red Bus label released a 1980 compilation entitled *Geordie Featuring Brian Johnson*, the band's logo in a similar typeface to that used by AC/DC for their famous thunderflash logo. A name change to Powerhouse made little difference and, after issuing an eponymous album on the Ambush label in 1986, they split up. They did re-unite with Johnson in 2001, during downtime for AC/DC, but this hasn't led to anything further.

At the time, bassist Dave Robson (who'd joined in 1977) remarked: "We've always kept in touch with Brian and when we all met up at a restaurant about two years ago, he said he'd really love to get the old band back together. We didn't really take it seriously at the time but he mentioned it again, and this year we started chatting about it in earnest and decided to do it.

"Brian really loved the band; when he left to go to ACDC he had tears in his eyes. He just wants to get back to his roots and give something back to the area, so we're planning on playing workingmen's clubs and pubs, assuming anyone books us.

"What's important is that we're going back to the venues where

we used to play and where
people came to support us.

*"The three of us still living on
Tyneside recently went back
into the studio to see if we could
still do it. After all, we hadn't
played together in 20 years. We
set up, had a cup of tea and then
just cranked it up. It was really
good – it was as if the 20 years
had just blown away. I'm really
excited about it and if it goes
well we may finish off the tour
in somewhere bigger."*

GET IT HOT

Track seven from the *Highway To Hell* album, this one
was written by Young, Young
& Scott. It has a good-time rock
'n' roll party theme and actually
name checks Barry Manilow
in the lyrics: Nobody's playin'
Manilow/Nobody's playin' soul/
An' no one's playin' hard-to-get/
Just a good ol' rock 'n' roll'. It's
not known what Manilow himself thought of this mention, nor
whether he ever thought about a
lyrical retaliation.

GET YOUR JUMBO JET OFF MY AIRPORT

Taking its title from a line in
the song 'Ain't No Fun (Waiting Round To Be A Millionaire)'
from *Dirty Deeds Done Dirt
Cheap*, this book, penned by one-
time *Kerrang!* and *RAW* magazine journalist Howard Johnson,
takes a very different tack to most
AC/DC books on the market, this
fine tome aside of course, which

tend to concentrate on the history of the band.

The clue is in the book's subtitle 'Random Notes For AC/DC Obsessives'. Johnson has interviewed a plethora of AC/DC fans; from one who owns some 500 AC/DC bootlegs, to those who work in the music industry, some of whom have been directly involved in the band's story themselves. These include an interview with original singer Dave Evans as well as entries from various AC/DC webmasters and fanzine editors, as well as a look at the band's recording of the 1996 VH1 session.

The end result is a curious but often amusing collection of anecdotes and tales about AC/DC and conveys the passion that the band seems to be able to instil in such a wide range of people. Not exactly essential AC/DC reading, but entertaining none the less.

GIMME A BULLET

A track from the *Powerage* album, this was recorded at Albert Studios in Sydney and written by the Young brothers with Bon Scott. It deals with the break-up of a relationship, with the protagonist admitting that neither drink nor drugs were going to help. There's no guitar solo in this song – a rarity for the band – and the US version actually lasts 20 seconds longer than the European one.

GIRLS GOT RHYTHM

The second track from *Highway To Hell* and written by the Young brothers and Bon Scott. This is typical of the clever way that Scott could play with words to create an experience: 'She's enough to start a landslide/Just a walkin' down the street'. It was released as a single in 1979 with 'T.N.T' on the B-side, and was part of a four track EP the same year, also featuring 'If You Want Blood (You've Got It)', plus live versions of 'Hell Ain't A Bad Place To Be' and 'Rock And Roll Damnation'.

GIVE IT UP

Twelfth and final track from the 2000 album *Stiff Upper Lip*. It was written by Angus and Malcolm Young and lyrically, it's a flexing of muscles. The king of the streets is strutting his stuff, and you'd better move out of his way: 'So if you can't stand the distance/You better disappear/Do I make myself clear?'

GIVEN THE DOG A BONE

Track four from the 1980 album *Back In Black*, written by the Youngs and Brian Johnson. Feminists didn't exactly react happily to lines like: 'She take you down easy/Going down to her knees/ Going down to the devil/Down down to ninety degrees/Oh, she's blowing me crazy/Till my ammunition is dry'. It's unlikely the band lost much sleep over claims of sexism.

GLASGOW

The Scottish city where Angus and Malcolm Young were born. They moved out of there (together with parents William and Margaret, plus the rest of their siblings, including older brother George) in 1963, re-locating to Sydney. Given the fact that the pair are Scottish by birth, and that Bon Scott was also born in Scotland, it may be claimed that the band are as much Scottish as they are Australian. In fact, Angus first started to play guitar when he was five years old, in 1960, although it has to be admitted he didn't take it up seriously until he bought a Gibson SG in Australia.

GLASGOW APOLLO

One of the most recognised and famed venues in Europe, it was here that AC/DC recorded most of the live album *If You Blood... You've Got It*. The gig took place on April 30, 1978, and Scott can clearly be heard to refer to the city of Glasgow during 'The Jack', when he asks, "Any virgins in Glasgow?" Two songs performed during the Apollo show, 'Dog Eat Dog' and 'Fling Thing', were left off the final running order of the record. One moment that will stick in the minds of all who were at the gig happened during the encore, when the whole band came back on wearing Scotland football jerseys. This was not only a clever move to get the locals going, but also expressed the Scottish roots of three members of the band – the

Youngs and Bon Scott, all born in Scotland. It also happened at a time when the Scottish football team had qualified for the World Cup that Summer, and some (misguidedly as it turned out) believed they could win the tournament in Argentina.

GOLDERS GREEN HIPPODROME

The location in North West London where AC/DC recorded a performance for the BBC's 'Sight & Sound In Concert' series. The show took place on November 27, 1977, and was simultaneously broadcast on both BBC TV and Radio 1 two days later. This was during the band's hugely successful 17-date UK tour, which included their first ever sold out gig at the Hammersmith Odeon in London, on November 12.

Footage from the 'Sight & Sound In Concert' show turned up on the *Plug Me In* DVD, specifically 'Hell Ain't A Bad Place To Be' and 'Rocker', both of which are on disc one of this release.

GONE SHOOTIN'

Track from the 1978 *Powerage* album, written by Angus and Malcolm Young plus Bon Scott. This is a song about heroin and overdosing, and pulls few punches: 'Packed her heart in a travellin'

bag/And never said bye bye'. The track is featured in the movie *Beavis & Butt-Head Do America*, and a clip of Johnson performing it in the studio is including on the DVD *Plug Me In*.

GO DOWN

Opening track from the 1977 album *Let There Be Rock*, written by Young, Young and Scott. The Ruby mentioned in the lyrics – 'Ain't no one I know/Do it good as you/Lickin' on that lickin' stick/The way you do' – is thought to be famed groupie Ruby Lipps, a woman who got that name for a rather obvious reason!

GO ZONE

Track four from the 1988 album *Blow Up Your Video*, written by the Young brothers and Brian Johnson. Lyrically, it's again to do with fun time. When Johnson sings 'When the beaver sing/Let me out I'm closin' in', he isn't discussing a visit to the zoo!

GOODBYE AND GOOD RIDDANCE TO BAD LUCK

A track from the 1990 album *The Razors Edge*, this was written by the Young brothers. The lyrics deal with always being positive, despite all the hits you take:

'Bad luck has changed/Broken the chains/Lay down a claim/For monetary gains'.

GORILLA

Before settling on his famed schoolboy costume, Angus tried many different outfits, including a gorilla one. It's hard to believe that he could have convincingly cavorted around the stage the way he has for decades while dressed as a gorilla, but footage exists of him performing with the band on Aussie television show *Countdown* dressed in such a suit. The programme's producer Paul Drane (below) recalls:

"Before the show, we got Angus into this gorilla suit and in this cage, which we elevated above the audience in the lighting, before the crowd actually came in. He's suspended up there in his gorilla suit – which couldn't have been very comfortable – with his guitar, and being really, really quiet. The other guys are somewhere on the studio set.

"So, the audience came in and they didn't even know Angus was there. And we dropped him down into the crowd after the intros – so he's probably been up there for nearly half-an-hour – and they just went absolutely berserk. It was incredible."

Other rejected costumes: Spider-Man, complete with a rope spider's web at the back of the stage, Zorro and Super-Ang (a piss-take on Superman) in which the band would have a telephone box on stage in which he could change.

GOT YOU BY THE BALLS

Track number eight from 1990's *The Razors Edge*, and written by Angus and Malcolm Young. The lyrics delve right into the world of high stakes prostitution, and don't pull any punches: 'Hey mister businessman/High society/She can play the schoolgirl/And spank you all you please'. The older they got, the more the Youngs seemed to enjoy being explicit in their lyricism.

CREG/PAUL

Bassist who stood in for Cliff Williams during part of the band's 1991 American tour. No official reason has ever been given for this decision, but it was purely temporary. Some believe Greg did as many as 25 shows on that tour, however it's more likely to be considerably less.

GRIFFITHS/RICHARD

The man who booked AC/DC's first shows in the UK. Here's what he has said of the band:

"It was clear to me it was Malcolm's band. Bon was a great guy. But even then, I sensed, off Michael (Browning, their manager at the time), that he wasn't sure that Bon was the singer to take the band all the way.
"Bon was sort of separate from the rest. Phil, he was off on his own, he was actually pretty obnoxious. Angus and Malcolm

were thick, obviously. And then Mark, you knew Mark wasn't going to last, he was just too much of a nice guy."

GTK TV SHOW

Australian TV programme which, in July 1974, showed a clip of the band, with vocalist Dave Evans, performing their debut single 'Can I Sit Next To You Girl' at the Last Picture Show Theater in Cronulla. At the time, GTK was the sole national rock music TV show in Australia. Screened by the Australian Broadcasting Company (ABC), the *GTK* stood for Get To Know. It premiered in 1969, and ran until 1974 with each show lasting just ten minutes and was broadcast at 6.30pm, Monday to Thursday, just before popular soap, *Bellbird*. Among the legends who appeared on the programme were Pete Townshend, Lou Reed and Marc Bolan.

GUNS FOR HIRE

Track six from the 1983 album *Flick Of The Switch*, this was written by the Young brothers and Brian Johnson. Lots of references to being the fastest and meanest gun around, with certain sexual intonations, as per usual: 'I'm a smooth operator a big dictator/ Gonna mark you with my brand/ My gun's for hire/Shoot you with desire'. Quite!

HAIL CAESAR

Track number seven from the 1995 album *Ballbreaker*, written by the Young brothers. Released as a single in 1996, it reached No. 56 in the UK, and was backed by 'Whiskey On The Rocks' and a live version of 'Whole Lotta Rosie'. Lyrically, it takes its theme from Julius Caesar: 'The senators rehearse the tale/Starring in the Coliseum/Tied upon the rack/Up comes the thumb of Caesar/To stab you in the back'.

The video has the band playing on large Coliseum-like steps, while crowds march past. Various movie clips are shown throughout, with Angus incorporated.

HAMMERSMITH ODEON

The iconic venue where AC/DC truly felt at home in the late 1970s and the first part of the next decade. They debuted there on November 10, 1976, and played a further 16 times up to 1982. Their first multiple date appearance was November 15/16 1978, while from November 1-4, 1979, they did four nights – the final London appearances for Bon Scott.

After a gap of 21 years, the band were chosen to open the newly refurbished venue (now known as the Hammersmith Apollo) on October 21, 2003.

HAMPTON COURT HOTEL

A venue in Sydney, where AC/DC frequently played in their early days. One show, from March 1974, has surfaced as a bootleg, titled *In The Beginning*. Featuring Dave Evans on vocals, Neil Smith on bass and Noel Taylor on drums the set includes covers of Chuck Berry, Little Richard, Free and the Rolling Stones, as well as originals like 'Soul Stripper', 'Rock 'N' Roll Singer' and 'Rockin' In The Parlour'. This is almost certainly the earliest known tape of a live 'DC show in circulation, and came in two vinyl volumes, each restricted to 200 copies. Since then, it's been made available on CD, and can be found on the internet.

For historical accuracy, the band's set list that night was:

'Soul Stripper'; 'No Particular Place To Go'; 'Stay For A While'; 'Carol'; 'It's All Over Now'; 'Jumpin' Jack Flash'; 'Rock 'N' Roll Singer'; 'Blue Suede Shoes'; 'Rockin' In The Parlour'; 'Bye Bye Johnny'; 'Lucille'; 'All Right Now'; 'Baby, Please Don't Go'; 'Honky Tonk Woman'.

HARD AS A ROCK

Opening track from the 1995 album *Ballbreaker*. Written by the Young brothers, it was released as a single in 1995, with 'Caught With Your Pants Down' on the B-side and reached No. 33 in September of that year. The lyrics...

well, this says it all: 'Her hot potatoes/Will elevate you/Her bad behaviour/Will leave you standing proud'. The video for the song was shot at Bray Studios in Windsor, South England, renowned as being the home of Hammer Films in its heyday.

HAVE A DRINK ON ME

The eighth track from the 1980 album *Back In Black*, written by Angus and Malcolm Young, plus Brian Johnson. This is said to be the band's tribute on the album to late singer Bon Scott: 'So join me for a drink boys/We're gonna make a big noise/So don't worry about tomorrow/Take it today'. The song was used in the 2006 comedy movie *Beerfest*.

HAYSEED DIXIE

As the name implies, this American band started life as something of an AC/DC tribute band, playing bluegrass versions of their songs and dubbing themselves a 'Hillbilly tribute' to 'DC.

They claim to be from the mythic Deer Lick Holler in the Appalachians and have been touring since 2001.

Their first album, called *A Hillbilly Tribute To AC/DC*, solely featured songs from the band, including 'Highway To Hell', 'You Shook me All Night Long', 'Dirty Deeds Done Dirt Cheap', 'Hells Bells', 'Have A Drink On Me', 'Let's Get It Up' and 'Big Balls'. Since then they've expanded their repertoire, not only doing covers by other bands, but also their own original material.

What appealed to Hayseed Dixie about 'DC, in the first place? Says frontman Barley Scotch:

"They were singing about stuff from the perspective of a working class guy who's reserving his right to fight the man and raise some hell!"

Incidentally, Hayseed Dixie have the AC/DC seal of approval. So enamoured were AC/DC bassist Cliff Williams and singer Brian Johnson with what they heard on *A Hillbilly Tribute To AC/DC* Williams asked the band to play a private end of tour party.

"They were doing their Stiff Upper Lip tour and Brian Johnson was going on about how great our album was and then I got a phone call from Cliff Williams asking me to play an end of tour party at this house he's got in the mountains of North

Carolina," says Scotch. "We went up there and they had a big pig roasting in the backyard and a load of beer and we just got drunk with them. You never know what people like that are going to be like but they were all really normal guys."

HEATSEEKER

The opening cut from the 1988 album *Blow Up Your Video*. Written by Young, Young & Johnson it was released as a single in '88, reaching number 12 in January of that year – the band's highest UK chart position at that time. 'Go Zone' and 'Snake Eye' feature on the B-side, although the latter only appeared at the time on the 12-inch single, having been recorded for, but eventually left off, *Blow Up Your Video*. Lyrically, it's about being ready to get up and rock, being a 'Heatseeker, charging up the sky'.

The video starts with Angus bursting out of a TV set, and triggering an intercontinental ballis-

tic missile, which traverses the globe, before burying itself in the Sydney Opera House. Cue Angus exploding out of the missile to play a guitar solo. It was directed by David Mallet, renowned director of the time, and forms the basis of the opening of the live show on the *Blow Up Your Video* tour, which featured the missile crashing through a back screen as AC/DC take to the stage to perform 'Heatseeker' itself.

HELL AIN'T A BAD PLACE TO BE

The seventh track from both Australian and International versions of the 1977 album *Let There Be Rock*. Written by Young, Young and Scott, it's about being dragged out of a rut by your partner: 'Don't mind her playing a demon/As long as it's with me/If this is hell then you could say/It's heavenly'. The song has proved immensely popular live, featuring in sets from both the Bon Scott and Brian Johnson eras, and is also the track where Angus would perform his famed Devil Horns sign.

HELL AIN'T NO PLACE TO BE

Biography of the band written by author Richard Bunton (who has also written books about Led

Zeppelin), published in 1983. This is long out of print.

HELL'S BELL

The bell that features on the track 'Hell's Bells', the opening song on 1980's *Back In Black* album. The bell itself was recorded by engineer Tony Platt in Leicestershire. In Loughborough, there's a monument called the carillon, dedicated to those from the area who died during both world wars. At the top of this 200 foot tower are 47 bells, the largest of which is the Denison Bell, a four tonner made by J. Taylor & Sons – and this was the one recorded by Platt.

'DC take a smaller replica of this bell on tour with them that weights 'just' one-and-a-half tons, a copy of which is rumoured to hang above the front door of Malcolm Young's house.

HELLS BELLS

The legendary opening track from the 1980 album *Back In Black*. Written by Young, Young & Johnson, it opens with the tolling of the bell four times, before the lengthy guitar intro begins to rumble over continued tolling as fans listening for the first time waited with baited breath to hear what new singer Brian Johnson sounded like – a teasing ploy by the band. It's said to be a tribute to Bon Scott, although the lyrics themselves ('I got my bell/I'm gonna take you to hell') don't necessarily support this view and in fact, refer to a violent storm that was raging when the band first arrived at Compass Point Studios in the Bahamas.

The song also appears in the film Maximum Overdrive, and is a popular track to air at various American sporting occasions, being used by several sports teams.

An all-female AC/DC tribute band from Seattle go under the name of Hell's Belles.

HELL OR HIGH WATER

Track number eight from the 1985 album *Fly On The Wall*. It was written by Young, Young & Johnson and is another song from the mean streets, with the lyrics proclaiming: 'Blood money, lying through your back teeth/Fighting on the main street, breathe your last breath on me'.

HIGH VOLTAGE

There are two versions of *High Voltage*. The first is the Australian one, which represents the band's debut, released in 1975 and featuring a red sleeve depicting an electricity unit behind barbed wire with a dog urinating over it. The second is the international edition, released the following year, and is a compilation of tracks from Australian version and from the follow-up, *T.N.T.*

The Aussie original features Bon Scott, Angus and Malcolm Young, plus drummer Tony Currenti, with George Young handling all the bass duties, as well as producing with Harry Vanda.

Work on the album took place in November 1974 at Albert Studios in Sydney. You can hear some of the naiveté one would expect from any young band (no pun intended), especially as they were still finding the right line-up, something that would happen in time for *T.N.T.* However, the sheer brilliance, focus and energy of the band still shine through. There were six songs here written by the main trio of Young, Young & Scott, with 'Soul Stripper' written by the Youngs, and a cover of Big Joe William's 'Baby, Please Don't Go' making up the list – or rather more than making up the list. Both of these were part of the Dave Evans era, although Scott readily made them his own. 'Baby, Please Don't Go' provided Scott with an early opportunity to shine brightly.

Listening now, it's easy to be critical, but even from the distance of so many years, and bearing in mind the basic production, there is still something special about songs like 'She's Got Balls' and 'You Ain't Got A Hold On Me'.

The full track listing is: *Baby, Please Don't Go/She's Got Balls/Little Lover/Stick Around/ Soul Stripper/You Ain't Got A Hold On Me/Love Song/Show Business.*

The international version of the record came out in May 1976, just as 'DC prepared for action in the UK. Oddly, most of the tracks come from *T.N.T.*, their second album. Quite why the record wasn't just called *T.N.T.* is a little odd. Only 'She's Got Balls' and 'Little Lover' survived from the original Australian edition, with the rest coming from *T.N.T.*, including the song 'High Voltage', which wasn't on the Australian album of the same title, but its follow-up. Confused?

The rather austere cover for the original *High Voltage* was altered, given a more garish, colourful sleeve, depicting Angus in full schoolboy mode as he's hit by a lightning flash – this was actually the sleeve used for the single 'It's A Long Way To The Top (If You Wanna Rock 'N' Roll)' in Australia. A third, almost disco-style

cover was used on the European version. Both of these editions feature fake letters written to the band in an attempt to convey the kind of moral outrage felt at the band's existence, a move also used by fellow Aussie rockers, Skyhooks on their 1975 album *Ego Is Not A Dirty Word*.

Despite this somewhat piece-meal approach, the second *High Voltage* has some classic moments, with 'It's A Long Way To The Top', 'The Jack' and 'High Voltage' being real winners. Of those tracks from the original *High Voltage* not used here, four would surface on *'74 Jailbreak*.

The full track listing is: *It's A Long Way To The Top (If You Wanna Rock 'N' Roll)/Rock 'N' Roll Singer/The Jack/Live Wire/T.N.T./Can I Sit Next To You Girl/Little Lover/She's Got Balls/High Voltage*.

HICH UOLTACE
(Song)

Track eight from the 1975 album *T.N.T.*, and also one that appears on the 1976 international release of *High Voltage*. Written by Young, Young and Scott, the song's lyrics give the vocalist a chance to offer up the fact that he

is high voltage rock 'n' roll: 'You ask me 'bout the clothes I wear'/ And you ask me why I grow my hair/And you ask me why I'm in a band/I dig doin' one night stands'. Lines that sum up the Bon Scott philosophy nicely.

For the musically minded, it should be pointed out that this song has a chorus which cunningly uses the chords A,C,D,C in progression. This was suggested by producer George Young.

HIGH VOLTAGE: THE ULTIMATE AC/DC TRIBUTE

A double CD released in 2007, this features a host of names covering 'DC songs, including Dave Meniketti (Y&T), Joe Lynn Turner (Rainbow), Phil Collen (Def Leppard), Pat Travers, Quiet Riot, Godflesh, Lemmy (Motorhead), Jake E. Lee (Badlands), Dee Snider (Twisted Sister), Scott Ian (Anthrax) and The Dwarves.

HIGHWAY TO HELL

A landmark album for AC/DC, this was released in 1979 and immediately stepped the band up a notch ore two. This was the first time they worked with any producer apart from the George Young and Harry Vanda team, with Robert John 'Mutt' Lange stepping into the band's life, to great effect.

Actually, the band's original choice this time around was Eddie Kramer, who'd worked in the past with such legends as Jimi Hendrix and Led Zeppelin, but he was fired without a single track having been recorded. They had already demoed all the material at Albert Studios in Sydney, and were clearly of a mind to find a man who could step up to the demands. Kramer wasn't to be the person in question.

With Lange onboard, the band went to Criteria Studios in Miami, and then Roundhouse Studios in London, delivering their most important album to date. Exactly what Lange brought to the project can't be pinned down. However, it's to be believed that he helped sharpen the band's songwriting, and develop their appreciation of sound.

Scott was certainly personally delighted with the way things had gone with Lange, and he felt the best was yet to come.

He said just before his death:

"I have the feeling we're a new band now. Anything's possible with this guy. He's got me thinking of fresh ways to approach old subjects. We're not gonna become lame, but we now know how to work the commercial angle without giving up anything."

Mind you, there was nearly a disaster at one point in the studio, as Angus told Phil Wilding and Phil Jupitus of BBC 6 Music:

"The engineer had all these strange ideas of what he wanted. Every day you'd come in and play and he'd go, 'I don't want to hear that shit!' One day he said he was off horse-riding, showing us these photos of his missus and his horses, and Bon said, 'Which one's the horse?' It was that kind of relationship. So he took the weekend off and we wrote most of Highway To Hell. He came in and got the cassette to hear what we'd been up to, and his kid pulled all the tape out. We were in a total panic but Bon got a pencil and managed to get it back together, thank God."

Highway To Hell is stuffed with classics, all delivered with high precision while never losing spontaneity. Released in July 1979, it quickly became a big seller, making it to number 17 on the US charts, easily their highest position at that stage. It made number eight in the UK, the first time they'd made the Top Ten. Pick out any song from here, and you're guaranteed to know the tune. Moreover any rock fan will be able to do the same thing. While *Back In Black* easily outstripped *Highway To Hell* in terms of sales, nonetheless this was the equal of its successor. Just look at the track listing – quite breathtaking. One can only surmise what the band would have gone on to achieve had Scott lived.

Incidentally, ever wondered: what are those weird words

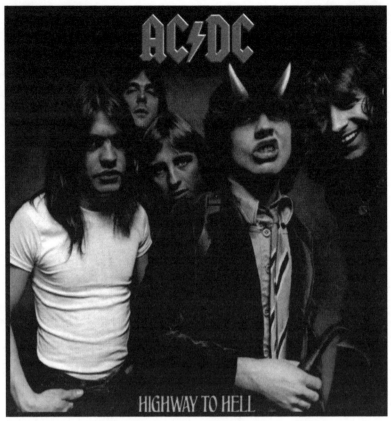

uttered by Scott at the end of the album? It's "Shazbot, na-nu na-nu", a phrase from the popular 1970s sci fi/comedy TV show *Mork & Mindy* – the catchphrase used in the series by Mork, the alien played by Robin Williams.

Full track listing: *Highway To Hell/Girls Got Rhythm/Walk All Over You/Touch Too Much/ Beating Around The Bush/ Shot Down In Flames/Get It Hot/If You Want Blood (You've Got It)/Love Hungry Man/ Night Prowler.*

HIGHWAY TO HELL
(Song)

Opening and title track from the band's 1979 album, written by the Young brothers and Bon Scott. Allegedly, the idea for the song came when the band were asked to describe what it's like on tour, and Angus replied that it was 'A fucking highway to hell'.

However, there is another, more prosaic explanation. *Highway To Hell* is actually the nickname given to the Canning Highway in Fre-mantle, Australia, where Scott once lived. At the bottom of this road is The Raffles bar, a well-known

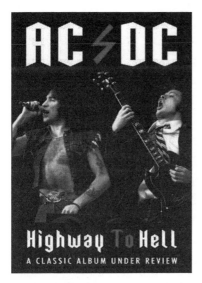

HIGHWAY TO HELL: A CLASSIC ALBUM UNDER REVIEW
(DVD)

Released in 2008, this is a critical analysis of the album, with experts and those who worked with the band as well as footage of AC/DC.

HIGHWAY TO HELL: THE LIFE AND TIMES OF AC/DC LEGEND BON SCOTT
(Clinton Walker)

Acclaimed biography of the singer, first published in 1994. This is an exhaustive look at the life and times of Scott, by an Australian historian who has also written about aboriginal music and the Australian independent music scene.

rock 'n' roll hangout in the 1970s. This would explain why Scott was 'going down, all the way', and also why he intones 'Ain't nothing I would rather do/ Going down, party time, my friends are gonna be there too'.

The song itself has long since passed into rock mythology. Apart from being covered by the likes of Marilyn Manson, Billy Joel, Slash's Snakepit and even Kiss, it has been used as a theme by wrestling body the WWE and appeared in an episode of *The Simpsons* as well as the movies *Little Nicky*, *House* and *School Of Rock*.

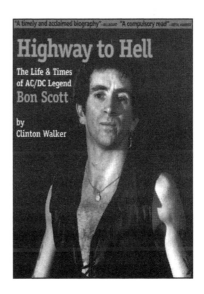

HIGHWAY TO HELL
(DVD)

Live performance by AC/DC from the Bon Scott era. Oddly, the cover depicts the current line-up. It lasts 64 minutes.

HOLD ME BACK

Fourth track from the 2000 album *Stiff Upper Lip*, written by Angus and Malcolm Young. It's a strutting song, with lines like 'I got a honk that'll blow the avenue' and 'Got a big fat momma who can hold a tune/Gotta slip that bone in hard and mean/A honky tonk woman get the best of me'. This might be something of a veiled piss-take of music business executives using their positions for sexual favours. Despite being titled 'Hold Me Back', the chorus is actually 'Can't hold me back'.

HOLLYWOOD ROCKWALK

This is outside the Sunset Boulevard branch of the famous Guitar Center in Los Angeles, and serves to pay tribute to rock musicians whose impact is undeniable. Artists are asked to put their handprints into blocks of cement, which are then displayed.

AC/DC were given this accolade on September 15, 2000. For once the entire band turned up to receive the honour. Of course, Bon Scott was absent, but during the ceremony Angus Young stated:

"I think Bon would be really happy, be really chuffed, you know, especially because he loved coming to LA. And I'll tell you what he loved best about L.A. He used to always say, 'I got to stop off at that little tattoo shop up on the Sunset Strip and get some new colours put on my tats, you know? So he would have loved it, I think."

At the same time, the band were given a special certificate to mark the occasion from the Mayor of Los Angeles Richard Riordan. The juxtaposition of such a local politician with AC/DC prompted

the event's host Jim Ladd, a local radio personality, to remark:

"I wonder how much Mayor Riordan knows about 'Giving The Dog A Bone'."

HOLTON/GARY

Singer and actor who was apparently considered as a replacement for Bon Scott. Holton first made his name with British band the Heavy Metal Kids, before taking up acting as the main thrust of his career. His biggest role came as Wayne Winston Norris in the successful 1980s TV series *Auf Wiedersehen, Pet*.

While not the generally held view, some maintain he was actually offered the chance to step into Scott's shoes, but turned it down. Holton died in October 1985 from an overdose of alcohol and morphine – in some ways mirroring what happening to Scott himself. Furthermore, he was 33 at the time – the same as Scott when he died. Strange indeed.

HOME

The first band to feature Cliff Williams, the group formed in 1970, quickly landing a deal with Epic. The line-up of Williams, guitarist Laurie Wisefield (who would go on to work with Wishbone Ash), singer Mick Stubbs,

keyboard player Clive John and drummer Mick Cook released their debut record in 1971, titled *Pause For A Hoarse Horse*. That same year they supported Led Zeppelin at the Empire Pool (now Wembley Arena) in London. With Jim Anderson in for Cook, they released a self-titled second album in '72 which gave them a semi-hit single in 'Dreamer' that peaked at number 41 in the UK.

A third album, *The Alchemist*, came out in 1973, to little fanfare. The group then metamorphosed into folk singer Al Stewart's backing band, although this was short-lived, with Williams departing in '74 for Bandit. In 2003 an album called *Live BBC Sessions 1972-1973* was released.

HONEY ROLL, THE

Track five from the 1995 album *Ballbreaker*, written by the Young siblings. The lyrics say it all: 'Honey roll over, and lettuce on top/Strap you to the bed, and make you rock/Run it up the flag, send it on home/Push you to the wall, and make you moan'. Oh, the wags!

HOUSE OF JAZZ

The third track from the 2000 album *Stiff Upper Lip*. Written by Angus and Malcolm Young, it's unlikely that the pair were envisaging a serious night listening to jazz music when they wrote the lines: 'Ball stripper/Big tipper/Got a slap 'n' tickler'!

HOWARD STERNS PRIVATE PARTS

Biographical movie about the famed New York shock jock Howard Stern, released in 1997, and starring Stern as himself. It's based on his 1993 autobiography and features AC/DC in a cameo appearance at Stern's rally in New York's Central Park. In the film Howard's wife, Alison, goes into labour to the sound of 'You Shook Me All Night Long'! The Ramones, Deep Purple, Van Halen, Cheap Trick and Ted Nugent also

have songs on the soundtrack, the album of which topped the US charts in 1997.

AC/DC also made an apperance on Stern's controversial radio show in 2003.

HOWE/BRUCE

The man who played bass in AC/DC very briefly in March 1975, replacing Paul Matters, before being replaced himself by Mark Evans. To be fair, most regard Howe as temporarily helping the band out, rather than looking to be a full-time member.

Howe, by this time, had already had a close association with Bon Scott as he was bassist with Fraternity from 1971-73, and had persuaded Scott to quit The Valentines to join them. The pair, together with other members of the group, lived in a rented two-story house in Jersey Road, Sydney, which was apparently renowned for its outrageous parties. It's been said that Scott learned to party hard through being in Fraternity. Howe once summed up their philosophy as: being straight was a state to be liberated from.

IF YOU DARE

The final track from the 1990 album *The Razors Edge*, this was written by Angus and Malcolm Young. Lyrically, it seems to push someone to see how far they'll go to prove their love, or lust: 'Woman if you love me/ Love me like you do/Love me like you say/Woman won't you come outside and play'.

IF YOU WANT BLOOD (YOU'VE GOT IT)

The first live album from AC/DC, released in 1978, and perfectly capturing the mood of the band at the time; they were on the rise, were full of confidence and charisma. At a time when the double live album was almost de rigeur, this lot proved on just one vinyl record that they were among the very best bands in the world.

Recorded during the 1978 *Powerage* tour, which lifted the band further up the food chain, much of the material was captured during a show at the Glasgow Apollo on April 30, 1978 (with some tracks being recorded in Munich later in the tour). A shrewd choice. Status Quo had already recorded a live album there (*Live!* in 1977), and the atmosphere had been electric. If anything, 'DC topped that, with a performance that was not only amazing, but also one can hear them in perfect synch with the ecstatic Scots. Listen to the way audience and band merge on 'Whole Lotta Rosie' – this could be the defining moment for that song. And Scott rises to the occasion during 'The Jack' by asking; "Any virgins in Glasgow?" Two songs from the Glasgow set are missing from the album, namely 'Fling Thing' and 'Dog Eat Dog'. The latter, though, did come out as the B-side to 'Whole Lotta Rosie' that year.

Of course, while the album is called *If You Want Blood (You've Got It)*, there is no song of that title, although one did appear on the next studio album, *Highway To Hell*.

If anyone ever needs testimony as to just how good 'DC were live at this juncture, refer them to *If You Want Blood...*, it says it all.

Full track listing: *Riff Raff/Hell Ain't A Bad Place To Be/Bad Boy Boogie/The Jack/Problem Child/Whole Lotta Rosie/Rock 'N' Roll Damnation/High Voltage/Let There Be Rocker/ Rocker/.*

The gig in Glasgow was also filmed, although it's never been released. 'Riff Raff' and the combination of 'Fling Thing' and 'Rocker' did get used on the *Family Jewels* DVD, while 'Rock 'N' Roll Damnation', 'Dog Eat Dog' and 'Let There Be Rock' appear on the 2007 DVD *Plug Me In* and some footage is included on the *Highway To Hell* DVD as well. Scottish TV have broadcast about 37 minutes of the film.

IF YOU WANT BLOOD (YOU'VE GOT IT)
(Song)

Seventh track from the *Highway To Hell* album from 1979 and written by Young, Young & Scott. This was the second time 'DC had recorded a song with a title the same as that of their previous album; earlier, 'High Voltage' had appeared on *T.N.T.*, the band's second long player, having been the title of their debut. Lyrically, it's all about how life throws you a curve ball, with spikes sticking straight into your veins. Wherever you turn, people demand more and more for less and less: 'Blood on the streets/ Blood on the rocks/Blood in the gutter/Every last drop'. The song title has a certain sense of bitter humour and irony.

ILLUSTRATED RECORD COLLECTORS GUIDE

This came in two separate volumes, and though self-published by AC/DC collector Chris Tesch, remain the only guides to AC/DC's releases that there have ever been. Volume one concentrated on all of AC/DC's singles, albums, 12" singles, CDs and promo releases. The second volume cast its eye over bootlegs, radio promo releases, releases by related bands and an index. Tesch published both volumes himself in the United States in 1992. Both have long since been deleted and are very hard to find, so essentially something of a holy grail for AC/DC fans. One noted AC/DC website states that Tesch was looking to have his work published by a major publishing company, but the work was stopped, although no reasons are given.

I'M A REBEL

A song made famous by Accept. In fact, it was the title track of the German metal band's second album, released in 1980. But there is a version in existence recorded by none other than... AC/DC.

What happened is that the band played a show on September 15, 1976 at the Factory in Maschener, Germany, and, as promoter Rudy Holzhauer (below) now explains:

"After the Factory gig we asked the boys to record a song for us. Shacht, the music publishing company, took over the studio expenses, because the song was written by one of their Hamburg authors: Alec Young - a brother of AC/DC's Malcolm and Angus Young. During the day after the gig, the band came in (at 6pm) to the Maschener studio, had breakfast (a bottle of whiskey)

and recorded the song in a few hours."

But it was never actually put out by the band. Again one has to ask why it wasn't included on *Bonfire.*

INJECT THE VENOM

Track number four from the 1981 album *For Those About To Rock (We Salute You).* Written by Young, Young and Johnson, some have taken lines like 'No mercy for the bad if they want it/No mercy for the bad if they plead' as a pro-capital punishment sentiment. But then you've got further lines like, 'Come choose your victim/Take him by surprise', which may be a comment on random violence.

IT'S A LONG WAY TO THE TOP (IF YOU WANNA ROCK 'N' ROLL)

The opening track from the T.N.T album, released in 1975, and also from the international version of *High Voltage,* issued the next year. This is notable for being one of the rare occasions when bagpipes are used in a rock song – but it works in creating the correct balance and atmosphere. Perhaps it harks back to Scott's days of playing in a pipe band.

Lyrically, it details the problems facing anyone out to become a rock star – from being robbed to getting ripped off, from being underpaid to breaking bones, all the pitfalls are here. Interestingly, there's no mention of unwanted pregnancy.

A video for the song was filmed on February 26, 1976 in Swanston Street, Melbourne. This is close to Corporation Lane, which was re-named AC/DC Lane in 2004. In the video, the band are standing on a flat-bed truck travelling down the street, with the Rats Of Tobruk Pipe Band also on board. The clip was shown on Aussie TV show *Countdown.*

Among those to cover the song are crooner Pat Boone and Aussie kiddie band The Wiggles.

JACK, THE

The third track from the *T.N.T.* album, released in 1975, and also from the international version of the *High Voltage* record, issued the following year. Written by Angus and Malcolm Young, together with Bon Scott, it's one of the band's cleverest uses of phraseology to talk about sexual matters. In this case about catching what is colloquially referred to as 'The Jack', which is the sexually transmitted disease Gonorrhoea. Apparently, this is based on a true story, wherein almost every member of the band caught a dose after they each slept with the same infected groupie.

The slow pace simply adds to the sleazoid factor, as Scott lets us into his boudoir, to relate: 'She was holdin' a pair/But I had to try/Her Deuce was wild/But my Ace was high'. This wordplay continues as a seeming card game is used to disguise what was really happening.

However on the live album *If You Want Blood (You've Got It)*, Scott changed the lyrics for a more explicit rendering of the situation:

'She gave me her mind/She gave me her body/But it seems to me she gave it to anybody'.

JACKYL

The wild, crazy American band who formed in 1990, and became renowned for the fact that frontman Jesse James Dupree would perform a buzzsaw solo on stage – literally cutting up a chair.

The band found fame in 1992 when their self-titled, debut album sold over a million copies in America, and in 1997 they got Brian Johnson in to guest on the song 'Locked And Loaded', which is on the *Cut The Crap* album. Johnson returned to the band in 2002, to guest on the *Relentless* record; he duets with Jesse James Dupree on the song 'Kill The Sunshine'.

JAILBREAK

The final track from the Australian version of the album *Dirty Deeds Done Dirt Cheap*, released in 1976. However, it was dropped from the running order for the international edition, only surfacing in 1984 on the *'74 Jailbreak* mini album. The song was also released as a single in '76 in Australia, the B-side being 'Fling Thing'.

Written by the Young brothers and Scott, it's about a man who is sentenced to 16 years in jail for killing his partner's lover. He manages to escape, only to be shot in the back. But does he live or does he die? In the video, filmed outside a prison in March 1976, Scott takes the lead character and does die, having been shot by Mark Evans and Malcolm Young, playing prison warders. The video appeared on the Australian TV show *Countdown*, and is included on the *Family Jewels* DVD.

In the song it's all left in the air, ending with the lines: 'Heartbeats they were racin'/Freedom he was chasin'/Spotlights, sirens, rifles firing/But he made it out/With a bullet in his back'.

The song itself is based on the true story of what happened to a friend of singer, Scott.

JAMES/CREC

A Fremantle sculptor, who was commissioned to make the life-size bronze statue of Bon Scott that was unveiled at Fisherman's Wharf in the town on February 24, 2008, as a tribute to the singer, who lived in the Australian town as a child.

Born in Western Australia in 1954, James based himself in Fremantle during 1987. Talking of the way he tackles commissions, he has said:

"The essential inspiration for my work is people. Some of my work is concerned with the artistic representations of individuals and or events based on historical fact, while other works concentrate on interpretations of various elements of the human condition."

JANUARY 27/1980

The date of the last ever AC/DC show with Bon Scott. It was at the Gaumont in Southampton (inevitably sold out), where they were supported by young British band Diamond Head. Scott was to make two more public appearances, both on TV. On February 7, AC/DC performed 'Touch Too Much' on BBC's Top Of The Pops, and two days later they played 'Beating Around The Bush' on Spanish programme *Aplauso* (above).

JASPER

Aussie band with whom Malcolm Young briefly played in early 1974 as he searched for a new drummer and bassist to join AC/DC. As a result, Jasper's rhythm section – drummer Noel

Taylor and bassist Neil Smith – joined 'DC, albeit only to be fired in April '74.

JEFFREY/IAN

AC/DC's tour manager at the time that Bon Scott died, the singer actually had dinner with Jeffrey that fateful evening (February 19, 1980), before he went down to the Music Machine and things went horribly wrong.

Respected in the music industry, Jeffrey worked with 'DC from 1976-1983, even becoming their personal manager for a time in 1982. He has also been tour manager for Def Leppard and Metallica.

Perhaps the biggest controversy surrounding AC/DC has always been whether Bon Scott's lyrics were used at all on the *Back In Black* album. Although the late singer was never credited, there are those who allege that a few lines do crop up on the record. Jeffrey claims to have a folder with lyrics for 15 songs Scott had been sketching out for the new album prior to his death, and has intimated that one or two phrases might have been used on songs which were eventually recorded for *Back In Black*.

However, it must be stressed that no-one has ever suggested that any recordings happened with Scott (Jeffrey has firmly scotched that rumour) and that the vast majority of the lyrics for the album were clearly written after Scott's death.

JOHN PEEL SHOW
Radio 1

AC/DC recorded one session for John Peel's acclaimed Radio 1 show, on June 3, 1976. It was produced by Tony Wilson at the Beeb's Maida Vale Studios in London, and aired on June 21 that same year. The band recorded four songs: 'Live Wire', 'High Voltage', 'Can I Sit Next To You, Girl' and 'Little Lover'.

JOHNNY B. GOODE

Yes, the classic Chuck Berry song, the hoary old chestnut covered by so many – including the Young brothers and Bon Scott jamming with Cheap Trick in 1979. The recording was included on a Cheap Trick Fan Club CD called *Bun E.'s Basement Bootlegs*, which was compiled by Cheap Trick drummer Bun E. Carlos. There are only 1000 copies of the CD in existence, at least officially anyway.

JOHNSON/BRIAN

In a way, you have to feel a little sorry for Brian Johnson. He's been AC/DC's singer since 1980, and yet somehow he's still overshadowed by the man he replaced, one Bon Scott. And yet he's made the position his own.

Despite rumours and stories down the years that he had been/was about to be fired or had quit, the affable Geordie is very much part of the AC/DC fabric. In fact, these days it's hard to believe that the band could ever contemplate working with any other frontman. So, what does Johnson bring to the table? A lot! He may not have Scott's earthy charisma, sly charm or capacity for excess. But what he does have is his own brand of working class heroics. With his flat cap and broad Newcastle accent, which doesn't seem to have softened over the years, he is everyone's fave uncle, while Scott was more the next door neighbour whom the girls hoped to bed, and

the fellas wanted to buy a drink. Scott was the man you were never quite sure you could trust, with your drink or your girlfriend, whereas Johnson is dependable, reliable and steady. Scott would lend you his last fiver, after borrowing a tenner off someone, while Johnson would give you the shirt off his back.

Who would you rather party with? Scott? Who would confide in? Johnson. That's a sweeping generalisation, and one that's a little harsh on both. However, it's the way they're perceived by the public, and why Johnson has never escaped the Scott legend.

So, who is Brian Johnson?

Born on October 5, 1947, to a father who was in the army (a sergeant-major, no less) and an Italian mother. He got the performing bug initially with the boy scouts, but really got his break with a band called Geordie. As explained elsewhere in the book,

they started out in 1971, trying to be exotic by adopting the name USA. But this soon changed to the more descriptive Geordie. With Johnson's sandpaper voice giving them a certain edge, Geordie happily existed in the slipstream of bands like Slade, who were enjoying considerable success at the time. They were a big local draw on the live scene, with one number – 'Geordie's Lost His Liggie' – being a major fave. This always climaxed with Johnson

carrying guitarist Vic Malcolm around on his shoulders, in the style of Bon Scott and Angus Young!

Recalls Malcolm of those days:

"Apart from us there were only three or four other bands getting regular gigs in our area. There were bands that had been around for years, which made us feel even better, as if success had just flown our way."

Johnson also has 'fond' memories of those times:

"I just wanted to be in a band. They were famous when I joined them. They were a great rock band at the time, but they got turned and twisted by the record company into a pop band. You know, all the big platforms shoes, all the silly shit I had to wear. And the trousers, I could've put a small African village in there. It was just terrible."

In March 1972, the band (who had still to change their name from USA) signed to the Red Bus label, and had a minor hit a few months later when, as Geordie, they reached the lower echelons of the chart with the single 'Don't Do That'. By April 1973 they'd hit the Top Ten with the single 'All Because Of You'. However, while they continued to get the occasional hit single, nonetheless their career hit the skids when punk zoomed over the horizon. Johnson was now struggling for work, even doing a voiceover for a vacuum cleaner commercial on TV, when AC/DC called – out of the blue.

Recalls Angus:

"I remember the first time I had ever heard Brian's name was from Bon. Bon had mentioned that he had been in England once touring with a band (Fraternity) and he had mentioned that Brian had been in a band called Geordie and Bon had said, 'Brian Johnson, he was a great rock and roll singer in the style of Little Richard' And that was Bon's big idol, Little Richard. I think when he saw Brian at that time, to Bon it was, 'Well he's a guy that knows what rock and roll is all about'' He mentioned that to us in Australia. I suppose when we decided to continue, Brian was the first name that Malcolm and myself came up with, so we said we should see if we can find him."

Interestingly enough, what impressed Scott when he first saw Johnson onstage was the way he writhed around on the floor as if in pain – apparently, though, the

singer was in genuine pain. Later the same night he was diagnosed as suffering from appendicitis.

Others might have been in the frame, but it was the Geordie man who came racing through, an outsider to many, but the man handed the toughest (or one of the toughest) tasks in rock – replacing the irreplaceable. For his audition, he sang 'Whole Lotta Rosie' and Ike & Tina Turner's classic 'Nutbush City Limits' – that convinced the rest of the band that he was the man.

Since then, Jonna (as he's affectionately known) has got on with the task in hand, even taking the knock of being told he was no longer allowed to contribute lyrics (after the 1988 album 'Blow Up Your Video') with good grace.

And while there have been increasingly long gaps between 'DC albums and tours, Johnson has taken the opportunity to involve himself in other projects. For instance, he's working on

a ballet inspired by Helen Of Troy, has helped out other bands like Jackyl and Neurotica as a songwriter/producer/mentor and raced vintage cars. He was also executive producer of the 2008 stoner comedy *Totally Baked*, for which he also produced three songs: 'Chain Gang', 'Chase That Tail' and 'Who Phoned The Law'

Although now living in Florida, Johnson is still down to earth, enjoying the simple pleasures in life:

"I live in Sarasota, and there's a pub called Watson's Pub. And they serve the beer like it is supposed to be served. These guys, when serving like Belgian beers, which are very prolific, but what they do is that they serve them in glasses that they are supposed to be served in different countries. Like German beer, real big Weiss beer, they are supposed to be served in

these beautiful steins, glasses. The Belgian beers come in big balloon glasses. It gives something extra to the pleasure of enjoying beer."

Early in 2008, Johnson turned up onstage with teenage band Bad Sara in his local town. Apparently, one of the band, 13-year-old Garrett Moore, spotted Johnson's wife Brenda in a parking lot. He grabbed the chance, and gave her a copy of their CD. The rest of the band are Alex Rappaport (who's 14) Mike Magazino (also 14), James Hyde (13) and Austin Bowman (an elderly 15!). Johnson heard it, liked the music and persuaded Paul Duffy, a friend, to give them a gig at a local venue called The Irish Rover.

"I heard 'em, I liked 'em, but there is no jumping off place in Sarasota for a rock band,"

said the AC/DC man at the time.

The band packed the venue, and Johnson joined them onstage for 'You Shook Me All Night Long' and 'Thunderstruck'.

"It's a dream to perform a duet with Brian; it's awesome, doesn't get any better," Moore said.afterwards. "It would be great to be a performer forever, but even if I'm not singing, I'll be in the business somewhere. I'll produce; I'll be a sound engineer."

Johnson, though, has little time for the rumours that so often spread about the band, especially through the internet. His comments in 2001 were:

"I gotta tell you, one of the troubles in the internet and some of the fanzine things, is rumours. These mischief makers. Like such and such is not going to make the gig this year, like Phil wasn't going to come on this tour. And we were looking at this and thought why would anybody want to put that down? There's no reason for it. Or I won't be there. You know, like in America, in 21 years – I missed one gig. Because I was so sick that the doctor wouldn't let me. He said, 'I can't let you on stage, Mr Johnson you're gonna mess the rest of the tour if you go tonight'. Blood pressure was that high, you know. We were just working too hard. So the doctor said, 'I can't let you go, you're gonna kill yourself'. And I cancelled the gig. Within 24 hours I had left the band, I had been sacked, I was going to join other band, etc.. I was like, 'Holy Shit', one gig in 21 years. It wasn't that bad in the '80s, the rumours were just hearsay, you know it goes in to your left ear and out from your right. But now with the internet, because the written word, people believe it. People believe anything that is written."

That's Brian Johnson – still down to earth and in touch with the roots of the music he loves. Still proudly sporting his cap – albeit mostly a baseball hat these days – despite not having a hair loss problem (of which he'd been accused by many music papers upon joining AC/DC), and getting on with life. And he is the singer on *Back In Black*, the biggest selling hard rock record of all time.

KENTUCKEE

The band featuring Angus Young just prior to the teenage guitar sensation teaming up with his brother Malcolm in AC/DC. Interestingly, it seems that original 'DC singer Dave Evans might well have been approached by Angus to throw in his lot with Kentuckee, before he joined 'DC.

Here's what the vocalist said in early 2007:

"I was visited at my Bondi home by Angus Young, who had a band called Kentuckee, and who had heard of me and was looking for a new singer. He had very long curly hair and was a tiny guy but very nice and polite. A month later I answered an advertisement in the Sydney Morning Herald for a rock singer with a strong voice and found Malcolm Young on the other end of the line."

Kentuckee never achieved anything of significance and only carries any interest as it was a passing phase for Angus (as was another band at the time called Tantrum).

KICKED IN THE TEETH

Track eight on the UK version of *Powerage*, but tenth and final track on the US and Australian versions. Written by Young, Young and Scott, it starts off with an acappella intro similar to Led Zeppelin's 'Black Dog'. Lyrically, it's about a woman who's exposed as being rather two-faced, leading on the hero: 'While ya been runnin' round town with every mother's son'. It also has the warning: 'You never know who's gonna win 'til the race been run'.

KING'S COLLEGE HOSPITAL
Camberwell

The hospital where Bon Scott was rushed on February 19, 1980, after being found unconscious in his car. Tragically, he was pronounced dead on arrival.

KING/STEPHEN

So, what's the connection between one of the modern masters of horror and AC/DC? Apart from the fact that King has often declared himself to be a huge fan of the band, the direct association comes with the 1986 movie *Maximum Overdrive*, the first – and, so far, only – film to be directed by the man himself. As a 'DC enthusiast, King took the opportunity to involve the band in this project by getting them to write and compose music for this, which led to the release of the *Who Made Who* album, featuring not just the title track but also two new instru-

mentals, namely 'Chase The Ace' and 'D.T.'.

The movie, though, is not regarded as one of King's finest moments, as he himself has admitted more than once since. However, the band themselves did make a cameo appearance in Maximum Overdrive, being seen on a boat in long shots during one scene. The famous AC/DC logo can also be spotted on the side of a truck in the same scene.

King and his wife, Tabitha, own three radio stations in the New England area, including WKIT, which is tagged as 'Stephen King's Rock 'N' Roll Station'.

King once said of his musical tastes:

"I don't have much use for pop music, and I refuse to listen to any musical artist who goes by a single name. Beyoncé? Go away. Jewel? Out of my face. Ashanti? Quit it. The only exception to this rule is Eminem. I love Eminem, partly because he's funny and savage, but also because he still admits that underneath it all, there is a person named Marshall Mathers.

"I like AC/DC, Metallica, Steve Earle, and the Dixie Chicks. I like Darryl Worley, although I have no use for his jejune political commentary. No, Darryl, I haven't forgotten, and I don't need you to remind me, okay?

"Ask me to name the greatest rock 'n' roll song of all time and I have to say it's a three-way tie between Slobberbone's 'Gimme

Back My Dog', Count Five's 'Psychotic Reaction' and Elvis Costello's '(What's So Funny 'Bout) Peace, Love And Understanding'. What I'm not interested in is ear candy. There's a place where you can put that, and it's not in your ear. I think that stuff should crawl right out of the radio speaker and get in your face. I think it should interrupt your life. Consequently I love the Jayhawks, like the White Stripes, and have no interest whatever in Celine Dion. If you like Celine Dion, you should write or e-mail the editors of this magazine and tell them that on no account should they hire Steve King to write commentaries, because Steve King thinks 'Who Let the Dogs Out' is better than all the songs Ms. Dion has recorded, put together."

KINNEAR/ALISTAIR

Does this man exist? Did he ever exist? Is it a pseudonym? Was he a drug dealer hiding from the authorities? Just some of the questions surrounding this figure after he was named as the person who discovered Bon Scott's body in his car in East Dulwich on February 19, 1980 – the fateful day when Scott died. In fact, Alistair Kinnear most definitely is real. And *Classic Rock* magazine tracked him down in 2005.

According to Kinnear, he got to know Scott through Silver Smith, a sometime girlfriend of the AC/DC singer. Kinnear and Smith moved into a Kensington flat in 1978, and Scott came to stay for a couple of weeks, at which point the pair (Kinnear and Bon) struck of a friendship. When Smith moved back to her native Australia, Kinnear moved to Overhill Road in East Dulwich.

On February 18, 1980, Kinnear and Scott went to the Music

Machine in London to see a band featuring the sister of Zena Kakoulli, the One Ones manager and wife of that band's mainman, Peter Perrett. Kinnear had originally invited Smith, once again back in London, along with him, but she suggested he take Bon, who'd earlier phoned her seeking something to do that evening. After a heavy drinking session during and after the gig, both Kinnear and Scott departed. Driving back to Scott's flat in Westminster, Scott passed out. Unable to get the vocalist into his own flat – nobody was home – Kinnear decided to go to East Dulwich, where, at about four or five in the morning, he thought it best to leave Scott in the car to sleep off the effects, having covered him with a blanket and left a note in case Scott woke early and wondered where he was.

"I slept till about 11, when I was awakened by a friend, Leslie Loads. I was so hung over I asked Leslie to do me a favour by checking on Bon. He did so, and returned to tell me my car was empty."

Assuming that Scott had gone home, Kinnear went back to sleep, only going to his car at 7.30 that evening (February 19), intending to drive to see his girlfriend who was in hospital.

"I was shocked to find Bon still lying flat in the front seat, obviously in a very bad way, and not breathing. I immediately drove him to King's College Hospital, where Bon was declared dead on arrival."

Kinnear insists that he never disappeared, but had lived in the Costa Del Sol for about 22 years, working as a musician and in touch with old friends across the globe. *"I am not hiding from anyone,"* he concluded.

Kirriemuir salutes rock star legend

KIRRIEMUIR SALUTED another of its famous sons at the weekend in a ceremony which drew visitors from Europe and interest from the opposite side of the world.

Fifty-five years after he emigrated to Australia with his family, Bon Scott was remembered by the town and hundreds of fans of rockers AC/DC with which he became a legend.

The appeal Scott and his fellow band members hold for all ages was evident in the range of generations which packed Kirrie's Cumberland Close under Saturday's sunny skies to see the unveiling of a Caithness stone slab commemorating the singer, which now sits alongside similar memorials unveiled to three other famed Kirriemarians—J. M. Barrie, Hugh Munro and Charles Lyell.

All the slabs have been carved by internationally renowned sculptor Bruce Walker, whose base is in Cumberland Close and Saturday's ceremony was led by Kirriemuir Community Council, which commissioned the Scott stone after an idea sparked by member Davie Milne.

Born Ronald Belford Scott on July 9, 1946, he spent his early years in Kirriemuir, where his father, Charles, worked in the family bakery in Bank Street.

Details of Bon's biography were delivered by community council chairman Major Ronnie Proctor, who revealed that he had been contacted just before the weekend event from Down Under by a lifelong friend of Scott's who wanted to pay his personal tribute to the musician, whose untimely death came in 1980.

Mr Proctor read a message from Vincent Lovegrove, who first met the then 19-year-old Bon in 1965 and forged an instant friendship which was to stretch right up until the Angus man's death.

Mr Lovegrove said "I spoke to his mother last week and Isa told me how proud she was of this plaque in Kirriemuir."

He continued. "The thing I loved most about Bon Scott was his almost unique self honesty. What you saw was what you got, he was a real person and as honest as the day is long.

"To my mind he was the street poet of my generations and of the generations that followed."

Among the crowd was Australian Darren Hill, who now owns a restaurant outside Forfar but travelled back home in 2005 to a memorial service at the singer's grave.

Mr Hill brought AC/DC memorabilia back for an exhibition mounted in Kirrie to coincide with the anniversary of the singer's death and revealed how this weekend's event had also sparked interest from his homeland.

"I was contacted by Australian Broadcasting Corporation radio on Friday night and did a live interview in which I was asked about Kirriemuir and my own interest in Bon Scott." said Mr Hill.

"Bon Scott's music speaks to many generations and I think it's great that they've made this memorial to him."

Janos Szedljak and his daughter Nikoletia travelled from Hungary for the event

Major Proctor surrounded by Bon Scott fans at the unveiling.

KIRRIEMUIR

Sometimes just called Kirrie, this is the burgh in Angus, Scotland where Bon Scott was born on July 9, 1949 and where he lived until he was six. Also born here were Peter Pan creator J. M. Barrie, but while film star David Niven often claimed this to be his birthplace, he was actually born in London.

Notorious for being a haven for witches in the 16th Century, Kirriemuir is twinned with French town Volvic.

More recently a Bon Scott tribute night has taken place at Kirriemuir Town Hall, featuring various AC/DC tribute bands, the third and latest of which being on May 19, 2008.

Museum's tribute to Kirrie rock star

Fiona Guest with some of the AC/DC memorabilia that forms the display commemorating the life of Bon Scott.

THE life of legendary rock musician Bon Scott is being commemorated in his Angus birthplace — with a display at Kirriemuir's Gateway to the Glens Museum.

From around the world, fans of AC/DC and their late lead singer, Bon Scott, have been enquiring about a commemoration of this legendary rock musician in Kirriemuir.

There have been numerous famous men and women associated with Kirriemuir, but few are as well known throughout the world as Bon Scott.

What is not as obvious is that his interest in music could be said to reach back to his birthplace and his father's involvement in traditional music in the town.

Ronald Belford 'Bon' Scott was born on July 9, 1946. Bon's family lived in Kirriemuir and his father Charles Scott worked in the family bakery in Bank Street and was also in the local pipe band.

In 1952, when Ronald was six years old the family emigrated to Australia, where Bon — as he was soon nicknamed — grew up.

He first joined pop-rock band, The Spektors and later played with The Valentines but it was with a young rock band from Sydney, led by two fellow Scots, Angus and Malcolm Young that he found fame.

AC/DC were to become one of the most famous rock groups in the world and it is a testament to their success that the recently released DVD — Family Jewels (described as a definitive history of the band) — has been hugely successful.

It is 25 years since Scott's tragic death in February 1980, and the display at the museum celebrates the career of this notable figure and will feature a host of objects, many lent by enthusiastic fans from around the world including rare vinyl albums, photographs, programmes and posters.

During the time the display is open, the museum would like to continue to develop its own collection of images, objects and stories about Bon Scott and his family here in Kirriemuir.

If anyone remembers the Scotts, or Kirriemuir Pipe Band, they are asked to get in touch with the museum and share their memories.

Artistic visitors to the museum during the display will be able to design their own album cover for display in the museum and fans can test their knowledge of Scott while new visitors develop their knowledge of this fascinating man and his music.

The display opened on Saturday and continues until August 20.

KISSIN' DYNAMITE

The fifth track from the 1988 album *Blow Up Your Video*. Written by Young, Young & Johnson, lyrically it's summed up by the following lines: 'She got a nasty reputation/She got a healthy appetite/When she needs some detonation/She sets the fuse alight, the fuse alight'.

KRAMER, EDDIE

Top engineer and producer, whose career stretches back to the early 1960s, when he worked with the likes of Sammy Davis Jr. and the Kinks. Later, he got the chance to record such legends as the Beatles, the Small Faces, the Rolling Stones and Jimi Hendrix. Moving from London to America, Kramer collaborated with Led Zeppelin on five albums, and recorded the Woodstock Festival, going on to work with Kiss, Curtis Mayfield, David Bowie, Twisted Sister, Anthrax, Dionne Warwick, Peter Frampton, the Red Hot Chili Peppers and Derek & The Dominoes.

But he can't add AC/DC to that illustrious list. Why? He was the original choice to produce Highway To Hell, but was fired before anything could be recorded.

LANDSLIDE

Track five from the *Flick Of The Switch* album, written by Angus and Malcolm Young, together with Brian Johnson. Lyrically, it's about breaking out of the monotony of conforming, and having a good time, although whether this is someone living the dream, or living in a dream, remains open to question: 'Well momma don't scold her son/For what he been doing upstairs/Daddy don't take him out no no/Sister just pull his hair'.

LANGE, ROBERT JOHN 'MUTT'

One of the greatest and most celebrated producers of the modern era, Robert John 'Mutt' Lange is almost a byword for success. The list of major artists who've benefited from his talents is impressive, taking in Def Leppard, Shania Twain (his third wife), Celine Dion, Michael Bolton, Billy Ocean, The Cars, Barbara Streisand, Bryan Adams, Foreigner... and, of course, AC/DC.

Born in 1948, in what is now Zimbabwe, Lange showed an enthusiasm for music from an early age, eventually starting his first band after moving to South Africa, ostensible to study. At the time he played rhythm guitar and sang. He and his first wife, singer Stevie Lange, moved to England in 1970, where they started the band Hocus. But with little success.

In 1976, Lange began what was to become a legendary production career, working in those formative days with the likes of City Boy (their self-titled '76 debut gave him his very first production credit), The Motors and the Boomtown Rats, in fact 'Mutt' (as he was nicknamed from an early age) got his first number one single in 1978 with the latter band's song 'Rat Trap'.

His association with AC/DC started in 1979, when he was asked to produce *Highway To Hell*, following an aborted attempt by the band to work with Eddie Kramer. He went on to collaborate with them on both *Back In Black* and *For Those About To Rock*. Aside from Harry Vanda and George Young, he has the distinction of being the producer who's worked on the most 'DC records.

Notoriously meticulous, sometimes it's said to the point of driving musicians insane, Lange's perfectionism has ensured he's been untouchable for many years as arguably the best producer in the world. Stories about his attention to detail are legion. As indeed are those about how he would dominate and control artists in the studio. One former associate once claimed that Lange would scrap tapes recorded with a specific band after they'd finished for the day in the studio, and then re-record all the parts himself – without the group ever knowing.

There are other rumours about how he'd painstakingly demand some singers record their lines syllable by syllable. Whatever the truth of these reports, there's no doubt that, almost without exception, the Lange name on an album (as producer and songwriter) is almost a guarantee of major sales. And he also seems to inspire genuine respect and affection from those with whom he's worked.

"I know there are those who think we were 'Mutt's puppets," Def Leppard vocalist Joe Elliott once said, *"but that's not true. Our relationship with him was more of a partnership. He listened to what we said and took our ideas on board. He didn't fashion our sound, but he helped massively to develop it."*

The same applies to AC/DC. What Lange did was enhance what was already there – and three albums on which he worked with them are among the finest of the band's career.

LANSDOWNE ROAD

Number six Lansdowne Road was where AC/DC based themselves from 1973-75 and is located in the St. Kilda area of Melbourne. The band worked there on the songs for the early albums. Some people have suggested that the group actually lived at number seven, but the current owner, Rosie Haas, has confirmed that it was indeed number six.

"It was a bit of a crazy place," bassist Mark Evans told Mojo magazine *"There was a brothel over the back fence, so we got to know the girls who worked there, and one of them started to go out with Bon. I remember realising how bad it was when one day I walked into his room and there were two girls going at it hammer and tong, and it didn't even shock me!"*

There have been suggestions that a plaque should be erected, to acknowledge the man not those two girls! So far, though, nothing has happened.

LAST ACTION HERO

1993 movie starring Arnold Schwarzenneger and Charles Dance. Seen as a satire on the action genre, the plot is about Danny Madigan (played by Austin O'Brien), a kid who, thanks to a

magic cinema ticket, ends up connected to his fictional idol Jack Slater (Schwarzenneger).

AC/DC's previously unreleased song 'Big Gun' features on the soundtrack, one that also includes contributions from Alice In Chains, Megadeth, Queensryche, Def Leppard, Anthrax and Aerosmith and reached number seven on the US albums charts.

LAUGHLIN/DENNIS

AC/DC's first proper manager, Laughlin was the original singer for Aussie band Sherbet, who started in 1969. However, he only appeared on their debut single, 'Crimson Ships' (1970), leaving long before they had huge success in Australia with replacement singer Daryl Braithwaite.

Laughlin became 'DC's manager very early on in their career, and would occasionally replace singer Dave Evans onstage towards the end of the latter's tenure with the band, when the relationship between the frontman and the Young brothers was breaking down. It has been suggested that Laughlin briefly replaced Dave Evans as AC/DC's frontman. However, this has been denied by Evans himself, who claims Laughlin just did one or two shows with the band when he was unable to perform.

In 1975 Laughlin was replaced as AC/DC's manager by Michael Browning.

LEBER-KREBS

Also known as CCC (Contemporary Communications Corporation), the Leber-Krebs organisation was among the biggest management companies in the rock world from the middle of the 1970s until the late 1980s. Steve Leber and David Krebs looked after Aerosmith, Ted Nugent, AC/DC, Scorpions and Def Leppard among others. 'DC joined them in 1979, after leaving Michael Browning, quitting three years later.

Steve Leber had started out with the massive William Morris Agency in 1964, actually establishing their music division. During the next eight years he handled artists such as Diana Ross, the Rolling Stones and the Beach Boys.

David Krebs had also begun his career at the William Morris Agency in 1964 – in the mail room. However, he quickly worked his way through to the Business Affairs department, and then on to working as an agent in the music division.

In 1972, the pair quit the William Morris Agency and formed Leber-Krebs Inc. Over the next 17 years they not only managed some of the biggest names in hard rock, but also founded the Texxas Jam and the California World Music Festival – two of the biggest annual events in America at the time (1970s).

Since their split, Leber has had success as a theatrical producer, and is now Director Of Corporate Strategy at musicvision.com. Krebs not only runs the non-profit organisation Uncommon Sense, which aims to educate Americans about energy, but is also currently involved in developing The American Rock Opera Repertory Company, fusing rock, theatre and the classics, and is managing Hanoi Rocks as well.

LET IT LOOSE

Track written by the Young brothers and Brian Johnson and recorded during the pre-production sessions for the 1988 album *Blow Up Your Video*, but omitted from the final track listing. Why? Because the demo was stolen, along with the song 'Alright Tonight', and bootlegged.

LET ME PUT MY LOVE INTO YOU

The fifth track from the 1980 album *Back In Black*, written by Young, Young and Johnson. This was cited by the PMRC (Parents Music Resource Center) in the 1980s as one of their Filthy Fifteen songs which were unsuitable for children, due the overt nature of its lyrics: 'Flying on a free flight/Driving all night / With my machinery/'Cause I got the power/Any hour/To show the man in me'.

LET THERE BE ROCK

Released in 1977, like albums before it this one came out with a different track listing in Australia to that of the rest of the world. The last to feature bassist Mark Evans, once more it saw the band stepping up their game. Like all the great names in rock history, 'DC have always had a knack of making the right record at the right time. When it was appropriate to make a quantum leap they would do so, although for the most part it was a case of developing their approach, finessing and driving it forward, without overtaking expectations and aspirations.

Compared to the band that had recorded *Dirty Deeds Done Dirt Cheap* the previous year, the quintet were perhaps more confident and cunning. The lyrics are more observed, the music more targeted – this was an international sound now from a five-piece who were more at ease with their own potential, and the growing demands all around them.

Let There Be Rock is leaner and hungrier than anything released before. The band could deal with sexual issues, as in 'Crabsody In Blue', a song about contracting a sexually transmitted disease that pulls no punches lyrically or musi-

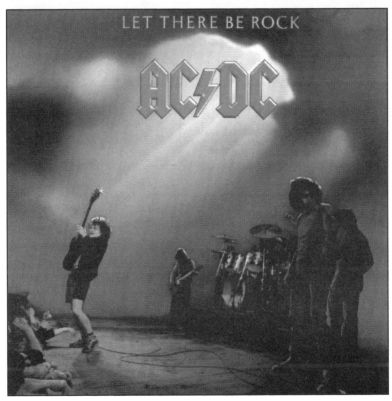

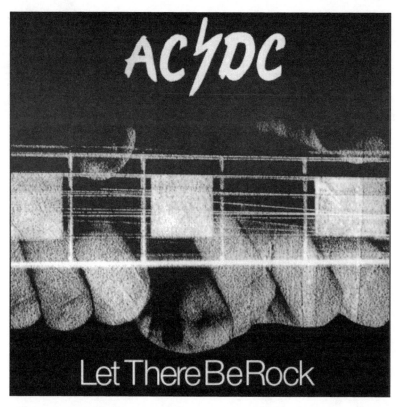

cally and was left off the US and Japanese versions, being replaced by 'Problem Child' (a track that first appeared on *Dirty Deeds Done Dirt Cheap*). They could stand back and observe greed in society ('Dog Eat Dog'). They deal with one-night stands ('Whole Lotta Rosie'), groupie havens ('Go Down'). 'Hell Ain't A Bad Place To Be' proves that hope of a better future can sometimes come from the most unlikely sources, while the title track is a celebration of the birth of rock 'n' roll and the way it swept the globe.

Here were AC/DC not collating songs, but coming up with a cohesive, coherent, cogent album. Every track is to count and punch its weight, each chord and word is carefully considered. But this is not an academic study – the energy and dynamic that had first gotten the band noticed was, if anything, more potent than before. Now, though, there was considerable weight and experience in the band's ranks, meaning the clinical studio setting was no barrier.

The Australian and international versions were given very different covers, with the former in a gatefold black and white sleeve featuring a guitar fretboard, with fingers in place, while the latter has a colour photo of the band in full flight.

The album provided the band with their first chart success outside of Australia and New Zealand. While in America it only reached a modest number 154, in the UK it made greater strides, peaking at number 17.

The full track listing for the Australian record is: *Go Down/ Dog Eat Dog/Let There Be Rock/Bad Boy Boogie/Overdose/Crabsody In Blue/Hell Ain't A Bad Place To Be/Whole Lotta Rosie.*

The full track listing for the international record is: *Go Down/Dog Eat Dog/Let There Be Rock/Bad Boy Boogie/ Problem Child/Overdose/Hell Ain't A Bad Place To Be/Whole Lotta Rosie.*

LET THERE BE ROCK
(Song)

Title track of the band's 1977 album, this was released as a single with 'Problem Child' on the B-side. Written by Young, Young and Scott, it celebrates the birth of rock 'n' roll in 1955, and references the Bible (in the way that Bon Scott intones the creation of the musical form by demanding let there be light… sound… drums… guitar… rock), and also some of the pioneers of the style, especially Chuck Berry. While the latter insisted in his classic 'Roll Over Beethoven' that someone should, 'Tell Tchaikovsky

the news', here Scott insists, 'But Tchaikovsky had the news'.

The song ends with the crescendo lyrical climax: 'One night in the club called the Shakin' Hand/There was a 42 decibel rockin' band/And the music was good and the music was loud/And the singer turned and he said to the crowd/Let there be rock'.

The band shot a video for this in a church, with Scott dressed as a priest, and the rest of the band made up as altar boys. This was one of the first public appearances from Cliff Williams, who replaced Mark Evans on bass soon after the album was released.

The song has been a staple part of AC/DC's live set since its inception, proving to be the centre point of many an AC/DC show. It would be during *Let There Be Rock* that Angus Young would leave the stage and set out, originally on the shoulders of Bon Scott, then later of a roadie, for a 'walkabout' through the crowd,

to be returned, stage side, on the shoulders of Bon and later Brian, to euphoric applause.

The track is now also part of the 'Rock Band 2' computer game set-up.

LET THERE BE ROCK
(Film)

Filmed at the Pavillon de Paris in France on December 9, 1979 during the band's *Highway To Hell* tour, this was shown in cinemas during September 1980, several months after the death of vocalist Bon Scott, and was also released around the same time on video.

It's essentially a live gig, although interviews with the band are included. The soundtrack was released as CDs two and three of the 1997 *Bonfire* box set.

The full track listing is:
CD1 - *Live Wire/Shot Down In Flames/Hell Ain't A Bad Place To Be/Sin City/Walk All Over You/Bad Boy Boogie.*
CD2 – *The Jack/Highway To Hell/Girls Got Rhythm/High Voltage/Whole Lotta Rosie/Rocker/T.N.T./Let There Be Rock.*

LET THERE BE ROCK: THE STORY OF AC/DC

AC/DC biography published in 2007, written by American jour-

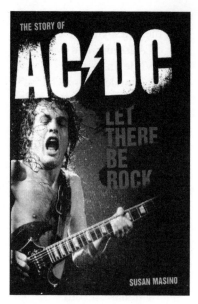

nalist Susan Masino, who first met the band on tour in 1977.

LET'S GET IT UP

The third track from the 1981 album *For Those About To Rock (We Salute You)*. This was released as a single with live versions of 'Back In Black' and 'T.N.T.' (the latter only on the 12 inch version) on the B-side. Written by Angus and Malcolm Young, together with Brian Johnson, the lyrics leave nothing to the imagination: 'Loose lips sink ships/So come aboard for a pleasure trip/It's high tide so let's ride/The moon is risin' and so am I'.

This was the first single to be released from the album and reached No. 13 in the charts, the band's highest UK placing to that date.

LET'S MAKE IT

Track from the 1990 album *The Razors Edge*. Written by the Young brothers, it's the band's usual sort of nookie thing: 'It's way past midnight/Why don't we take a ride/We'll make some honey as we're cruisin' real slow'.

LIVE

The first live album of the Brian Johnson era, this was released in 1992. It was recorded at the band's record breaking third headlining appearance at Monsters Of Rock in 1991 on *The Razors Edge* tour, and produced by Bruce Fairbairn.

The full track listing is: *Thunderstruck/Shoot To Thrill/Back In Black/Who Made Who/ Heatseeker/The Jack/Moneytalks/Hells Bells/Dirty Deeds Done Dirt Cheap/Whole Lotta Rosie/You Shook Me All Night Long/Highway To Hell/T.N.T./ For Those About To Rock (We Salute You).*

A two-CD collector's edition was issued a month after the single CD, the full track listing for this being:
CD1 – *Thunderstruck/Shoot To Thrill/Back In Black/Sin City/ Who Made Who/Heatseeker/Fire Your Guns/Jailbreak/The Jack/ The Razor's Edge/Dirty Deeds Done Dirty Cheap/Moneytalks.*

CD2 – *Hells Bells/Are You Ready/That's The Way I Wanna Rock 'N' Roll/High Voltage/You Shook Me All Night Long/Whole Lotta Rosie/Let There Be Rock/ Bonny* (traditional Scottish folk song, dedicated to Bon Scott)*/Highway To Hell/T.N.T./ For Those About To Rock (We Salute You).*

The single CD version reached Number Five in the UK charts.

LIVE AT DONINGTON

This was shot on August 17, 1991, at the band's third and last headlining appearance at the Monsters Of Rock – AC/DC remain the only act ever to headline Monsters Of Rock three times.

Aside from the live performances, the DVD also has special footage of certain songs where the camera is on one band member only, plus audio commentary from the Young brothers and a discography.

Altogether 26 cameras were used to capture the gig, including one in a helicopter. Subsequently, it's been released in Blu-ray disc format (October 2007).

The full track listing is *Thunderstruck/Shoot To Thrill/Back In Black/Hell Ain't A Bad Place To Be/Heatseeker/Fire Your Guns/ Jailbreak/The Jack/Dirty Deeds Done Dirt Cheap/Moneytalks/*

Hells Bells/High Voltage/Whole Lotta Rosie/T.N.T./Let There Be Rock/ Highway To Hell/For Those About To Rock (We Salute You).

LIVE / BON PLEASE DON'T GO

It's a Korean live album, but totally official. This was released in 1992, but features recordings from 1976-79. It's said to be very collectible, although how much any copy is worth is open to question. It was released on the Hee Gee/Golden Records label.

LIVE FROM THE ATLANTIC STUDIOS

Album included in the 1997 box set *Bonfire*, this was actually recorded on December 7, 1977 in New York. AC/DC did a special set

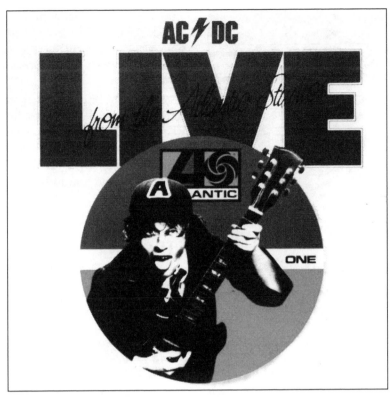

at the famed Atlantic Studios, in front of a select crowd. The results were mixed by George Young and then sent out – along with a letter and a 'DC postcard – to radio stations across America as a promotional tool to boost the band's standing over there, on the back of the *Let There Be Rock* album and their first ever US tour.

Until its inclusion in the aforementioned *Bonfire* set, the album was never officially available as a commercial record. However, there had been bootlegs around for years, one of which was on the Impossible Recordworks label and is said to be the first ever AC/DC bootleg, available in 1978.

If you've got the original promotional vinyl copy, together with the letter and postcard, it could be worth up to $200. Oddly the bootleg mentioned above is valued at twice that amount!

The full track listing is: *Live Wire/Problem Child/High Voltage/Hell Ain't A Bad Place To Be/Dog Eat Dog/The Jack/ Whole Lotta Rosie/Rocker.*

LIVE '77

This unofficial DVD was released in 2003 and features a show filmed at the Golders Green Hippodrome in North West Lon-

don on October 27, 1977 during the *Let There Be Rock* tour.

The full track listing is: *Let There Rock/Problem Child/Hell Ain't A Bad Place To Be/Whole Lotta Rosie/Bad Boy Boogie/Rocker/T.N.T.*

'Hell Ain't A Bad Place To Be' and 'Rocker' both appear on the 2007 two-disc DVD set *Plug Me In*, while 'Let There Be Rock' is included on the third disc in the deluxe edition of the same release.

LIVE WIRE

Track number four from the *T.N.T.* album in 1975, and also appeared the next year on the international version of *High Voltage* (also as track four). Written by Young, Young and Scott, this was a regular set opener during Scott's time with the band.

In 1982, Brian Johnson performed the track for the very first time onstage and sang the second verse twice – he's not performed it again since.

Lyrically, to a great extent it reflects Bon Scott – a magnet for women, but someone of whom men could be wary: 'I'm as cool as a body on ice/Or hotter than a rollin' dice/Send you to heaven/Take you to hell'.

LITTLE LOVER

The third track from the Australian debut AC/DC album *High Voltage*, released in 1975. It was one of only two songs from this record to make it onto the international version the following year, along with *She's Got Balls.* Written by Angus and Malcolm Young and Bon Scott, it's about the guitarist in an unsigned band picking up a girl at a gig, whom he spots grooving down at the front. At one point it refers to her having his picture on her bedroom wall, next to Gary Glitter – which these days would not be something of which to boast! There's also a commercial reference: 'Killed me when I saw/The wet patch on your seat/Was it Coca Cola?'

Some have suggested that *Little Lover* is, in fact, a veiled reference to underage girls, which, along with the aforementioned Glitter reference, would not only be inadvisable in today's overtly politically correct climate, but enough to have the band up on charges –

the suggestion has, however, never been substantiated.

LOCK UP YOUR DAUGHTERS

The sly name given to the band's first proper headlining tour of the UK. There were 19 dates in all, and it's worth recalling them. They were as follows: Glasgow City Hall June 11, Edinburgh Leith Theatre 12, Southport Floral Hall 13, Sheffield Top Rank Suite 14, Bradford St. George's Hall 15, Bedworth Civic Hall 17, Liverpool Stadium 19, Douglas Palace Lido 20, Cardiff Top Rank Suite 22, Swansea Brangwyn Hall 23, Corby Festival Hall 24, Guildford Civic Hall 26, Birmingham Mayfair Suite 27, Southampton Top Rank Suite 30, Gravesend Woodville Halls July 1, Plymouth Top Rank Suites 2, Yeovil Johnson Hall 3, Brighton Top Rank Suite 4, London Lyceum Ballroom 7.

The tour was sponsored by UK weekly music magazine *Sounds*, and the support bill included both bands and films! Not all of the dates were well attended. Only five people turned up in Swansea. Problems of a different sort happened in Glasgow, where the crowd were too boisterous, and seats were ripped out, being hurled around the venue.

The last in London also featured a 'Best Dressed Schoolgirl/ Schoolboy' contest.

LOVE AT FIRST FEEL

The second track from the international version of the 1976 album *Dirty Deeds Done Dirt Cheap*. It was one of two tracks not featured on the original Aussie version of the record, the other being 'Cold Hearted Man', which eventually surfaced on *Powerage*. 'Love At First Feel' was also released in 1976 as a single in Australia, with 'Problem Child' on the B-side.

Written by the Young brothers and Bon Scott, again there's a definite feel (no pun intended) of underage sex, as on 'Little Lover', with the protagonist variously described as being disgusting and committing a sin: 'I didn't know if you were legal tender/But I spent you just the same'.

LOVE BOMB

Track from the 1995 album *Ballbreaker*. Written by Angus and

Malcolm Young, it uses a bombing raid as a metaphor for sex: 'Cruisin' the sky, let's fly/Blowin' all night and day/Open your bays, get ready, it's bombs away'.

LOVEGROVE/VINCE

One of those who briefly managed AC/DC in their early days, Lovegrove (below, with Bon Scott) resigned to spend more time with his family. He was also a member of The Valentines, alongside Bon Scott.

Lovegrove, who managed both Cold Chisel and The Divinyls as well, is probably most famous for the 1978 TV documentary *Australian Music To The World* – the first international documentary on Aussie music. He's also produced two acclaimed AIDS documentaries, 1987's *Suzi's Story* (about his wife, who died from the disease) and another in 1994 about his son Troy (another victim).

Based in London, another of his works is a biography on late INXS frontman Michael Hutchence, titled *Shining Through – Torn Apart*.

LOVE HUNGRY MAN

Ninth track from the 1979 album *Highway To Hell*, written by Angus and Malcolm Young and Bon Scott. The lyrics say it all: 'Oh baby you're such a treat love/I'm a love-hungry man/And a man's got to eat'. There's also a reference to 'Bon appetite', which would seem to suggest that Scott empathised with the sentiments of the song.

LOVE SONG (OH JENE)

Track seven from the Australian version of 1975's *High Voltage* album, it was written by the Young brothers and Bon Scott and has never been released outside of Australia. It evolved from a song titled 'Fell In Love', which had been written by Malcolm Young and Dave Evans.

Interestingly, Malcolm Young plays the lead guitar on this song, with Angus chipping in on the acoustic.

For Scott, the lyrics are surprisingly tender: 'If you leave me you'll make me cry/When I think of you saying good bye'.

This was also AC/DC's first hit single in Australia, although it was the B-side, 'Baby Please Don't Go' that picked up most of the airplay. Released on March 3, 1975, it peaked at number ten on the Australian charts. Most of the sales for the single were generated in Melbourne and Adelaide.

MCFARLANE TOYS

A company started in 1994 by Todd McFarlane, an artist, designer, comic book writer and toy manufacturer. McFarlane Toys makes detailed models of characters from movies, comics and video games as well as famous musicians and sporting personalities.

There is an Angus Young figure, with the guitarist dressed in his classic schoolboy outfit (shorts, jacket, white shirt and tie) and, of course, complete with his famous Gibson SG six-string.

KnuckleBonz. Inc released Angus and Malcolm Young sculptures in 2006, with Angus in

his trademark schoolboy uniform and Malcolm in his usual onstage stance. This was part of the company's 'Guitar Hero' series. Tony Simerman, President of the company, said at the time:

"The dual attack of the Young brothers is one of the all time greatest pairings in rock. Angus is the ultimate combo of chops and showmanship and Mal's rhythm work has always been AC/DC's secret weapon. It is only fitting that they be created as a tandem for the series."

MALLET, DAVID

The acclaimed video director who's worked on a number of AC/DC projects. While the producer of any album is always a vital part in the process, when the arrival of MTV in the 1980s immeasurably increased the importance of promo clips, people like Mallet

became almost as central to the success of any record.

Aside from doing the promotional videos for a number of songs, including 'Moneytalks' and 'Heatseaker', Mallet was also the director for the long-form releases *Live At Donington* in 1992 and *No Bull* four years later.

His work is also features on the *Clipped* collection of promos from *The Razors Edge* era. This obviously included 'Heatseeker' and 'Moneytalks', plus 'Thunderstruck', 'Are You Ready' and 'That's The Way I Wanna Rock 'N' Roll'.

As well as AC/DC, Mallet has worked with artists like Def Leppard, David Bowie, Asia, Queen and Rush and has also been a TV producer – one of his big successes was *The Kenny Everett Video Show*.

MARQUEE, THE

The famous London club in Wardour Street, where AC/DC played on no less than 11 occasions. They first made an appearance there on May 11, 1976, opening for a band called Crawler (who in a previous incarnation had been Back Street Crawler, and had then featured ex-Free guitarist Paul Kossoff) – the general consensus of opinion was that the hot young Aussies were the star attraction on that night, eclipsing the more venerable headliners. Their last appearance was on September 8,

1976, so all of their shows at the venue were squeezed into just four months.

The club first started in 1958, then situated at 165 Oxford Street. During its six-year tenure at this location, a number of major names appeared. Some of the most notable were the Rolling Stones, who played their first ever show there on July 12, 1962 as well as The Who and the Jimi Hendrix Experience.

The club moved to Wardour Street in Soho during 1964 and, over the next 24 years so many of the biggest names in rock played there it's almost easier to list those who didn't! Now established as one of the most famous clubs in the world, The Marquee was forced to move to Charing Cross Road in 1988, after the Wardour Street site was sold for redevelopment.

Subsequently, there have been several failed attempts to re-activate the venue at various locations, the most recent being in August, 2007, when it was housed in Upper St. Martin's Lane, Covent Garden. But this particular venue had shut in less than six months.

Evans. Matters joined AC/DC at the suggestion of George Young, who had seen him performing in the band Armageddon.

Matters had previously been with New South Wales band Armageddon, whose brand of heavy blues with pop sensibilities helped them to pick up a strong local following.

Formed in 1969, they won two local battle of the bands contests (both allegedly under controversial circumstances), but Matters quit in '74, and the band never subsequently achieved any significant standing.

After his brief tenure with AC/DC, Matters joined The Locals, before deciding that perhaps he wasn't going to be a rock star after all.

MATTERS/PAUL

Bassist Matters was briefly a member of AC/DC around the time of the *High Voltage* album, and even appeared in some promotional band photos, although he was soon replaced by Mark

MAXIMUM OVERDRIVE

Horror movie directed by author Stephen King. This 1986 film is generally regarded as being somewhat tongue-in-cheek – though others claim it to be downright rubbish – and was based, at least

in part, on King's own story, *Trucks*.

It's King's only attempt at directing any film to date, and is something of an embarrassment. The man himself was at least disgusted enough with his efforts to state he would never direct another movie.

The plot's all about the radiation from a passing comet bringing to life machinery across the globe, all of which have strangely genocidal aspirations. A group of psychotic trucks trap people in a roadside café in Wilmington, Carolina, which is where the action is set.

Emilio Estevez, Pat Hingle and Yeardley Smith (the voice of Lisa Simpson) star – not that they'll thank anyone for the reminder – while AC/DC supplied the soundtrack, which was released as the album *Who Made Who* in 1986. This features new compositions 'Who Made Who', 'D.T.' and 'Chase The Ace' (the latter pair being instrumentals), plus 'You Shook Me All Night Long', 'Sink The Pink', 'Ride On', 'Hells Bells', 'Shake Your Foundation' and 'For Those About To Rock (We Salute You)'.

AC/DC are one of King's favourite bands, so at least in this sense getting them involved with *Maximum Overdrive* made the project worthwhile for him. In fact, when he bought the radio station WKIT (100.3FM) in Bangor, Maine several years ago, one of his principle goals was to have the group being blasted out regularly.

MEANSTREAK

The third track from the 1988 album *Blow Up Your Video*, this was written by Young, Young and Johnson, and, along with the decidedly heavy 'This Means War', one of the heaviest tracks the band have ever recorded, a nod no doubt to the emergence of thrash metal at the time. It's about someone who's been there, done it, and isn't quite sure what he wants. It name checks the Count Of Monte Cristo and the Sheik Of Arabi: 'I'm the perfect culture vulture in the face of poverty/An' I ain't met no one who told me I got class/Say never feed the animal the boys got to much flash'.

MELDRUM, IAN 'MOLLY'

Ian 'Molly' Meldrum is an Australian music critic, producer and talent spotter, and was the man responsible for booking all the acts onto the popular Aussie music TV show *Countdown* form 1974-1987, it's entire lifespan. He also had an on-air role in the programme from 1975 to '86. AC/DC made several appearances on the show.

Openly gay, Meldrum is renowned for wearing a trademark Akubra hat and for championing the Australian music scene.

An interview Meldrum recorded with Bon Scott in 1978 is included on the *Plug Me In* DVD. During the course of this, both try and fail to recall the name of the bassist in Kiss (Gene Simmons).

MELTDOWN

Track from the 2000 album *Stiff Upper Lip*, written by Angus and Malcolm Young. Wanna know what the song's about? This will give you a clue or two: 'I look at my watch to find out the right time of the day/I look at her libido hey hey hey'

MENSCH, PETER

At one time co-manager of AC/DC with Cliff Burnstein, Mensch is among the most respected and successful music managers in the world. Under the name Q. Prime Inc., Mensch and Burnstein have guided the careers of the Rolling Stones, Madonna, Metallica and Def Leppard, to name just a few.

After graduating from Brandeis University with a degree in Urban Studies, Mensch gained an M.A. in marketing at the University Of Chicago.

He began his music career as Aerosmith's tour accountant, working for Leber-Krebs, a company that in the 1970s was among the biggest management operations in rock music. It was at this juncture that he became AC/DC's management representative, taking over from Michael Browning on July 1, 1979. However, in June 1982, the relationship ended with the band taking on their old tour manager Ian Jeffery as their personal manager.

In 1982, Mensch teamed up with Burnstein to start a new company, taking clients such as Def Leppard with them. At first, the fledgling organisation was run from two flats: Mensch's in Earl's Court, West London and Burnstein's in Hoboken, New Jersey. Today, they have offices in Manhattan and look after the Red Hot Chili Peppers, Metallica, Jimmy Page and Snow Patrol among others.

MESSIN' WITH THE KID

A track supposedly recorded for the *Flick Of The Switch* album, but then excluded. This has turned up on a rare AC/DC bootleg called *Aftershock*, which purports to feature not only this song, but also alternative versions of various tracks which were featured on the final record. What you get are three takes of 'Guns For Hire' and 'Nervous Shakedown' and two jam sessions.

MICHIGAN AM 600 WTAC

The first radio station in America to play AC/DC on air. Station manager Peter Cavanaugh also booked the band to play at the Capitol Theater in Flint, Michigan, supported by legendary proto-punks MC5.

In the 1960s and '70s, it was regarded as a major outlet for rock bands, also being the first station in the country to play anything from The Who. In 1980 it became a country station and, oddly, is now known as WSNL, whose output is exclusively religious music.

MILTON KEYNES NATIONAL BOWL

The scene for AC/DC's last outdoor gig in the UK, at least at the time of writing this book. The event took place on June 8, 2001, when 'DC were joined on the bill by The Offspring (pop-punks), Queens Of The Stone Age (stoner) and Megadeth (metal) – a diverse bill indeed, which reflected the fact that the headliners were attracting fans from across the rock divide.

Megadeth were the opening band, and they kicked into a ferocious rhythm, although the blustery conditions mitigated against them getting a strong response.

Queens Of The Stone Age were just beginning to make their mark as a commercial force to be reckoned with, but they weren't at their best on this day. Perhaps it was also the case that the crowd wasn't exactly populated with the sort of people who took to their music. But, they still gave it their all, and in the end got a warm reception.

Much to everyone's surprise, The Offspring did really well. Concentrating on their best known songs helped. However it was clear their presence on the bill had been a shrewd move.

But it was clearly AC/DC's night. As has been the case for decades, it doesn't matter how strong any other band in the line-up is, they won't upstage 'DC. David Lee Roth and Van Halen tried in 1984 at Donington, when the Halens were arguably the hottest rock band on the planet, and they came unstuck. So, it was true at Milton Keynes. The band mixed and matched classics from

the past with material from then new album *Stiff Upper Lip*. They pulled out the Hells Bell, the cannons are lit up. This is a triumph. Or is it? Here's what journalist Ian Winwood said about the band in a review for Kerrang! magazine at the time:

"Saying bad things about AC/DC is a bit like waiting outside the gates of a nursery school and telling the crying kids there's no such person as Santa Claus. But, as the band chug open a four-and-half-hour version of 'The Jack' – unreconstructed sexism concerning a girl who has the clap, in an age where men and women have AIDS – a couple of thoughts spring to mind. The first is that AC/DC are not always very good and the second is that on the contrary, sometimes AC/DC can

be very bad, and very boring indeed.

"There are some parts of this Milton Keynes show that are simply amazing, most of them in the last 45 minutes. So that'll be 'Highway To Hell', 'Whole Lotta Rosie' and 'Let There Be Rock', in that order. 'Rock 'N' Roll Ain't Noise Pollution' and 'You Shook Me All Night Long' are also damn fine songs. But that's not really the point any more. As Brian Johnson swings on the giant Hell's Bell, as Angus Young duckwalks up the walkway that parts the crowd and up the staircase at the side of the stage, you realise in terms of a production, this is exactly the same show they played at Wembley Arena in December, at Sydney Opera House in January and at New York's Madison Square Garden in May.

"You realise that this could be anywhere, and that AC/DC don't really care where they are. Worse still, as Brian Johnson tells the crowd they're the loudest of the tour so far, you know that just like Bruce Forsyth, he's lying, and that he'll say exactly the same thing to the crowds in Germany or Holland. And in that sense, AC/DC don't really care that you're here either.

"They close, of course, with 'For Those About To Rock' – even though people have just finished rocking, so surely that should be 'For Those Who Have Just Rocked'. The cannons fire

and the fireworks explode. And still everybody loves AC/DC, even though AC/DC were really not very good tonight. Thing is though... you just don't say those type of things out loud, now do you?"

Incidentally, AC/DC were one of several big bands to play at this venue in a matter of two months. Black Sabbath, Bon Jovi and Robbie Williams were also there between May 26 and July 22.

AC/DC's set that night was: *Stiff Upper Lip/You Shook Me All Night Long/Problem Child/Thunderstruck/Hell Ain't A Bad Place To Be/Hard As A Rock/Shoot To Thrill/Rock 'N' Roll Ain't Noise Pollution/What Do You Do For Money Honey/Bad Boy Boogie/Hells Bells/Up To My Neck In You/The Jack/Back In Black/Dirty Deeds Done Dirt Cheap/Highway To Hell/Whole Lotta Rosie/Let There Be Rock/TNT/For Those About To Rock (We Salute You)*

MIRAVAL STUDIO
France

The studio where the band recorded the *Blow Up Your Video* album, with returning producers Harry Vanda and George Young. It's also the place Pink Floyd recorded *The Wall* and Judas Priest forged the *Painkiller*

record. The Cranberries have also worked there.

Talking about their choice of studio, the band said:

"In December 1986, we'd had a break for some time. Under the direction of Vanda and Young, the conditions were the best to get up a spontaneous album that would remind (you) of the early ones. That was a very important step for our spirits."

MISTRESS FOR CHRISTMAS

Track from the 1990 album *The Razors Edge*. Written by Angus and Malcolm Young, it's a salacious Xmas dream, what the 'DC guys want in their stocking: 'Jingle bells, jingle bells, Jingle all the day/I just can't wait till Christmas time/When I can grope you in the hay (When I can roll you in the hay)'.

The track was also released as the B-side of the single 'Moneytalks'. In all honesty, not one of Yuletide's more memorable ditties.

MONEYTALKS

The third track from 1990's *The Razors Edge* album. Written by the Young brothers, it was released as a single in December 1990 in seven inch, 12 inch and CD formats, with 'Mistress For Christmas' on the B-side of each one. In the UK, 'Borrowed Time' also features on the single, while 'Down On The Border' figures on the Australian version. This was a Top 40 hit for the band in the UK, US and Australia, though surprisingly only reaching No. 36 in the UK.

Lyrically, it's a song about those who use money to replace personality, talent and hard work: 'A French maid, foreign chef/A big house with king size bed/You've had enough, you ship them out/

The dollar's up-down, you'd better buy the pound'.

MOUNTAIN STUDIOS
Montreux

The studio where AC/DC recorded the *Fly On The Wall* album. Located in Montreux from 1975 to 2003, it's now in Attalens, Switzerland. From 1979 to 1993, the studio was owned by Queen, who recorded six albums there, including *Jazz, Hot Space* and *A Kind Of Magic.*

Other acts to work at the studio include David Bowie, the Rolling Stones, Yes, Magnum and Iggy Pop.

MUSIC MACHINE

The venue in Camden, North London where Bon Scott spent the evening of February 18, 1980 – the night he died. At the time it was a renowned location for rock and metal gigs, as well as a place where many musicians would hang out.

Opened as the Camden Theatre in 1900, the BBC recorded many famous radio shows there from 1945 to 1972, at which point it became the Music Machine.

A name change to the Camden Palace occurred in 1982, before being re-developed as Koko in 2004.

MYER MUSIC BOWL

The venue in Melbourne where a riot happened when AC/DC played there in February 1988, as part of their first Australian tour in seven years. About 60 people were arrested that night.

a series of free shows just after recording their second album, *T.N.T.* However, the band's rapidly growing stature by this juncture worked against them. At the first of these gigs, thousands of school-girls turned up and stormed the place, desperate to get a glimpse of their heroes. 'DC managed to get through two songs, before the whole plan was abandoned, as massive damage was caused.

There are some who believe that Phil Rudd broke his thumb during this fracas, and therefore had to sit out a few gigs. This is not actually the case. Rudd broke his thumb shortly after, during an incident at the Matthew Findlers

MYER MUSIC STORE

A record store in Melbourne where AC/DC were due to play

Hotel in Melbourne. To allow them to carry on fulfilling gig commitments, the band brought back Colin Burgess.

NAMUR

The Belgian town where AC/DC played their first show with new singer Brian Johnson. The gig took place on June 29, 1980 and was part of a six-date warm-up package touring around the Benelux countries, to give the new man a chance to settle in, before being unleashed properly and formally on the world.

NERVOUS SHAKEDOWN

Track number four from the 1983 album *Flick Of The Switch*, the song tells a cautionary tale of being arrested by a bent police force and then, when standing in the dock, the court authorities deciding to send the individual down regardless. Written by Young, Young and Johnson, there may be an element of truth behind the song, as several members of AC/DC have had scrapes with the authorities over the years, especially Bon Scott, who even served time in both Fremantle Prison and Riverbank Juvenile Institution in Perth in the early '60s.

The song was released as an EP in August 1984, backed by live versions of 'Rock And Roll Ain't Noise Pollution', 'Sin City' and 'This House Is On Fire', all recorded in Detroit in 1983. It reached number 35 in the UK singles chart.

NEUROTICA

A Florida rock band best known for featuring Kelly Schaeffer from death metallers Atheist, and for having Brian Johnson produce their 1998 debut album *Seed* and co-writing and singing backing vocals on the song 'Deadly Sin'.

The story goes that Johnson was having a pint of Guinness in a Florida bar one evening when Neurotica were there to play a show. Suitably impressed with the band's hard-driving performance, Johnson introduced himself and offered to help them in any way he could.

"I just wanted to help," Johnson told Metal Edge magazine at the time. *"It was not so much producing, I just went in and helped them as much as I could. It was done at a little 16-track studio. They had some great songs but I was basically showing them how to arrange them and just make them exciting by having highs and lows and drama. They're great kids; I think they've got a big future."*

The album was co-produced by engineer Mike Fraser (another with AC/DC connections), and Johnson also helped the band sign a deal with his friend Doug Kaye's indie label, who released the band's second album, *Neurotica*. This was produced by Kaye and mixed by Kevin 'Caveman' Shirley, best known for his recent work with Iron Maiden, in 2002.

Alongside Schaeffer, Neurotica also feature Shane Bowen (guitar), Chris Rollo (guitar), Migwell Pryzbyl (bass) and Jason West (drums).

NICK OF TIME

The sixth track from 1988's *Blow Up Your Video* album. Written by Malcolm and Angus Young and Brian Johnson, the song takes a typically anti-establishment stance about living life as hard as you want to and getting through by the skin of your teeth. Lyrics like 'Wrong track, wrong line, Fast train to run on time/ Bad blood, bad news, hangin' by a rope got nothin' to lose' help convey the sentiment.

One of four tracks from *Blow Up Your Video* that were aired on the subsequent world tour.

NIGHT OF THE LONG KNIVES

The penultimate track from 1981's *For Those About To Rock (We Salute You)* and co-written by Malcolm Young, Angus Young and Brian Johnson, it plays on the semi-gladiatorial theme behind the album – the title of which came from a book about Roman Gladiators being read by Angus Young at the time, entitled *For Those About To Die, We Salute You*.

Historically the Night Of The Long Knives is the name given to a purge that took place in Nazi Germany between June 30 and July 2, 1934, in which Hitler moved against the SA and their leader Ernest Rohm, and some 85 people were killed. The phrase has been equally applied to a Saxon massacre of British chieftains in 436AD, the assassination of the British traveller and explorer Alexander Burns in Kabul in 1861, and even British Prime Minister Harold MacMillan's sacking of seven cabinet ministers in 1962.

This AC/DC song almost certainly uses a more general reference, with lines like 'Who's your friend, who's your foe/Who's your Judas, you don't know'.

NIGHT PROWLER

The dark, brooding final track on AC/DC's *Highway To Hell* album was penned by Bon Scott, Angus Young and Malcolm Young, and almost certainly plays on the old bogie man ethos with lines like 'A rat runs down an alley/And a chill runs down your spine/Someone walks across your grave/And a chill runs down your spine/Cause no one's gonna warn you/And no one's gonna yell attack/And you won't feel the steel/Til it's hanging out your back'.

The song caused some controversy for AC/DC in 1985, some six years after it was recorded, when an American serial killer, Richard Ramirez, was nicknamed 'The Night Stalker'. When it was discovered that Ramirez was also a big fan of AC/DC, the police let it be known that not only was he a fan of the song

'Night Prowler' but wore an AC/DC T-shirt while committing his crimes, and even left an AC/DC hat at the scene of one of them. Ramirez added to the controversy by shouting 'Hail Satan' and displaying a pentagram carved into his palm at his ensuing trial. The US media, already whipped into an anti-rock frenzy by the pro-censorship lobby PMRC (Parents Music Resource Center) and TV evangelists, at the time went into hysterical anti-AC/DC overdrive, causing several of the band's live shows to be picketed. AC/DC responded to the allegations when they were the subject of VH1's *Behind The Music*, claiming that while the song had become embroiled in the controversy, it was, in fact, about a boy creeping into his girlfriend's room at night. Ramirez, who killed or attacked at least 24 people between 1984 and 1985, is currently on death row in San Quentin state prison in California.

Richard Ramirez leaving court after being charged with a murder attributed to the 'Night Stalker'.

'Night Stalker' suspect charged with murder

Incidentally, 'Night Prowler' is one of the few AC/DC songs not recorded in 4/4 time, but rather uses a 12/8 time signature, with the Young brothers' guitars also down tuned a half step. Bon Scott certainly helps lift the mood a little by stating 'Shazbot, na-nu, na-nu', the catchphrase from the popular sci fi comedy *Mork And Mindy,* at the songs completion.

nO BULL

No Bull is the title of the 1996 live AC/DC video (and later DVD) recorded at Madrid's Plaza de Toros de Las Ventas on July 10, 1996 and produced by long-time video director David Mallet. Coming in the middle of the band's *Ballbreaker* tour, the show features props like the huge inflatable Rosie character, and a finale

with a whole array of canons on 'For Those About To Rock (We Salute You)', instead of the usual two guns used at regular shows. The VHS version also includes backstage footage, something of a rarity with AC/DC, and the DVD carries the promo video for 'Hard As A Rock' and a Making Of 'Hard As A Rock' documentary. This was the band's second live long-form effort, following on from the 1980 film *Let There Be Rock.*

Full tracklisting: *Back In Black/ Shot Down In Flames/Thunderstruck/Girls Got Rhythm/Hard As A Rock/Shoot To Thrill/ Boogie Man/Hail Caesar/Hells Bells/Dog Eat Dog/The Jack/ Ballbreaker/Rock And Roll Ain't Noise Pollution/Dirty Deeds Done Dirt Cheap/You Shook Me All Night Long/Whole Lotta Rosie/T.N.T./Let There Be Rock/ Highway To Hell/For Those About To Rock (We Salute You).*

Initial UK copies of No Bull featured an extra live CD with 'Hard As A Rock', 'Hail Caesar' and 'Dog Eat Dog'.

O'BRIEN, BRENDAN

One of the most celebrated producers of recent times, O'Brien was brought in by AC/DC for their crucial 2008 album, on which he worked alongside Mike Fraser.

Born in Atlanta, O'Brien started out playing guitar with a local band called the Pranks, regarded in the late 1970s as the best covers band in the city. He then moved on to Samura Catfish, but when they split up, he began to engineer and produce other local bands, as well as briefly playing bass for the Georgia Satellites.

It was the debut album from the Black Crowes, *Shake Your Money Maker*, in 1990 that first got him national and international attention. O'Brien was the engineer on that project, and from there his career took flight. His work with Pearl Jam, the Stone Temple Pilots and Pete Droge got him a reputation as one of the pre-eminent studio masters of the grunge era. In reality, though, his diversity can be seen through collaborations with Bruce Springsteen, The Offspring, Limp Bizkit, Rage Against The Machine and The Music.

Brian Johnson has said of working with O'Brien:

"He's a great guy. He knows exactly what we want, and so far, it sounds really good. I'm well pleased."

O'Brien himself has said of the way he works with artists:

"I do make a lot of records with a lot of people, and sometimes they overlap, and sometimes I have two or three things going at once. Everybody I work with is the most important person

I work with, while I'm with them. But sometimes I have to compartmentalize and move on for a few days and do something else. Obviously with Bruce Springsteen – with really any artist – I'll do whatever I can to move things around. But it's funny... I remember the first day that Bruce and I met. I said, 'Hey man, I've gotta tell you. We had a great day together. I'm excited about doing this.... But I've just got to tell you, I'm worried. You have a history of recording things and not putting them out'. I don't know any of this stuff, but I had always heard, and I said, 'That scares me to death, man. I don't want to do that'. And he just kind of went, 'Well, I don't know what to tell you, man'. There was no reassurance, at all, like, 'Oh, it's gonna be okay'. He just goes 'Yeah, I don't know what to tell you – we'll see how it goes'. And I thought, I guess I can accept that."

O'LOUGHLIN, ALEX

Australian-born actor, who made his name in two US TV series, *The Shield* and *Moonlight*. In the latter, O'Loughlin played private detective and vampire Mick St. John, while in the former he was Detective Kevin Hiatt. O'Loughlin was also tested for the role of James Bond in *Casino Royale*, but lost out to Daniel Craig.

OK, so what has he to do with AC/DC? Well, in 2007, a rumour started on the internet that O'Loughlin was actually Bon Scott's son. Quite why this began remains a mystery. The two do look similar, and there have been stories for years than the late singer did have children in various parts of the world – knowing Scott's deserved reputation for enjoying female company, this would come as no surprise. However, there appeared to be no foundation for this at all. O'Loughlin eventually said:

"I don't know how that started. I got a phone call from a friend of mine and I Google-searched it, and it was all over the internet. It was on IMDB and the

tabloids. It's not that it was a negative rumour. It's just so interesting to me that something that was completely fictitious could actually make it that far that quickly."

In reality, the actor's father is a science teacher in Sydney. But O'Loughlin (who was born in 1975, 1977 or 1978, depending on what source you access) does have a love for the sort of music his rock 'n' roll 'dad' sang:

"I love rock and blues and I play the guitar, but I never practiced enough to be good enough to do anything with it. But it's something that brings me great joy. I write songs for personal reasons. It's an expression. It's yet another expression of my art and that helps me be clear about what I'm doing in my chosen profession."

OVERDOSE

The opening fractured guitar lines that punctuate the sixth track on the 1977 album *Let There Be Rock* build effectively into a driving rocker typical of AC/DC at the time. The song had originally appeared as the fifth track on the Australian edition, released three months earlier, in March of the same year.

Penned by Bon Scott and Malcolm and Angus Young, the song itself tells the tale of a man whose love for his woman has gotten the better of him, although given the title, this could also be (mis)construed as being about addiction to drugs. Bon Scott was no stranger to various forms of narcotics, although never to the extent of addiction, and given his predilection for writing semi-auto-biographical songs, this may lie behind the meaning of lyrics such as: 'You gave me something I never had/Pulled me down with you/Pulled me up, think I'm in love/Hope you can pull me through'.

To the authors' knowledge the song has not featured live, even on the band's lengthy world tour in support of *Let There Be Rock*. It was, however, covered by US thrash band Exodus, on their 1989 album *Fabulous Disaster*.

Cemetery. It can be reached by taking the 176 bus from Central London towards Penge, alighting just opposite the Lordship Lane Estate in East Dulwich. Overhill Road is situated on the left hand side of the road, travelling north.

Inevitably, number 67 still attracts visits from curious AC/DC fans, and the walls feature graffiti in honour of the late singer, in a similar manner to his grave at Fremantle Cemetery in Western Australia.

OVERHILL ROAD
East Dulwich

Overhill Road in London's SE22 area, is the road in which Alistair Kinnear lived, the friend Bon Scott was drinking with the night he tragically died, to be precise at number 67. The road runs between Lordship Lane and Underhill Road, which borders the west side of Old Camberwell

OXFORD POLYTECHNIC

Worth mentioning as a venue that banned AC/DC in October 1976. Why? Because of their lewd lyrics. Not that this stopped the band from playing in the fair city. On November 15, right at the end of their UK tour, they turned up at the Theatre in Oxford.

Full tracklisting: *Live Wire/Shot Down In Flames/Hell Ain't A Bad Place To Be/Sin City/Bad Boy Boogie/The Jack/Highway To Hell/Girls Got Rhythm/High Voltage/Whole Lotta Rosie/ Rocker/Let There Be Rock*

PARIS PAVILLION
1979

An unofficial live DVD that was released in 2007, filmed at the Pavillion venue in Paris on December 9, 1979, during the *Highway To Hell* tour. Footage of the show itself was actually shot for the cinema release *Let There Be Rock*, which has never been made available on DVD. The unofficial nature of the title was compounded by the fact that the cover features an image of the band from the Brian Johnson era.

PART ROCK MANAGEMENT

A company run by Stewart Young, who signed up AC/DC as a management client in September 1985, thereby replacing Crispin Dye in that position.

Young was a vastly experienced and respected manager, with a formidable track record. He'd been involved with some major artists, form Emerson, Lake & Palmer to Gary Moore, Billy Squier to Cyndi Lauper, Foreigner to the Scorpions. He also helped to launch the Manticore label, which is most known for ELP's involvement.

These days, he's part of the TBA Entertainment Corporation, a multi-faceted international company, and still looks after the careers of ELP, Gary Moore and Scorpions.

PLATT/TONY

Tony Platt is a producer and engineer who worked as 'Mutt' Lange's engineer on AC/DC's *Highway To Hell* and *Back In*

Black albums; he also worked with the band on their self-produced *Flick Of The Switch* record.

Platt's career began at Trident Studios in London, where he worked as an assistant engineer with the likes of Led Zeppelin, The Who and the Rolling Stones. Progressing to full engineer status, he worked with Paul McCartney, Free and Mott The Hoople before moving to Island Studios (again in London) and working with Bob Marley on his breakthrough albums *Catch A Fire* and *Burnin'*.

Platt was instrumental in helping both Thin Lizzy and The Stranglers secure record deals having worked on demos with these bands. Following the *Highway To Hell* sessions, AC/DC also asked Platt to engineer the sound on their cinema film (and later VHS release) *Let There Be Rock*.

As well as *Flick Of The Switch*, Platt was a regular name on rock and metal releases throughout the '80s and '90s, working as an in-house producer for Zomba, working with the likes of Motorhead, Manowar, Billy Squier, Y&T,

Cheap Trick, Dio. Krokus and Bonham amongst others.

More recently Platt has been active as a producer in the jazz genre. And he has his own philosophy towards the way music and record labels should interact in the 21st Century, as he lends his vast experience to ensuring music survives and prospers: "What happens now is that record companies come up with artist development budgets and they give too much money to a bunch of kids that have never experienced that sort of money before. The kids buy a load of equipment and set up a home studio where they work in a complete vacuum creating songs from computerised tape loops. I'm not saying these kids are incapable of coming up with good music or that there is anything wrong with using computers in home studios – it's just that they are not receiving any third party objective direction, which is drastically important at that stage in their career. What they should do is go into a studio where they have access to a producer and to other people who can help them interpret their ideas in a more interesting way. A good studio has a special atmosphere that encourages creativity by relaxing the band and providing a whole support structure which is invaluable.

"Record companies could do a lot to help this situation if they thought seriously about re-introducing staff producers.

At the moment what happens is that a few producers get offered all the work – even when they are not suitable for the project – because the record company looks through the Music Week *charts and allocates projects to the producers who have had the most recent hits. That's ridiculous – A&R should be about fitting a team together to make it really work, not about relying on someone who is flavour of the month.*

"Another point – and it's one I often have to make to young bands I work with – is that being a musician and song writer is fine, but ultimately you also have to be an entertainer. If you spend your entire artistic life locked away in a bedroom with a rack of computers, you are not going to have any contact with an audience and you will never learn how to project yourself to that audience. This is becoming such a common problem; every week on Top Of The Pops *you see bands that are scared witless because they've no idea how to respond – not even to a camera."*

PLAYING WITH GIRLS

The sixth track on AC/DC's 1985 album *Fly On The Wall*, written by Brian Johnson, Malcolm Young and Angus Young. It's the typical stream of smut and innuendo one would expect

from AC/DC, but, much like the album it came from, falls somewhat short of the level of quality and thought most fans expected from the band.

Take a look at lyrics like: 'I like a tall girl, but I'll take 'em small/I want them all up front I like them all/I wanna see them strut their stuff/Lose their social grace/You play your cards right and you'll deal yourself an ace'. See what we mean?

PLUG ME IN

The most recent DVD release from AC/DC, *Plug Me In* is a double disc that saw the light of day in October 2007, and like its predecessor, *Family Jewels*, plundered the AC/DC vaults for even more rare recordings. Some may have been somewhat surprised at the wealth of material on offer (early versions of *Plug Me In* even came with an additional third disc of treats) not least when one considers the announcement that there was nothing left to release following 2005's *Family Jewels*.

Again the band opted to feature Bon Scott material on disc one and the Brian Johnson era on the second, with the extra disc carrying a mixture of material. The Bon Scott disc includes some rare television slots and unreleased live tracks, whilst the Johnson one is all live material except for a version of 'Gone Shootin'', recorded at London's VH1 studios in 1996.

The extra disc features a mix of TV, live and rehearsal footage and a 1983 gig from Houston in Texas.

Full track listing:

Disc One
High Voltage (King Of Pop Awards1975)/*It's A Long Way To The Top (If You Wanna Rock 'N' Roll)* (Bandstand, 1976)/*School Days* (St. Albans High School, 1976)/*T.N.T.* (St. Albans High School, 1976)/*Live Wire* (Super Pop/Rollin' Bolan, 1976)/*Can I Sit Next To You Girl* (Super Pop/Rollin' Bolan, 1976)/*Baby Please Don't Go* (Myer Music Bowl, Melbourne, 1976)/*Hell Ain't A Bad Place To Be* (Sight And Sound In Concert, London, 1977)/*Rocker* (Sight And Sound In Concert, London, 1977)/*Rock 'N 'Roll Damnation* (Apollo Theatre, Glasgow, 1978)/*Dog Eat Dog* (Apollo Theatre, Glasgow, 1978)/*Let There Be Rock* (Apollo Theatre, Glasgow, 1978)/*Problem Child* (Rock Goes To College, Colchester, 1978)/*Sin City* (Rock Goes To College, Colchester, 1978)/*Bad Boy Boogie* (Rock Goes To College, Colchester, 1978)/*Highway To Hell* (Countdown, Holland, 1979)/*The Jack* (Countdown, Holland, 1979)/*Whole Lotta Rosie* (Countdown, Holland, 1979) Extras: Interview at Sydney Airport, 1975/Interview, Covent Garden, London, 1976/ *Baby Please Don't Go* (Szenne '77, Germany, 1976)/*Problem Child* (Myer Music Bowl, Melbourne, 1976)/Interview – *Dirty Deeds Done Dirt Cheap* (Melbourne Radio promo film 1976)/Bon Scott Interview (Countdown, 1977)/*Rock 'N' Roll Damnation* (Top Of The Pops, London, 1978)/Live And Interview (Australian Music To The World, Atlanta, GA, 1978)/Live Super 8 Bootleg Film (Theatre du Verdue, Nice, France, 1979)

Disc Two
Shot Down In Flames (Budokan, Tokyo, 1981)/*What Do You Do For Money Honey* (Budokan, Tokyo, 1981)/*You Shook Me All Night Long* (Budokan, Tokyo, 1981)/*Let There Be Rock* (Budokan, Tokyo, 1981)/*Back In Black* (Budokan, Tokyo, 1981)/*T.N.T* (Capital Centre, Landover MD, 1981)/*Shoot To Thrill* (Capital Centre, Landover MD, 1981)/*Guns For Hire* (Joe Louis Arena, Detroit MI, 1983)/*Dirty Deeds Done Dirt Cheap* (Joe Louis Arena, Detroit MI, 1983)/*Flick Of The Switch* (Capital Centre, Landover MD, 1983)/*Bedlam In Belgium* (Capital Centre, Landover MD, 1983)/*Back In Black* (Tushino Airfield, Moscow, 1991)/*Highway To Hell* (Tushino Airfield, Moscow, 1991)/*Whole Lotta Rosie* (Tushino Airfield, Moscow, 1991)/*For Those About To Rock (We Salute You)* (Tushino Airfield, Moscow,

1991)/*Gone Shootin'* (VH1 Studios, London, 1996)/*Hail Caesar* (Sydney Entertainment Centre, 1996)/*Ballbreaker* (Sydney Entertainment Centre, 1996)/*Rock And Roll Ain't Noise Pollution* (Sydney Entertainment Centre, 1996)/*Hard As A Rock*/ (Stade de France, Paris, 2001)/*Hells Bells* (Stade de France, Paris, 2001)//*Ride On* (Stade de France, Paris, 2001)/ *Stiff Upper Lip* (Circus Krone, Munich, 2003)/*Thunderstruck* (Circus Krone, Munich, 2003)/ *If You Want Blood (You've Got It)* (Downsview Park, Toronto, 2003)/*The Jack* (Downsview Park, Toronto, 2003)/*You Shook Me All Night Long*(Downsview Park, Toronto, 2003)

Extras - Beavis & Butt-head *Ballbreaker* intro film/*Hells Bells* – Interview and Live (Countdown, Brussels, 1981)/ Interview (Monsters Of Rock, Castle Donington, 1984/*Gone Shootin'* (Rehearsal, VH1 Studios, London, 1996)/*Rock Me Baby* (Rolling Stones with Angus and Malcolm Young, Leipzig, Germany, 2003)

Disc Three: *She's Got Balls* (St. Albans High School, 1976)/*It's A Long Way To The Top (If You Want To Rock 'N' Roll)* (St. Albans High School, 1976)/*Let There Be Rock* (Sight And Sound In Concert, London, 1977)/*Bad Boy Boogie* (Apollo Theatre, Glasgow, 1978)/ *Girls Got Rhythm* (Top Pop,

1979)/*Guns For Hire* (Band rehearsals, 1983)/*This House Is On Fire* (Joe Louis Arena, Detroit MI, 1983)/*Highway To Hell* (Dublin, 1996)/*Girls Got Rhythm* (Sydney Entertainment Centre, 1996)/*Let There Be Rock* (Stuttgart, 2000)/*Angus Statue Intro* (Stiff Upper Lip tour film, 2001)/*Guns For Hire* (Summit, Houston, 1983)/*Shoot To Thrill* (Summit, Houston, 1983)/*Sin City* (Summit, Houston, 1983) / *This House Is On Fire* (Summit, Houston, 1983)/*Back In Black* (Summit, Houston, 1983)/*Bad Boy Boogie* (Summit, Houston, 1983)/*Rock And Roll Ain't Noise Pollution* (Summit, Houston, 1983)/*Flick Of The Switch* (Summit, Houston, 1983)/*Hells Bells* (Summit, Houston, 1983)

The three DVD version also features a poster, some replica backstage passes and stickers.

POWERAGE

The fifth AC/DC album, released on Atlantic Records on 25 May, 1978, it also happens to be the band's fourth International release, but was the first to come out simultaneously in Australia and around the rest of the world. It was also the first time the same sleeve was used in every territory, as well as the first of the band's records to feature new bassist Cliff Williams. On top of all these 'firsts', it was also the last studio album to be produced by the George Young and Harry Vanda partnership.

A long-time favourite with many fans, *Powerage* is one of the band's rawest, most powerful offerings, capturing the live energy for which they were well known. It also features some of their best known songs; 'Rock 'N' Roll Damnation', 'Sin City' and 'Riff Raff' all swiftly became live favourites, the last-named proving to be an effective show opener, as featured on the live album *If You Want Blood*, which would follow *Powerage* in 1978. This song allowed Angus, atop the speaker stacks behind the drum riser, to appear, teasing out the intro to the delight of the crowd, before leaping down onto the stage as the rest of the band kicked in.

In truth there are no dud tracks among the ten that make up *Powerage*, and the likes of 'Gimme A Bullet', 'Kicked In The Teeth', 'Up To My Neck In You' and 'What's Next To The Moon' are unquestionably amongst the more explosive AC/DC songs, and 'Gone Shootin'' highlights the bluesier side to the band.

Ironically it was the raw sound of *Powerage* that led to Atlantic Records deciding a change of producer was needed, in the hope of attaining a more polished sound that would be easier to sell to the American market, hence the arrival in the world of AC/DC of 'Mutt Lange' for the next studio album, *Highway To Hell*. With hindsight, the move paid huge dividends, but the love for *Powerage* felt by many AC/DC fans merely serves to show how far removed they and their beloved band really are from the cut-throat and often ignorant music business.

Powerage reached No. 26 in the UK album charts and a lowly 133 in America, but it was the very first AC/DC album to reach Gold status (selling 500,000 copies) in the States. In typically irreverent style Bon Scott refused to be overawed by the band's increased success, telling the Melbourne *Daily Herald* at the time:

"All that has changed is my intake of alcohol. I can now afford to drink twice as much".

Somewhat typically with early AC/DC releases, there was some variation as to which tracks appeared in which territories. Early European versions omitted 'Rock 'N' Roll Damnation', and also boasted a harsher sound mix, whilst 'Cold Hearted Man' has only ever featured on the European versions of the album. And a Canadian version, which was released on cassette only, features 'Sin City' as the first track on side one and 'Rock 'N' Roll Damnation' as the first track on side two.

Full track listing:
Rock'N' Roll Damnation/ Gimme A Bullet/Down Payment Blues/Gone Shootin'/Riff Raff/Sin City/Up To My Neck In You/What's Next To The Moon/ Cold Hearted Man/Kicked In The Teeth

POWER/PAUL

The commercial artist responsible for the cover of the debut AC/DC album, *High Voltage*. Power worked at EMI in Australia at the time, and the label weren't impressed with what he came up with. In fact, they were ready to scrap it, when... well, let's leave the story to Power himself:

"I recall a few people in higher positions who were giving me shit about my lack of taste in rendering such offensive album cover art. I nearly told the three nameless EMI honchos to get fucked. I was under a lot of pressure. I thought I'd nailed

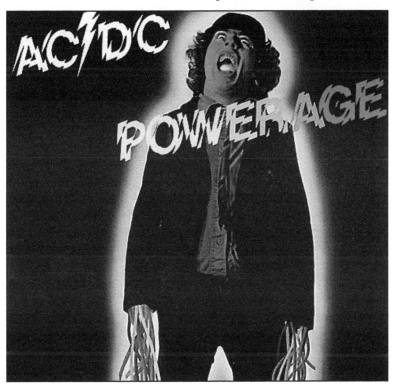

what the band was about. I was about to get fired, I could feel it, when who should turn up? Bon Scott! I guess he heard the fiasco in the hallway. He put his arm around me and said, 'Isn't this great? You've really caught what the band is all about! I love it!'

"The three execs were gob-smacked! You could have heard a pin drop! Bon said to them, 'I'm taking Paulie out for a beer. You don't mind, do you? I mean, artwork this fucking good should be rewarded, right?' The three execs mumbled, 'Right'. We waited until we were outside EMI and laughed our arses off. He saved my job and the High Voltage album cover."

PROBLEM CHILD

The fourth track on the Australian version of *Dirty Deeds Done Dirt Cheap*, as well as the fifth track on the International version, 'Problem Child' is a slice of pure anti-establishmentism from the joint pens of Bon Scott, Angus Young and Malcolm Young.

'What I want I take/What I don't I break/And I don't like you/With a flick of my knife/I can change your life/There's nothing you can do', leers Scott on a rough, tough yet memorable rocker.

The songs was a massive live favourite with Scott, who would often introduce it on stage by announcing that it was about Angus Young, and features on the live albums *If You Want Blood* and *Live At Atlantic Studios*. 'Problem Child' was resurrected for the live set on the *Stiff Upper Lip* tour and is included on the *Stiff Upper Lip* live DVD as well.

The song strangely also appears on some versions of 1977's *Let There Be Rock*, on which it replaced the slightly controversial 'Crabsody In Blue'.

PROUD, JOHN

John Proud was the drummer for AC/DC in November 1974. He had also featured in George Young and Harry Vanda's Marcus Hook Roll Band, alongside Angus and Malcolm Young, and appears on their *Tales Of Old Grand-Daddy* record. He was replaced in AC/DC by Tony Currenti, who would record the original *High Voltage* album with the band.

PUT THE FINGER ON YOU

The second track from AC/DC's *For Those About To Rock (We Salute You)* album, 'Put The Finger On You' is a typical slice of AC/DC-esque smut and innuendo. Written by Brian Johnson, Angus Young and Malcolm Young, even Bon Scott would have been proud of lines like: 'I put the finger on you for sure/It's the key to unlocking your door/Don't you know I've broken through your security/My hands ain't tied no more'.

Q.PRIME

The management company set up by Peter Mensch (below, left) and Cliff Burnstein (right), who looked after AC/DC for just under three years between 1979 and 1982, and who had first met when they were involved with the mighty CCC Management company, responsible for acts like Aerosmith, Ted Nugent and the Scorpions.

Mensch had majored in Urban Studies at Brandeis University, before getting a masters degree in Marketing from the University of Chicago. He began his music career as Aerosmith's tour accountant.

Burnstein had started out as an A&R man for Mercury Records; one of his first signings being cult hard rockers Legs Diamond. But it was at CCC that he cut his managerial teeth.

In 1982, Mensch and Burnstein decided to split from CCC and head out on their own. At first, the business was run from two flats: in Hoboken, New Jersey (where Bunstein was based) and Earl's Court, London (home for Mensch). Their clients included Def Leppard, whom Mensch had persuaded to join CCC.

Mensch took over as AC/DC's personal management representative within CCC in July 1979, and looked after their interests until June 1982, when band and management went their separate ways; one assumes because AC/DC felt they wouldn't receive the kind of attention they required from the fledgling company. They instead appointed their old tour manager Ian Jeffrey as their personal manager, in effect then, managing themselves.

Today, Q. Prime (as the company is now known) manage a raft of top names, including Jimmy Page, Metallica, Shania Twain, Muse, Garbage and Snow Patrol. And, over the years, some of the biggest names in the world have passed through their offices, including the Red Hot Chili Peppers, Madonna and the Rolling Stones. Madonna worked with them on her 1998 album *Ray Of Light*, and the Mensch-Burnstein axis is credited with helping to make this such a huge success. The Stones hired them as consultants for their 1989 album *Steel Wheels* and the subsequent tour.

Over the years, Mensch and Bunstein have had to deal with some significant problems within bands. The death of Bon Scott in February 1980 threw AC/DC into a state of potential turmoil, yet the pair also presided over the band when they released the phenomenally successful *Back In Black* album, as well as seeing *For Those About To Rock* hit the Number One slot in the US, the band's only American Number One. Def Leppard drummer Rick Allen lost an arm in a road accident at the end of 1983, and the death of Metallica bassist Cliff Burton in 1986 was a landmark tragedy that could have torn the band apart. But the pair's managerial policy has always been the same: allow the band to make their own decisions. In fact, this has always been the hallmark of the Mensch-Bunstein ethos – they never smother their artists in cotton wool.

RACE, THE

The Race was a 2006 Sky One reality TV show in the UK, in which two famous Formula 1 racing drivers, Eddie Irvine and David Coulthard, under the watchful eye of presenter Denise Van Outen, put a series of celebrities through their paces at the world famous Silverstone circuit, pitching a team of women against a team of men to find out who was the best race car driver.

A long-time fan of motor racing, Brian Johnson is well known for racing vintage cars in his adopted home of America, and was part of the men's team, alongside actor Nick Moran, ex-boxer Nigel Benn, footballer Les Ferdinand and electro pop star (and failed pilot) Gary Numan. Representing the ladies team were pop star Ms. Dynamite, Tamara, daughter of F1 boss Bernie Ecclestone, pop star Jenny Frost, film star Melissa Joan Hart and Ingrid Tarrant, wife of disgraced celebrity Chris.

During the week-long series, Johnson was involved in a clash with Ms. Dynamite when he clipped the back of her car resulting in her having to spend a night in hospital, although she was relatively unscathed, and also staged a mini-revolt complaining about conditions after a bad first night's

sleep for everyone. Johnson went on to win the programme in a final with Gary Numan, although he received far less media coverage compared with some of the other celebrities taking part, and relatively little fanfare over his victory.

RAINBOW

The celebrated group formed by Ritchie Blackmore after he quit Deep Purple, and by 1976 established as one of the biggest bands in rock. Blackmore had been joined by then by vocalist Ronnie James Dio, drummer Cozy Powell, bassist Jimmy Bain and keyboard player Tony Carey – the line-up that recorded the seminal *Rising* album, and the one regarded by many as the best of this band's chequered and peripatetic career.

In 1976, the band offered AC/DC the chance to support them on 19 shows around Europe. Apparently, the Aussies got the offer as a direct result of their residency at The Marquee Club in London, which had seen them grow immeasurably in stature. The tour kicked off in Stockholm on September 20, and finished in Erlangen, Germany on October 28.

The two bands played together in America during October 1978 and what was arguably the most infamous gig of this American jaunt happened at the Palladium in New York on August 24. Rainbow ended their set after three numbers! It was claimed that the band were having problems with the PA system, but there were strong reports at the time that Blackmore had thrown one of his famous tantrums, stormed offstage and refused to go back on. Some put this down to the guitarist's irritation at the way AC/DC had won over the crowd.

Amusingly Blackmore would later dismiss AC/DC in the press, claiming that as a musician he failed to be amused by what he asserted was the band's failure to progress musically.

RAMIREZ/RICHARD

Known as 'The Night Stalker', Ramirez was an American serial killer who murdered or attacked at least 24 people during a spree which began with the death of Jennie Vincow on June 28, 1984, and finally ended when Ramirez was cornered a day after his identity was made known to the public, on August 31 1985. He was tried and convicted on 13 counts of murder, five attempted murders, 11 sexual assaults and 14 burglaries. On 7 November 1989 Ramirez was sentenced to death in California's gas chamber. He is currently on death row in San Quentin State Prison.

The connection with AC/DC comes from the fact that Ramirez was dubbed 'The Night Stalker', which led some to make the link with the AC/DC song 'Night Prowler' when it was made public knowledge that the alleged perpetrator of the crimes was an AC/DC fan, and that an AC/DC cap had been found near the site of one of the crimes. In fact, Ramirez was initially dubbed 'The Midnight Stalker' by the media before it was changed to 'The Night Stalker', although the only evidence that he was a fan of any heavy metal was found at the scene of the murder of Peter and Barbara Pan, where Ramirez had scrawled an inverted pentagram on the wall and underneath it had written the line 'Jack the knife', which is actually a line from the song 'The Ripper' by Judas Priest.

In the early to mid-'80s AC/DC were very much in the firing line of TV evangelists and the PMRC lobby group, the latter led by Tipper Gore, wife of politician Al Gore, with some proclaiming the letters AC/DC stood for 'Anti Christ Devil Child'. Ironically, Judas Priest would themselves become embroiled in a court case equally feverishly covered by a rabid media when it was alleged that two Californian teenagers, James Vance and Ray Belknap, had forged a suicide pact over supposed subliminal messages hidden behind the track 'Better By You, Better Than Me', itself actually a cover of a Spooky Tooth song.

RAVE ON

Recorded during sessions for 2000's *Stiff Upper Lip*, 'Rave On' would have been cut between July and October 1999 at the Bryan Adams-owned Warehouse Studios. It did not make the album's final track list however.

RAZORS EDGE, THE

The 12th AC/DC studio album was released on 24 September, 1990 and immediately went a long way to re-establishing the band as a major force in heavy rock after the barren years of the mid-'80s. *The Razors Edge* was also something of a departure for AC/DC in both their choice of producer and a shift in focus of some of the band's material.

Their previous album, 1988's *Blow Up Your Video*, had been the one that acted as a springboard back to the immense success they would garner in the wake of *The Razors Edge*, but as an album overall it seemed to lack the cohesiveness of 1983's *Flick Of The Switch*, even if it was considerably better than 1985's *Fly On The Wall*. With *The Razors Edge* however, AC/DC seemed to take everything to a completely new level.

First, their choice of producer Bruce Fairbairn might have raised a few eyebrows. Whereas the tried and tested team of George Young and Harry Vanda helmed *Blow Up Your Video*, the band turned to the more overtly commercial ears of the man who'd previously

overseen work on Bon Jovi's *Slippery When Wet* and Aerosmith's *Permanent Vacation, Pump* and *Get A Grip.* However with hindsight the move seems to have made perfect sense. AC/DC had, after all, worked with the legendary 'Mutt' Lange on their three most successful albums, *Highway To Hell, Back In Black* and *For Those About To Rock*, and Lange wasn't exactly known as a man who lacked finesse in the studio.

The Razors Edge was recorded at Fairbairn's own Little Mountain Studio in Vancouver, Canada, and his appointment seemed to make even more sense when you consider that he was a fan of the band.

"Bruce is a big fan of our older albums," said Angus at the time. *"His name got called out a lot, so Malcolm went over to Vancouver to meet him. Bruce told Malcolm that he didn't want to change AC/DC. And he didn't want us to do anything we'd feel uncomfortable with. These days its hard to find producers who are rock producers. A lot of people say they are, but as soon as you start working with them they'll push their ballads at you."*

Although there would be no ballads on *The Razors Edge*, it certainly had a more commercial sound than the last few AC/DC albums, typified perhaps by the hit single 'Moneytalks'. In open-

ing cut, 'Thunderstruck', the band managed to surpass the invective of *Blow Up Your Video*'s opening track 'Heatseeker', and also come up with a perfect song that would kick off all their shows on the forthcoming *The Razors Edge* tour. And whilst the likes of 'Are You Ready' and 'Fire Your Guns' are typical, no-nonsense AC/DC rockers, perhaps the best on offer is the title track. An ominous, Eastern sounding, slow-building rocker that was unlike anything the band had committed to tape for many years, it showed that despite their reputation for always delivering in their own distinctive style, they were not afraid to continue trying out new ideas.

It wasn't all sweetness and light, however. *The Razors Edge* was the first AC/DC album to feature more than ten tracks (an extra burden imposed by record companies eager for bands to fill out the entire 78 minutes of the CD format), and even thought its 12 tracks meant just two additions, aside from the aforementioned songs, there seems to be more than a fair amount of filler material on the record, not least the misfiring, tongue-in-cheek Christmas message of 'Mistress For Christmas', whilst the likes 'Let's Make It' and 'If You Dare' are throwaway at best.

The Razors Edge is the only AC/DC studio album to feature drummer Chris Slade; though he'd also appear on 1992's *Live*. Slade had replaced Simon Wright in 1989, initially as a temporary fill-in, but so impressed Malcolm and Angus Young during the recording of the album that he was asked to join the band full time. It is also the first AC/DC album not to feature lyrical contributions from Brian Johnson. Johnson was going through a divorce at that point and didn't have the time to devote to working on the lyrics so Angus and Malcolm Young alone looked after that side. Initially this led to rumours that Johnson was on his way out of the band, but the singer was swift to allay such fears.

"I just said, 'Gee guys, this is great. I'm not going to fix what isn't broken'," he said at the time. *"So I didn't write on this album. It doesn't matter with AC/DC. You're all together and whatever happens, happens."*

The Razors Edge was AC/DC's best performing album for almost a decade. It reached number two in the US charts, the first time the band had been in the US Top 10 since *For Those About To Rock* hit the top spot in 1981, and reached number four in the UK. 'Thunderstruck', 'Moneytalks' and 'Are You Ready' were all successful singles. The ensuing world tour was another massive success also. AC/DC were back near the top of their game.

Full track listing: *Thunderstruck/Fire Your Guns/Moneytalks/The Razors Edge/Mistress For Christmas/Rock Your Heart Out/Are You Ready/Got You By The Balls/Shot Of Love/Let's Make It/Goodbye And Good Riddance To Bad Luck/If You Dare*

RAZORS EDGE, THE
(Song)

"We had the main riff and there was something ominous about it. And for that reason alone we decided to go ahead with it. In the past we'd stay away from things that sounded too musical."

So says Angus Young of the title track from the band's 12th studio album, *The Razors Edge*. The fourth track on the album, it was written by Angus and Malcolm Young alone, and as Angus' comments suggest, represents something of a departure for the band.

There is indeed an ominous feel to the brooding opening that builds over eerie vocal effects before exploding into the song proper. A tale relating the dangers of living life on the edge is best summed up with lyrics like: 'You're livin' on the edge/You don't know wrong from right/They're breathing down your neck/You're gonna die of fright'.

Without a doubt one of the latter-day highlights of the AC/DC canon.

Reading Festival

AC/DC played at the famous event only once, in 1976, the three days running from August 27-29 and were on the bill during the last day (a Sunday). The first day had been headlined by Gong, a slightly surreal hippy inspired outfit, with reggae star U Roy and Supercharge also worth mentioning.

The second day was headlined by Rory Gallagher, the famed Irish blues-rock guitar hero, with Eddie And The Hot Rods and Pat Travers also representing the full-on, high energy rock approach. Against this, were set the progressive bands such as Van Der Graaf Generator, Manfred Mann, Camel and Jon Hiseman's Colosseum.

On the final day, AC/DC were set right in the middle of the bill, going onstage at 5.30 in the afternoon. Also playing that day were headliners Black Oak Arkansas, Ted Nugent, Sutherland Brothers & Quiver (all of whom were on after 'DC), Brand X, Sassafras, Backdoor, A Band Called 'O', The Enid, Aft and Howard Bragen.

For the record AC/DC's set that day at the first outdoor show they'd done in the UK was: *Live Wire/Rock 'N' Roll Singer/She's Got Balls/The Jack/School Days/Rocker/High Voltage/Baby, Please Don't Go.*

Now, it would be tremendous to be able to report that the band stole the limelight and were the highlight of the event, but that simply wasn't the case. Perhaps because they were following the genteel prog of The Enid and the jazz rock noodlings of Brand X, but for some reason nothing truly kicked in that day for 'DC. The crowd was lethargic and this reflected back onto the performance. Try as they might – and you couldn't fault the effort put in by the five onstage – the tyros couldn't get close to top gear.

Part of the problem was that the festival itself was changing. Having been dominated for so long by the more intellectual, progressive elements, a new vision of hard rock was creeping in, reflecting the fact that the trends were altering. By the following year, punk and new wave would take over. This, though, was a transitional year. Many of the crowd represented the old guard, and were slightly immune to the charms of bands that came from the other end of the musical spectrum. So, the reaction to 'DC, and to be fair others such as Eddie And The Hot Rods, wasn't as enthusiastic as it might have been.

There were even some who wondered whether AC/DC had been sacrificed, their set being used as a buffer, so that the big names right at the top of the bill, again not representing the tradi-

tional Reading fare, would find it easier to get the crowds going.

Whatever the truth of this, and it is highly unlikely to be the case, this was the only time the band ever played at the Reading Festival. While they were to dominate the Monsters Of Rock event at Donington in the 1980s and 1990s, a return to this festival has never happened. They've been rumoured to be appearing on a number of occasions, but as the band became ever more connected to the metal world, so they would cease to be part of the Reading plans.

RED COW

The Red Cow was a pub in Hammersmith where AC/DC played their first ever UK show in April 1976. The band had been booked as support act to British band Backstreet Crawler on a nationwide tour, but owing to the recent passing of their guitarist, ex-Free man Paul Kossoff, the headlining band had pulled some shows. Left

without any gigs for what would have been the opening of the tour, 'DC took what they could find on their first visit to the UK and ended up playing this pub on the Hammersmith Road in West London. They would return for a further show on May 20, but the band's debut gig also set up a run at the nearby Nashville Rooms, now known as The (Famous) Three Kings or F3K near West Kensington tube station, as well as further dates at two other venues in London: the Marquee Club in Wardour Street (this location closed in 1988), where they would get to play a residency, and the Fulham Greyhound, which still exist to this day.

The Red Cow played host to many bands, having evolved from a country and western style pub to becoming known for putting on punk bands such as The Lurkers and even The Jam. The pub stopped featuring live music in 1978 and was demolished in 1981, and a new pub was incorporated into the office block which now stands on the site at 157 Hammersmith Road. It was initially again named The Red Cow, but a year later was changed to Latymers, as it's known today. Only a large ceiling mirror exists from the days when AC/DC performed there.

RIDE ON

The eighth track on both the Australian and International versions of *Dirty Deeds Done Dirt Cheap*. Written by Bon Scott, Angus Young and Malcolm Young, 'Ride On' represents something of a departure from the usual cut and thrust of AC/DC's relentlessly rocking material.

A delightful slow blues tune, telling the tale of the life of a drifter, moving from woman to woman and from town to town, the song is very much a showcase for the lyrical and vocal talents of frontman Scott, as well as for the intricate blues soloing of the then 21-year old lead guitar player.

The drifter telling the story is often interpreted as being Bon Scott, giving the other side of the picture about being in a touring band. While the party-hard attitude came through in so many other songs, here he opens up about how lonely such a life can be. It's arguably the man's most introspective lyricism.

The track was not available in the United States until *Dirty Deeds Done Dirt Cheap* was released there in 1981. The song also appears in identical form on the *Volts* compilation from the *Bonfire* box set. It has rarely, if ever, been performed live by the band.

R.I.P.
(ROCK IN PEACE)

The seventh track from the Australian edition of *Dirty Deeds Done Dirt Cheap*, 'R.I.P. (Rock In Peace)' was omitted from the International versions of the album for reasons unknown.

The song, written by Bon Scott and Angus and Malcolm Young, is a simple call for someone to be left alone to get on with what they want to do without any hassle, as typified by lines like: 'Leave me alone/Like a dog with a bone/Like a stone that's been thrown/Let me be on my own' as well as name checking some of the band's rock 'n' roll heroes like Little Richard, Jerry Lee Lewis and Chuck Berry.

The song has never been officially released outside of Australia.

RISING POWER

The opening track from AC/DC's 1983 album *Flick Of The Switch*, and written by Brian Johnson and Angus and Malcolm Young, 'Rising Power' goes a long way to firmly establishing the raw qualities of the new record, something of a shock in the face of the slightly over-produced feel of 1981's *For Those About To Rock*.

The track slips effortlessly into its groove and is chock full of the band's trademark tongue-in-cheek innuendo in lyrics such as: 'I've got my feet up, like to love/Through the dawn till I've blown/All I want's her lovin' down/Love the way she move around'.

ROCK AND ROLL AIN'T NOISE POLLUTION

The tenth and final track from AC/DC's 1980 album *Back In Black*, this song, much like 'Let There Be Rock' before it and 'For Those About To Rock (We Salute You)' that would follow it, is the kind of unashamed homage to the music AC/DC play that the band have loved to indulge in over the years.

Written by Brian Johnson, Angus Young and Malcolm Young, this loose limbed, laid back rocker extols the virtues of both rock and roll in lines like: 'Heavy decibels are playing on my guitar/We got vibrations coming up through the floor/We're just listenin' to the rock/That's giving too much noise/Are you deaf, you wanna hear some more', although this being AC/DC they also find time for a little salacious sex to be thrown in for good measure in the second verse with: 'I took a look inside your bedroom door/You looked so good lyin' on your bed/Well I asked you if you wanted any rhythm and love/You said you want to rock and roll instead'.

'Rock And Roll Ain't Noise Pollution' was released as a single, backed with the song 'Hells Bells', and reached Number 15 in the UK Top 40, at the time AC/DC's highest charting UK single and making it the most successful single from the *Back In Black*

album. According to Brian Johnson, the lyrics to the song were pretty much improvised in the studio as the track was being recorded. The song was used in a 2006 Nike Air Max television advert.

ROCK AND ROLL AIN'T NOISE POLLUTION
(Korean album)

One of the rarest and most unique of AC/DC collector's items, this Korean only compilation bizarrely united songs from the albums *Dirty Deeds Done Dirt Cheap* and *Back In Black*. It came housed in the international *Dirty Deeds* sleeve but used the famous *Back In Black* track 'Rock And Roll Ain't Noise Pollution' as the compilation's title.

The main reason for such a release lies with the Korean Ministry of Culture, who, at this time, monitored almost all official record releases in their country and have a policy of removing any tracks they deem inappropriate or too explicit for their own society, often, it seems, replacing them with tracks from other albums at will. That almost certainly seems to be the case here. *Dirty Deeds Done Dirt Cheap* had just been released in America in 1981 (although it had, of course, been released throughout the rest of the world in 1976) whilst *Back In Black* would have been AC/DC's most recent studio album at the time. The record was released by Atlantic/Oasis Records, and it is interesting to note that some of the songs deemed worthy of inclusion include the sleazy 'Love At First Feel' and the charmingly ribald 'Big Balls' from *Dirty Deeds Done Dirt Cheap*, whilst the lurid double entendres of 'Given The Dog A Bone' and the more blatant 'Let Me Put My Love Into You" from *Back In Black* are also given the official nod, proving that AC/DC's love of smut and innuendo doesn't always translate literally or remains beyond the comprehension of some of the world's more restrictive societies.

Back In Black itself has been released, in pirate form, at least eight times in Korea regardless of this official release, something of which both the authorities and the record company must surely have been aware, but a release such as *Rock And Roll Ain't Noise Pollution* must have been an attempt to gain at least some fiscal reward from the release.

Nevertheless, the record remains a highly prized item amongst AC/DC collectors.

Full track listing: *Love At First Feel/There's Gonna Be Some Rockin'/Let Me Put My Love Into You/Rocker/Ain't No Fun (Waiting Round To Be A Millionaire)/Rock And Roll Ain't Noise Pollution/Given The Dog A Bone/Big Balls/Shake A Leg/ Ride On.*

ROCK AND ROLL HALL OF FAME

AC/DC were inducted into the legendary Rock And Roll Hall of Fame at a celebration at the Waldorf-Astoria hotel in New York on Monday 10 March 2003. At the ceremony the band were inducted by Aerosmith vocalist Steven Tyler who referred to their sound as, "The thunder from down under that gives you the second most powerful surge that flows through your body". Tyler also provided backing vocals with the group as they performed 'Highway To Hell' and 'You Shook Me All Night Long'. Brian Johnson also quoted from the band's 1977 album *Let There Be Rock* during his acceptance speech.

The event was not without controversy however. Bassist Mark Evans, who played on *T.N.T.* and *Dirty Deeds Done Dirt Cheap,* had originally been included on the list of nominees along with the current line-up and the late Bon Scott. However in January 2003 his name disappeared from the list. No announcement has ever been forthcoming from AC/DC, nor an explanation from the Rock And Roll Hall of Fame, although unsurprisingly Evans himself had something to say (see Mark Evans entry).

ROCK IN RIO

One of the biggest events of its type in the 1980s, this was a true extravaganza. In fact, the first Rock In Rio in 1985 is claimed to have been the biggest ever rock festival, attracting an astonishing 1.5 million fans.

The event took place from January 11-20, and was headlined by AC/DC (who appeared on January 15), Queen, Yes, Rod Stewart and George Benson. Other notable rockers to play were Scorpions, Ozzy, Whitesnake and Iron Maiden.

AC/DC's set was: *Guns For Hire/Shoot To Thrill/Sin City/ Shot Down In Flames/Back In Black/Have A Drink On Me/Bad Boy Boogie/Rock 'N' Roll Ain't Noise Pollution/Hells Bells/The Jack/Jailbreak/Dirty Deeds Done Dirt Cheap/Highway To Hell/Whole Lotta Rosie/Let There Be Rock/For Those About To Rock (We Salute You)*

ROCK 'N' ROLL DAMNATION

The opening track from AC/DC's fifth album *Powerage*, 'Rock 'N' Roll Damnation' has long been a live favourite of the band's and has been performed with both Bon Scott and Brian Johnson (most recently on their 2003 world tour). Written by Bon Scott, Angus Young and Malcolm Young, the song is a typical shout out for the joys of rock 'n' roll against those that decry the sort of behaviour the Bon Scott era line-up revelled in. 'They say that you play too loud/Well baby that's tough', intones Scott at the beginning of the song.

'Rock 'N' Roll Damnation' also features on the Bon Scott era live album *If You Want Blood,* but has suffered something of a chequered history when it comes to

studio albums. A Canadian cassette version of *Powerage* moved the song to track one, side two, whilst it was totally omitted from very early versions of the European edition of the album.

The track was released as a single, backed with 'Sin City' in June 1978, reaching number 24 in the UK Top 40, their first UK hit single; the band appeared on BBC1's *Top Of The Pops* for the very first time to play this song.

ROCK 'N' ROLL SINGER

Yet more unashamed tributes to the joys from rock 'n' roll arrived in the second song from AC/DC's second album *T.N.T.* (which was also the second song that featured on the International version of *High Voltage*). Penned by Bon Scott and Angus and Malcolm Young, the track is a rarity in that it actually contains profanity – the word 'shit' cropping up in the lines 'And you can stick your golden handshake/And you can stick your silly rules/And all the other shit/That you teach to kids in school/Cause I ain't no fool'. Amazingly, AC/DC have rarely used swear words in their lyrics.

A version of 'Rock 'N' Roll Singer' was recorded with original vocalist Dave Evans, during the same sessions as debut single 'Can I Sit Next To You Girl' and 'Rockin' In The Parlour'.

ROCK 'N' ROLL TRAIN

The first single from the 2008 album *Black Ice*, this has been described by Metal Hammer magazine as, "Classic AC/DC and, as good a record as *Stiff Upper Lip* was, this blows anything from that record clean out of the water. With a pace that's in the same vein as 'Highway To Hell', 'Rock 'N' Roll Train' has a huge chorus." (The book went to press before the authors were able to assess it). A video was shot in London, with 150 lucky fans invited to be extras.

ROCKER

A self-explanatory song that appeares as track number six on *T.N.T.* as well as being track number four on the International version of *Dirty Deeds Done Dirt Cheap.*

With lines like 'Got slick back hair/Skin tight jeans/A Cadillac car/And teenage dreams' Bon Scott, who co-wrote the song with Angus and Malcolm Young, easily sets himself and his band mates up as rebellious icons for Australia's rock loving youth.

ROCKIN' IN THE PARLOUR

The B-side to AC/DC's first ever single 'Can I Sit Next To You Girl', which was recorded with original singer Dave Evans. With lines like 'I met her in Caroline/Right about '69/Well she came up to me and said 'Hi there honey/How'd you like to come along' it's hardly MENSA fare, as would befit a young band just starting out.

ROCK GOES TO COLLEGE

A BBC2 series that ran from 1978 to 1981, featuring a succession of up and coming bands performing 50-60 minute sets at Universities and Polytechnics around the country, which were then broadcast simultaneously on television and radio. Each programme was introduced by a notable BBC DJ.

AC/DC appeared at the University of Essex on November 10, 1978, during their *Powerage* tour. Introduced by the BBC's Pete Drummond their set list was: *Live Wire/Problem Child/Sin City/Bad Boy Boogie/Whole Lotta Rosie/Rocker/Let There Be Rock*.

The set has long been bootlegged, while the version of 'Whole Lotta Rosie' can be found on the AC/DC DVD *Family Jewels*. The whole set has also been aired on VH1 Classic's programme *BBC Crown Jewels*.

ROCK YOUR HEART OUT

Track number six from the 1990 album *The Razors Edge*, this song, written by Angus and Malcolm Young, is something of a return to the open displays of the joys of rocking out which the band used to specialise in during the Bon Scott era, and the acknowledgement of their fan base, typified by songs such as 'For Those About To Rock'. Lines like 'Throw your fist up/Shout your mouth off/Beat the walls down/Get tough, freak out' perfectly encapsulate this spirit.

ROLLING STONES

The legendary rockers have long been favourites of AC/DC, and the band broke their 'support no one rule' when asked to open for the Stones on three German tour dates in June 2003. The bands appeared together at Oberhausen (June 13), Leipzig (June 20) and Hockenheim (June 22). The two acts also appeared on the bill for the Molson Canadian Rocks For Toronto show to raise money for

SARS victims, in front of 450,000 fans at Downsview Park, Toronto on 30 July the same year.

Previously, Angus and Malcolm Young had appeared with the Stones at Sydney's Enmore Theatre (one of Mick Jagger, Keith Richards et al's legendary club gigs), jamming on a version of B.B. King's 'Rock Me Baby' in January 2003, and also in London's Twickenham on 30 September '03, when Richards managed to persuade Malcolm to solo on the same song. Some of these jamming performances were captured on the four-disc DVD box set *4 Flicks* released in November 2003.

ROUNDHOUSE STUDIOS
London

Studios where AC/DC and 'Mutt' Lange recorded some of *Highway To Hell,* between March and April 1979. The studios, located in an old railway turntable house in London's Chalk Farm, form part of the legendary Roundhouse complex, which once saw acts like The Doors, Jimi Hendrix, Led Zeppelin, Rolling Stones and David Bowie perform. The venue, which was closed down by Camden Council in 1983, was recently refurbished and reopened in 2006.

RUBIN/RICK

Rick Rubin is a record company executive and producer, who helmed the console for AC/DC's 1995 album *Ballbreaker.*

Long credited with being the brains behind the melding of rap and rock music, Rubin formed the Def Jam label whilst still at school, and his first release on the label was his university band Hose, for whom he played guitar. He then formed a partnership with DJ Jazzy Jay from Zulu Nation, and began learning hip-hop recording techniques. Jay in turn introduced Rubin to hip hop promoter Russell Simmons, with whom he formed a more professional Def Jam label. They signed LL Cool J, and later Public Enemy helped put the label on the map whilst Rubin's continued fusion of rap and rock won plaudits through the Beastie Boys, as well as his pioneering move to have Run DMC and the renewed Aerosmith join together for the groundbreaking 'Walk This Way' collaboration of 1986. However in 1988 both Simmons and Rubin split, the former remaining in control of Def Jam, the latter starting the more rock orientated Def American label (later American Recordings), to whom he signed the likes of Slayer, The Black Crowes, Masters Of Reality and even plucky Brit rockers Wolfsbane.

Rubin earned recognition for his production work with Trouble, Danzig, Tom Petty and the Red Hot Chili Peppers, and specifically his work with a rejuvenated Johnny Cash. He earned less applause for The Cult's 1987 album *Electric*, which some critics noted was 'possibly the best AC/DC album the band have never recorded'. And yet, he was the choice of the Young brothers to produce AC/DC's 13th studio album *Ballbreaker,* having passed the Young test when he oversaw the recording of the track 'Big Gun' from *The Last Action Hero* soundtrack. There were fears that as a massive AC/DC fan, Rubin may prove too close to the band to achieve the necessary sound they would require. Five years had passed since the commercial sound of *The Razors Edge,* and the musical climate had shifted somewhat.

In the end, *Ballbreaker* was regarded as an even stronger album than its predecessor, thanks in no small part to the sound, which was rawer and bluesier in tone, harking back to the days of *Powerage*, a style older fans had long yearned for. Yet Rubin has been well known for being great with coaxing the right sound at the right time from a band, and his suggestions that AC/DC use older speakers, heavier gauged guitar strings and flatwound bass strings played with a pick, certainly seemed to do the trick as far as this album was concerned. On top of that, Rubin is noted as a producer who gets on well with bands that he works with. And if Brian Johnson is to be believed that was certainly the case here:

"He's more a fan than producer," he said. *"So it was like having another pair of ears, which is what you need when you're making an album. I think the songs on [*Ballbreaker*] ended up sounding like the old AC/DC than anything we'd done since* For Those About To Rock.*"*

Rubin himself had this to say about his enduring passion for the band:

"When I was in junior high in 1979, my classmates all liked Led Zeppelin. But I loved AC/DC. I got turned on to them when I heard them play "Problem Child" on The Midnight Special. Like Zeppelin, they were rooted in American R&B,

but AC/DC took it to a minimal extreme that had never been heard before. Of course, I didn't know that back then. I only knew that they sounded better than any other band.

"For AC/DC, rock began with Chuck Berry and ended around Elvis. They poured their life-blood into that groove, and they mastered it. Highway To Hell is probably the most natural-sounding rock record I've ever heard. There's so little adornment. Nothing gets in the way of the push-and-pull between the guitarists Angus and Malcolm Young, bassist Cliff Williams and drummer Phil Rudd. For me, it's the embodiment of rock 'n' roll.

"When I'm producing a rock band, I try to create albums that sound as powerful as Highway To Hell. Whether it's The Cult or the Red Hot Chili Peppers, I apply the same basic formula: Keep it sparse. Make the guitar parts more rhythmic. It sounds simple, but what AC/DC did is almost impossible to duplicate. A great band like Metallica could play an AC/DC song note for note, and they still wouldn't capture the tension and release that drives the music. There's nothing like it.

"The other thing that separates AC/DC as a hard-rock band is that you can dance to their music. They didn't play funk, but everything they played was funky. And that beat could really get a crowd going. I first saw them play in 1979, before their singer Bon Scott died and was replaced by Brian Johnson. They were opening for Ted Nugent at Madison Square Garden (New York). The crowd yanked all the chairs off the floor and piled them into a pyramid in front of the stage. It was a tribute to how great they were.

"I got the chance to work with AC/DC on the 1995 album Ballbreaker. The best thing was the return of Phil Rudd, who had left the band in 1982. To me, that made them AC/DC again. You can hear it in how he drags behind the beat. It's that same rhythm that first drew me to them in junior high.

I'll go on record as saying they're the greatest rock 'n' roll band of all time. They didn't write emotional lyrics. They didn't play emotional songs. The emotion is all in that groove. And that groove is timeless."

RUDD/PHIL

54-year old Phil Rudd is widely regarded as being the finest anchor man that AC/DC have ever had, and has held the position, over two stints. The first was for the longest period ever by a drummer in this band, between 1973 and 1983, and the second from 1994 to the current day. His no-nonsense attitude to his craft, allied with a metronomic approach to time keeping, has proved near essential to underpinning the classic AC/DC sound.

Born Philip Hugh Norman Witschke Rudcevecuis in Melbourne on 19 May, 1954, Rudd cut his teeth playing in a variety of local bands before hooking up with local skinhead group Colored Balls, alongside noted Australian guitarist Lobby Lloyd and frontman Angry Anderson (who would later front AC/DC contemporaries Rose Tattoo). The band did not fare well, their skinhead image attracting a rowdy element and gigs were often marred by violence, but they did manage one album, *Ball Power* in 1973 and two singles in 'Liberate Rock' and 'Mess Of Blues'. However it would be good

grounding for the young Rudd, for the days when he would head out on Australia's notoriously hard pub circuit with AC/DC.

"That was a one gig career, that one," Rudd told www. cyberdrum.com in a rare interview of his time with the Aussie rockers. *"I was really young and they asked me to do a show one night and rehearsal was like, uh, six joints and the biggest can of beer."*

It wasn't long before Colored Balls had morphed into Buster Brown, a more hard rock orientated outfit who seemed like they were going to make more headway, managing to release one album, 'Something To Say' on the Mushroom label, until bassist Geordie Leach (who would also feature in Rose Tattoo with Angry Anderson) mentioned to Rudd that the fast-rising AC/DC were unhappy with their current drummer Pete Clack, and were interested in auditioning interested parties for the role. An eager Rudd begged Leach to accompany him to the audition, but the bassist declined. Had he known that AC/DC were equally unhappy with bassist Rob Bailey, (although that was allegedly because he was both married and towered over the diminutive Young brothers rather than for any lack of talent, an amusing rumour that almost certainly has no truth in it) Leach may have cared to join his drum partner and might never have featured in Rose Tattoo at all. However it was Rudd who turned up alone to the audition, and subsequently it was Phil Rudd who got the job.

According to his future bass partner Mark Evans, Phil Rudd was born to play for AC/DC in much the same way that Keith Richards was born to play for the Rolling Stones, whilst Evans' successor, Cliff Williams states that, "Phil's playing is exactly what we need. He's got a sixth sense".

Equally, Rudd himself, a master at an understated style which is often confused as being too simplistic and yet, much like AC/DC themselves, is very difficult to replicate, points out that he is merely a cog in the wheel of what keeps AC/DC on maximum overdrive.

"The rhythm section is Cliff, Malcolm and myself. And we all lock together to get the groove. We all listen to each other to lock and be tight because if one person decides to go by himself, it doesn't mean anything. We are all looking for the pocket, and search for the real feel of the thing, and that is the essence of what we try to do."

Rudd featured on every AC/DC album from *High Voltage* to *Flick Of The Switch*, and initially slotted into his newfound roll with ease,

even being prepared to up sticks and move to the UK in 1976, and undertake the pressurised work load which AC/DC embraced – as their rapid climb up the ladder to rock superstardom took shape.

The relationship between Rudd, who had been particularly affected by the death of Bon Scott, and rhythm guitarist Malcolm Young, had always been slightly fractious. With both members in thrall to alcohol during the '80s, things were destined to come to a head, and they did so during the recording of *Flick Of The Switch*.

Mystery has always surrounded Rudd's actual departure from AC/DC, one rumour suggesting the pair came to blows before Rudd was duly fired. The notoriously reluctant AC/DC have never officially commented on the reason, although at the time Angus merely stated;

"He was thinking about leaving for a while. He didn't mind the studio side of it, it was the touring that did it. He likes toying with his yachts better."

A MySpace page currently exists that claims to be for Phil Rudd, drummer of AC/DC, although much like the recent page claimed to be officially owned by Angus Young, and later found to be owned by a young female Australian, it may not be as official as it claims. Either way, of Rudd's departure from the band, it states:

"Rudd's sacking from the band was partly as a result of his own problems with alcohol, and also growing conflict between him and band leader Malcolm Young, which eventually became physical".

True or not, this tends to tie in with the accepted, although never completely explained, reasons why Phil Rudd and AC/DC parted ways back in 1983. However a later claim that Rudd went on tour with AC/DC around the time of *TheRazors Edge* and made sandwiches back stage seems to stretch the bounds of believability.

Rudd has not, as indeed neither has either of the Young brothers or any member of AC/DC for that matter, commented on the true reasons for his departure from the band. He has, however, gone on record as saying:

"It's something we enjoy doing. We get to the show and 15,000 people there give you the horse-power to do it and you just do it. The whole thing just comes up because you know what you are doing is simple, but hard to do. We've been doing this a long time and we've all come to appreciate each other now. In the past we were more fired up and much more aggressive and now, we just enjoy what it is we can do and there are no restrictions and limits, everything is still one hundred per cent. We do still battle to get that raw sound on stage and you need to be able to feel it to enjoy it. Some nights you do enjoy more than others because it does happen when the overall sound might be swirling, and you may have a problem hearing someone and instead you hear indirectly from the hall and when this happens you must work hard to try and keep everything together where it's supposed to be."

Either way, despite having his name on the credits of *Flick Of The Switch*, Rudd was gone, ex-Procol Harum drummer B.J. Wilson being drafted in to help complete any drum parts on the album, before ex-Tytan/AIIZ drummer Simon Wright was called upon to join the band full-time and appear in promo videos for the album's singles – the first real indication to fans that Rudd was no more.

Rudd retreated to New Zealand, where he sought to shy away from over-zealous AC/DC fans. He set up a helicopter charter company and generally busied himself with non-musical activities.

"I raced cars, flew helicopters, became a farmer, planted some crops," he said, failing to mention anything about yachts. *"I lived in New Zealand, which was great, nice, quiet, with nobody bothering me."*

However Phil Rudd continued to play drums intermittently, and had also built his own recording studio, keeping his hand in with music whenever he felt like it. With AC/DC losing his replacement Wright to Dio in 1989, and perhaps finding that his successor Chris Slade should always have been a temporary fill-in, it seemed inevitable that something would happen between the old band mates. In 1994 it did.

"We hadn't seen Phil for about ten years, so when we were playing in New Zealand we thought we'd give him a call," explained Malcolm of Rudd's eventual return. *"He seemed just like the old Phil. Then around May me and Angus were jamming and we just said, 'Let's jam with the guy and see how it goes'. We'd already decided we wanted to try and get back to where we were on those old records and Phil was the missing ingredient."*

And so Phil Rudd returned to AC/DC to drum, thus far on *Ball-breaker, Stiff Upper Lip* and the

band's long-awaited 15th studio album. The machine that makes certain the AC/DC engine runs as best it can is back in business.

RUFF STUFF

Track eight on AC/DC's 1988 album *Blow Up Your Video*, 'Ruff Stuff' is a rather crude and blatant attempt to recreate the style of writing, though certainly not the infectious groove, of older AC/DC songs like 'Whole Lotta Rosie'.

Written by Brian Johnson, Malcolm Young and Angus Young, lines like: 'I like 'em big and I like 'em small/If I took the oath I would take them all/Gimme that ruff stuff that's what I want' give some indication why, despite impressive sales at the time, *Blow Up Your Video* is no longer considered quite as good an album as it once was.

'74 JAILBREAK

Originally released for the North American and Japanese markets in October 1984, *'74 Jailbreak* is a collection of five early AC/DC tracks that had long been only available in Australia. All recorded between 1974 and 1976, the set featured some of the band's more bluesy, rock 'n' roll moments, most of which had appeared on their debut album *High Voltage*, as well as 'Jailbreak' from the Australian version of *Dirty Deeds Done Dirt Cheap*, which had been left off of the international edition of that album, itself only released in America in 1981. *'74 Jailbreak* was finally released in Europe in 1990, and also formed part of Epic Records' 2003 re-issues set. It reached number 74 in the US charts upon release.

Full tracklisting: *Jailbreak/ You Ain't Got A Hold On Me/ Show Business/Soul Stripper/ Baby, Please Don't Go*

SAFE IN NEW YORK CITY

The fifth track from AC/DC's 14th album *Stiff Upper Lip*, 'Safe In New York City' was written by Angus and Malcolm Young. The song itself seemingly warns of the dangers of taking a night time tour through the famous American city, with lines like: 'All over the city and down to the dives/ Don't mess with this place it'll eat you alive/Got lip smackin' honey to soak up the jam/On top of the world ma I'm ready to slam' suggesting the pitfalls. However, the later 'Take a look at that thing in the tight ass jeans/Comin' your way now you may be in luck/ Don't you fret boy she's ready to buck' gives the song a more typically salacious vibe, indicating it may be nothing more than one of AC/DC's tawdry tales of night time fun. Given that New York has famously been made a much safer city in the last 20 years than it was in the '70s would seem to suggest the latter is more the case, although the events of 9/11 added a certain delicate nature to the subject matter.

The song was released as a single, but failed to chart in either the UK or the US.

SALT PALACE ARENA

On January 18, 1991, the band played a show at this venue in Salt Lake City. Tragically, three fans were killed.

Curtis Child (aged 14), Jimmie Boyd (14) and Elizabeth Glausi (19) got caught up in a frightening crush among a crowd of 13,294. The first two named were killed on the spot, but Glausi died after her parents requested her life-support be turned off.

Curtis Child's family launched an $8 million law suit against AC/DC, the concert promoters and county officials. Glausi's parents subsequently sued the band as well.

On February 10, an inquiry into the matter cleared 'DC of any culpability in this sad situation, although it would be some little while before these suits were finally settled and cleared up.

This was the start of yet more problems for the band, ones that would seemingly crop up through-

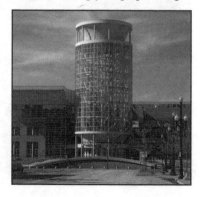

out the year. On September 28, AC/DC headlined the Rock Around The Bloc free concert at Tushino Airfield, just a few days after a failed Communist coup.

The Russian authorities were very touchy about the situation, concerned that with an expected attendance of anywhere between 500,000 and a million people, trouble might erupt. In the end, there were isolated skirmishes that led to 53 fans being hospitalised, with injuries mainly caused by night sticks being wielded by the police.

On November 13, two fans were stabbed at a show in Wellington, New Zealand, as the band reach the end of the world tour. There were also reports of several drugs overdoses at the same gig, following which a minority of fans went on what was claimed to be a rampage, with 50 arrests made.

SATELLITE BLUES

The eighth track from AC/DC's 2000 album *Stiff Upper Lip*, 'Satellite Blues' is the song wherein the band finally seem to acknowledge the technological advances that have been made during their 35-year career. Although typically they manage to find a blatantly sexual avenue through which to do so.

Written by Angus and Malcolm Young, 'Satellite Blues' tells the tale of a man settling down to

enjoy some pornography via his satellite television, only for his ultimate satisfaction to be ruined by a systems malfunction, his disgruntlement all too evident in the final stanza of the song: 'This thing's nothing but a load of crap/ I'm gonna send it right back/ You can stick it where it hurts Mac/ I've got the satellite blues'.

The track was released as the third single from *Stiff Upper Lip*, and managed to reach number 23 in Australia but did not chart anywhere else. Brian Johnson had originally wanted to release 'Can't Stand Still' as the single, but was outvoted.

SCHOOL DAYS

A cover of the Chuck Berry (below) song, sometimes also known as 'School Days (Ring! Ring! Goes The Bell)', this appeared as the ninth and final

track on AC/DC's second album *T.N.T.* It was the only cover song on the album and did not feature on the international version of *High Voltage*, which was a compilation of AC/DC's first two albums. It does, however, appear on the *Volts* collection in the *Bonfire* box set.

The song is very much a rock 'n' roll standard, having been a 1957 single for Berry and also appeared on his very first album, titled *After School Session*. Lyrically it deals with the boredom of having to attend school and looking forward to cutting loose at the local dance, something with which the youthful AC/DC, who were all major Chuck Berry fans and hardly the greatest fans of school, would have felt great empathy.

The song has also been covered by the likes of The Beach Boys, Gary Glitter, Lil' Rob and has even featured in an episode of the popular TV cartoon series *The Simpsons*.

SCHOOLKIDS WEEK

This took place at the Hard Rock Café in Melbourne during May 1975. The idea was to organise daytime shows for those too young to get along to regular gigs. AC/DC were among the bands on the bill – presumably it helped having the man who manages the band, Michael Browning, also running the Hard Rock Café. Scott was forced to miss one of these dates, with Angus and Malcolm taking over lead vocals.

SCHWARZENNEGER, ARNOLD

The beefcake one-time Terminator turned Governor of California, appears in the video clip for the AC/DC single 'Big Gun'. The reason? He was the main star of the 1993 movie *Last Action Hero*, in which the above song is featured. So when the plot was put together for the video, it seemed logical to get the man himself involved.

In fact, the video opens with Schwarzenneger kicking down the door of the band's dressing room, walking in and eyeing each member in turn. Suddenly, Angus kicks his schoolboy cap towards the muscle-bound Austrian-born star. Putting it on, Schwarzen-

neger becomes Angus, even with the trademark Gibson SG guitar!

Angus Young told FHM about his first encounter with Arnie:

"I remember when I met him, he picked me up with one hand, lifted me to eye level and said 'Hullo Ang-goose'. We had done a track for his movie, Last Action Hero, *and the film studio wanted him to be part of the video. I said to him, 'It'd be cool if you were in the school suit like me'. So they had a big school suit made for him. And the director said, 'Arnold, see that little runaround Angus does? It'd be good if you could copy it'. So I showed him how to do it."*

It's not actually known if the man himself has a penchant for AC/DC, or even rock music, but he did also appear in the video for Guns n' Roses' 'You Could Be Mine' and Bon Jovi's 'Say It Isn't So', therefore he might be a closet rocker of sorts.

For trivia hounds, the AC/DC clip was directed by David Mallet and filmed at Van Nuys Airport Hangar in Los Angeles on May 6, 1993.

SCOTT/BON

How do you define a rock star? Go on, try it? The problem is that there is no scientific, sociological, economic or psychological profile of such a beast. It's down to instinct and impact – which is why Bon Scott is regarded by so many as one of the ultimate examples of the species.

If you ever met the man, you knew he was special. Scott had a way of entering a room or bar that made everyone aware of his presence, without the need to actually do anything different or remarkable. He was a tornado, a tidal wave, yet a lot more subtle than either of these two other forces of nature. He had the gift of being able to take an audience of hundreds and make it seem like everyone had been transported into a stadium. Conversely, he could address tens of thousands as if each were his pal in a club. If he talked to you, he had your attention, and you had his.

"For me, playing in clubs and also the bigger places... both are amazing," Scott once said. *"I love being able to walk out of a crowd and onstage. Being one of the guys at the bar, and then*

getting up to entertain people whom you can reach out and touch. But nothing beats playing in front of a huge stadium audience – the bigger the better. It's a challenge for me and the band. The bigger the occasion, the better and harder we play."

Bon Scott was an enigma in some respects, yet also remarkably straightforward. He had none of the pretensions and affectations that blight so many who regard themselves as rock stars. He had no need of bodyguards and VIP treatment, not that he'd turn down a free drink, or an available woman. He'd happily stand you a drink at the bar any time, but would expect you to buy the next one. In other words, he'd treat you as a friend, but would demand the same attitude from you.

Self-confident to the point where it didn't need to be displayed or mentioned. Talented as both a songwriter and performer to a degree that put him in a league on his own. A man who didn't sing a lyric, so much as tell a story... Scott was a bon viveur, a raconteur, a team player who was also singularly individual. But mostly he had a zest and fire for life which was overpowering and inspiring. There are those people who literally fizz with vibrancy, energy and a restive, creative spirit. Scott was one of these. He once confided:

"Sometimes I don't know what drives me. It's as if I've been plugged into a huge generator and been given the chance to spread its power to everyone. I am no more than a wire through which this force is running. I don't know where it's gonna lead, and sometimes it gets me in trouble, but I love having that ability. I love being Bon Scott – even though I often can't figure him out!"

Ronald Belford Scott was born on July 9, 1946 in Kirriemuir, Scotland to Charles and Isabelle Scott. His parents had met when Charles (more commonly known as Chick) was stationed in Kirkcaldy, Scotland, while in the army during the Second World War (Bon's dad was working as a baker). Chick married Isabelle Cunningham in 1941, and Bon arrived five years later.

In 1952, the Scott family – including Bon's brother Graeme and sister Valerie – emigrated to Australia, at first staying with Isabelle's sister in the Melbourne district of Sunshine. Bon was enrolled in the local primary school, getting his first taste of education – and the educational system got their first glance at a kid who might not have been academically assiduous, but stood out from the crowd, because he seemed fearless. He once said of his early days at school:

"My new schoolmates threatened to kick the shit out of me when they heard my Scottish accent. I had one week to learn to speak like them if I wanted to remain intact. Course, I didn't take any notice. No-one railroads me, and it made me all the more determined to speak my own way. That's how I got my name, you know. The Bonny Scot, see?"

While some children make their mark through laughter and jokes, and others excel at traditional sports, the young Bon was the one who'd take on any dare imaginable. From diving off the highest board, to fighting anyone who'd challenge him – he was a born leader, because he would do something first, and then expect others to follow.

In 1956, the Scott family moved to the hotter, dryer climate of Fremantle, a port in Western Australia close to Perth, on doctor's advice. Bon's brother had developed asthma and it was felt a change in environment would do him some considerable good. And Bon got his introduction to music, by joining the Fremantle Pipe Band, alongside his father. It was here that he learnt to play the drums and also the bagpipes. Now, the latter skill would come into its own on the AC/DC track 'It's A Long Way To The Top (If You Wanna Rock 'N' Roll), but the former would be used to good effect with his first proper band, The Spektors. However, before he took his first steps down the path to becoming a rock legend, Bon ended up in legal trouble. By 1963, he'd dropped out of school and moved into the house

of Olive and Jim Henderson. But his wayward character and daredevil behaviour quickly attracted the wrong sort of attention. At the age of 16, he was up in Fremantle Children's Court charged with stealing 12 gallons of petrol (quite what he planned to do with this remained a mystery, although arson probably wasn't on his mind), having 'unlawful carnal knowledge' (shagging an underage girl; rape was never implied), running away from legal custody and giving the police a false name and address.

He pleaded guilty on all counts, and spent a short time in Fremantle Prison for assessment, before being handed over to the Riverbank Juvenile Institution until he was 18. There are those who believe this to be a major turning point in his life. Because of his custodial situation, Scott was

unable to see his grandparents when they came over on a visit to Australia. Moreover, he believed he'd let down his parents badly – and was now determined to be a success, in an effort to make it up to them and prove he was far from a deadweight with little future beyond lawless activities. Scott would always feel that, while he was skirting on the edges of the law in his younger days, he really had no interest in becoming a hardened criminal; he loved the notion of being a rebel and outlaw, but in a strange way would never sanction illegal activities for their own sake.

After drifting through various dead-end jobs – from postman to bartender and truck packer – in 1964, now aged 18, Scott teamed up with Wyn Milson, John Collins and Brian Gannon in The Spektors. Bon was on drums and vocals, with Milson on guitar,

Gannon on bass and Collins on vocals and drums; while Collins would be the main singer in the band, when Scott stepped up, then the former would take his place behind the kit.

Playing purely covers – especially from the Beatles and Rolling Stones – the Spektors toured the local Perth club scene and picked up a decent following, even winning a Battle Of The Bands contest. But by early 1966, Milson and Scott had left and teamed up with members of another local band, The Winstons, to start The Valentines. Interestingly, Scott now shared the vocals with former Winstons frontman Vince Lovegrove. For a time, this combination worked.

In May 1967, the band released their debut single, 'Everyday I Have To Cry', which was to be a Top Five hit for The Valentines in the local area – no mean feat. They were to put out six more singles, including 'She Said', 'Peculiar Hole In The Sky' and 'My Old Man's A Groovy Old Man', all of which were co-written by the Easybeats duo of Harry Vanda and George Young – two people who would play a major role in Scott's life a few years further down the line.

The Valentines' last single was 'Juliette', released in February 1970, and written by Scott. Despite re-locating to Melbourne and achieving considerable status on the national Australian touring circuit – for a time they were regarded as bigger than even the

hugely popular Easybeats – the band split up in August, 1970. There were rumours at the time of excessive drug-taking and major musical differences among the members, as some within the group – possibly Scott – objected to their squeaky clean, bubblegum pop approach.

Whatever the truth, Bon was soon back in action. A group called Levi Smiths Clefs had only just split up, and one or two of their number stayed together as Fraternity. But they needed a vocalist, until bassist Bruce Howe suggested the ex-Valentines man – the pair were friends by now. Scott was back in business.

Fraternity signed to the Sweet Peach label, but their debut album (1971's *Livestock*) was not a success, despite the fact they'd become a major draw on the live circuit. A hard album to track down these days, *Livestock* was just too drippy to make an impact. It all sounded too much like a poor copy of Canadian giants The Band.

Fraternity soon left Sweet Peach and teamed up with the Raven label for a series of singles and '72's

superior album *Flaming Galah,* which was a much harder hitting record than its predecessor. But still major success eluded them.

In an effort to kickstart things, the previous year Fraternity had used the prize money from winning Headley's National Battle Of The Sounds to travel to London, and from there tour across the UK and Europe, in a similar manner to the way AC/DC would do things four years later. But it didn't work well; the only gig of note happening when Fraternity supported Geordie – Bon Scott opening for Brian Johnson!

Depressed, and now for some reason called Fang, (even though the *Flaming Galah* album would come out under the 'Fraternity' name) the band returned home, and the various members started drifting apart, having lost faith in the whole project. A loose alliance of Fraternity/Fang members worked under the name of the

Mount Lofty Rangers, with whom Scott recorded briefly. But after one session, the singer fell out badly with the other musicians. Depressed, angry and drunk, he got on his Triumph motorbike, roared off... and suffered a serious crash, which put him in a coma for three days, during which time Irene – the wife he'd married just prior to Fraternity's disappointing trip to England (they divorced in 1978, Thornton now lives in Melbourne) – never left his side. It was the end of Scott's relationship with the Fraternity members in any shape or form.

John Bissett, who played keyboards in the early days of the band, recalls Bon fondly:

"Bon was a natural-born daredevil. He entertained the local kids in one town by jumping off a high point on a pier into a swarm of jellyfish in the ocean below. He would ride a trolley down an embankment at the Adelaide Hills property into a small lake at the bottom. When the trolley hit the bottom

he would be projectiled into the lake. He suffered some painful injuries on his trail bike, but never lost his spirit. He was dubbed 'Road Test Ronnie' by the band as he usually was the first to try a new type of acid or weed. He seemed able to cope with any drug that science or nature could come up with. Only Datura (a hallucinogenic), which he road-tested in London, got the better of him. He had a bad couple of days and the rest of us avoided it.

"I think Bon learned his 'sex, drugs and rock 'n' roll' attitude and lifestyle in Fraternity. Some commentators saw us as a bunch of clean-living hippies, into lentils and sandals. Nothing could be further from the truth. Fraternity was very much a 'sex, drugs and rock' outfit, though I would put booze at the front of that list – particularly cheap South Australian brandy. We had our share of groupies, though some of us indulged more than others. Bon would sign autographs for girls in very intimate places, but was not much into casual sexual relationships from my observation."

By 1974, on the suggestion of former bandmate Lovegrove, Scott was working as an occasional roadie for AC/DC, driving their van. At the time, Dave Evans was fronting the band, but the Young brothers – Angus and Malcolm – had decided that he wasn't right for them. Their attentions turned to the experienced Scott.

"I kept telling them I wanted to play drums for the band," insisted the singer years later. *"But they were having none of it. 'We don't need a drummer', they'd say, 'we need a singer'."*

Eventually, 'DC got their man, and fates were sealed.

Over the next six years, the band released six studio albums and the live *If You Want Blood...You've Got It.* As their stock rose, so did Scott's reputation. His clever use of words, that unmistakable, swaggering vocal delivery were to prove so crucial to their success. He was at ease onstage, at home in the studio and loved people. He also became an unofficial guardian for Angus, looking out for the guitarist in a very protective manner. Said Scott:

"I always say to Angus, 'You see what I do? Don't you do any of that. It's not healthy'. I think he listens."

Yet for all his love of partying to excess and going the extra metre in search of bacchanalian fun, Scott worked hard in the band and was intensely proud of what had been done. He was also someone who embraced the challenge of working with 'Mutt' Lange as the producer on the Highway To Hell *album.*

"Harry Vanda and George Young are great, and they're mates. But Lange... I think he's brought something extra out of us. I believe he'll help to really open the potential of this band. What we can achieve in the next few years could be startling. Just wait and see."

Tragically, Scott wasn't to live to see his words come true. On February 19, 1980, he died in a car parked in East Dulwich. The circumstances have given rise to many theories about the death, lots, it seems, revolving around the so-called mystery man Alistair Kinnear. Some suggested he deliberately delayed calling the ambulance. Others that this was a pseudonym for a drugs dealer, trying to hide his identity. There was even an utterly reprehensible claim that the Young brothers had paid someone to kill their singer, having badly fallen out with him.

Sorry, but the fact is that Scott's death can be put down to no more than a horrendous accident. And Alistair Kinnear did, and does, exist. As previously stated, Classic Rock magazine tracked him down in 2005 and he talked them through what occurred on that

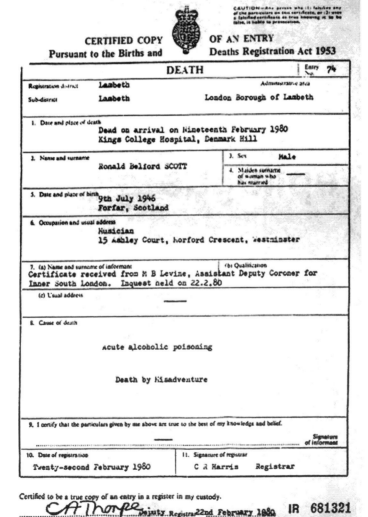

dreadful night (see earlier entry for details).

The coroner delivered an open verdict on Scott's death, but there were no traces of drugs found in his body, which ruled out a heroin overdose as some speculated.

Bon Scott's ashes were interred in Fremantle Cemetery, and his grave is said to be the most visited in Australia, having become a shrine for AC/DC fans from across the world. Many turn up to 'have a beer with Bon', something that would have amused and delighted the man himself. In 2006, the National Trust Of Australia declared Scott's grave important enough to be classified as a heritage place. Sadly, the plaque erected to commemorate this honour was stolen on July 9, 2006 – which would have been Bon's 60th birthday.

Fremantle further honoured one of their favourite sons by putting up a bronze statue of him in February 2008. Sculpted by local artists Greg James, it stands at Fisherman's Wharf in the town. The Bon Scott Project also ran there, from May 17 to June 29, 2008. This was a collection of works from 19 Australian and internationally-based artists inspired by the intense 'taking life by the balls' spirit of the man and his music. The works were often irreverent, unconventional and exciting, and explored ideas of masculinity, remembrance and rebellion. Curator Jasmin Stephens selected artists who were interested in the man, but not necessarily fans.

"Scott's fans have shared codes and vocabularies. We wanted artists who are not necessarily fans to break open some of these conventions with a range of responses."

Inevitably, there have been retrospective compilations of recordings Bon did with both The Valentines and Fraternity. The former feature on 1987's *The Valentines*, re-issued the next year as part of *Seasons Of Change The Early Years 1967-72* in 1988. This itself was again released three years later, this time as *Bon Scott - The Early Years 1967-1972*. Fraternity had the double album *The Complete Sessions 1971-72* released in 1997.

AC/DC themselves released the *Bonfire* set in 1997, to celebrate his

memory. However, they did mysteriously include a re-mastered version of *Back In Black*, which of course features Scott's successor Brian Johnson. It fuelled speculation that Bon might have had more to do with the album than has ever been admitted by 'DC themselves. Did any of his lyrics get used posthumously? The band firmly deny this, and yet the stories won't go away. It's not for the authors to speculate on the truth or otherwise of this situation, although it must be pointed out that Scott's last girlfriend, Anna Bara, has also insisted that he wrote down some of the lyrics for the album in a book that then 'mysteriously' disappeared. She further insists that Scott came up with the title of 'Rock And Roll Ain't Noise Pollution', which was used on the *Back In Black* album. However, such

allegations must be taken with a massive pinch of salt.

What can definitely be dismissed is the claim made by some more zealous fans that Scott actually recorded some songs for the album just prior to his death. For years it was said tapes existed, although strangely none ever came to light. In more recent times, the advent of the internet has led to people uploading songs which they insist are those elusive demos. On all occasions these have turned out to be recordings from tribute bands, or other acts who might sound like Scott era AC/DC, but are patently not to the real deal.

Finally, in 2003 when AC/DC were inducted into the Rock & Roll Hall Of Fame, Scott was included alongside the current line-up (the only former member to be so honoured), with members

of his family accepting the accolade on his behalf.

Although there have always been rumours that Bon might well have fathered children around the globe, this remains in the realms of speculation. However, in 2007 it was claimed that he was the father of Australian actor Alex O'Loughlin, who starred in the US series *The Shield*. This has since been denied by O'Loughlin, who said:

"The rumour started about me in the last year. It started with a friend of mine calling me, my best buddy here actually, Vince, he called me very upset. He was using words that I won't use today, and he was cursing and saying, 'What's your problem, man?' And I was like, 'I don't know what you're talking about.' And he said, 'Have you got something you need to tell me?' And I said, 'No, I don't think so.' And he asked me to go and Google search my name, and the rock band AC/DC, of which he's a giant fan, and apparently according to the rest of the world and several big newspapers back where I'm from, I'm the son of the late Bon Scott, the late singer of AC/DC.

"And I was shocked, and then I was thrilled. I rock. Secretly I rock all the time. You didn't know that because I kind of keep it to myself. But I do rock, just so you know. And I play music very badly, but AC/DC was a big part. I'm Australian so I grew up with AC/DC, and they are a big part of the songs that you learn on the guitar, the first ones. But then my mom called me and she was very upset and that sort of thing. Publicly, you know, labelled a groupie and therefore a hussy and a harlot, which isn't true at all. My mom is a very wonderful woman and very respectable. And so I suppose it's probably a good time to say, since he's passed on and he can't speak the truth, I should speak for Bon and say that I'm pretty sure he's not my dad."

Bon Scott's legacy and legend have grown over the years. He is now more iconic than ever – and can only become increasingly important. What might he have gone on to achieve? One can only guess. Certainly greater triumphs with AC/DC, and perhaps some solo records, exploring other sides of his artistry. Who knows, he might have turned his hand to acting… but he'd have always been the one propping up the bar, telling the stories and keeping us all enthralled. That was Bon Scott – flesh and blood made myth, and myth made flesh and blood.

"The thing I loved most about Bon Scott was his almost unique self-honesty," said Vince Love-grove in 2006. *"What you saw was what you got; he was a real person and as honest as the day is long. To my mind, he was the street poet of my generations and of the generations that followed."*

Yet, if the man does come across as something of a subscriber to the bacchanalian school of excess and be damned, then that is just part of his appeal. Sure, the man would always appreciate any opportunity to indulge in the pleasures offered. But he was never less than fully professional in his dealings with, and on behalf of, the band. In his time with AC/DC, he only missed one show – and that was down to circumstances out of his control. Moreover, he was a diligent songwriter who'd always log ideas for future reference, and would work on his lyrics until he felt that they flowed in a style and manner that captured what he wanted to say. Often it was the spontaneity of the moment that gave him inspiration – from an empty bottle to an attractive passing female. Others might have been equally witty, but what he could do was capture that spirit and ensure it was there for future reference.

One of the stories with which he's most associated happened when a wag once asked him whether he was AC or DC. His response? "No mate, I'm the lightning flash in the middle!" – followed by a hefty blow to both the culprit's ego and physical well-being. This has often seemed to be an apocryphal story. However, it would be typical of Scott, who'd never indulge idiots out to wind him up.

Over the years, there have been several rumours of movies in the pipeline based on Scott's life and actions. So far though, nothing has come of any of these vague ideas. Scott himself once remarked:

"If there was to be a movie about me – and I can't think why anyone'll wanna do that – then I reckon I'd have to play the part myself. I can't think of an actor who could do me justice!"

Naturally, you'd have to take such a statement with a slight pinch of salt. But Bon Scott knew his worth, and also realised how far it extended. Anything that would have interfered with his determination to lead his life the way he wanted was to be spurned.

Scott was also said to keep notes that were the basis for possible short stories, or even a novel. There's little doubt that he had a unique way with words, one that was both insightful yet also very much of the street. He related directly to the audience, and his blue collar performances were actually surprising for a man who liked to give the impression that working for a living was never an option. While he wanted people to think this all came naturally to him, Scott actually had a strong work ethic. He believed that anything achieved must be earned, and that nothing came for free. Again, he expressed this side of his personality better than anyone else might have been able: "I want what I have to last, and I want to appreciate what it all means. So I work at getting better. I don't believe anyone'll come and take it away – let them try! – but I have to be the best at what I do, and who I am. I'm not gonna be one of those 'I could have been a contender' types, the ones who moan about how life lets them down.

I aim to fulfil every last bit of potential, to do every goddamn thing I can and try to do everything that comes my way."

And let's leave the last word to Bon Scott himself:

"I've never had a message for anyone in my entire life. Except maybe to give out my room number."

SEND FOR THE MAN

The final track from the band's 1985 album *Fly On The Wall*. Written by Brian Johnson, Angus Young and Malcolm Young, the bravura lyric is a shameless boast of sexual prowess, the kind of thing that Bon Scott used to revel in, although dispatched with a little less finesse than the late singer might have used, in lines like: 'You're like a dream/You're low dirty and mean/You're good enough to eat/Sticky hot and sweet'.

SHAKE A LEG

The ninth track from AC/DC's groundbreaking sixth album *Back In Black*, 'Shake A Leg', written by Brian Johnson, Angus Young and Malcolm Young, boasts one of the record's most impressive yet unheralded riffs.

The song itself seems to relate the semi-autobiographical tale of a restless youth growing up on the streets and trying to avoid trouble, before hitting pay-dirt by landing the women of his dreams, culminating with these scene-setting lines: 'Magazines, wet dreams, dirty women on machines for me/Big licks, skin flicks, trickey dicks are my chemistry/Goin' against the grain, trying to keep me sane with you/So stop your grinnin' and drop your linen for me'.

The song was rumoured to have been performed on one or two of the very earliest warm-up shows Johnson performed with AC/DC in Belgium and Holland, prior to the *Back In Black* world tour, but is sung in such a high register (it features some of the highest notes Johnson has committed to vinyl) that the band were forced to drop it from the set and it has not been performed since.

SHAKE YOUR FOUNDATIONS

The second track from AC/DC's ninth studio album *Fly On The Wall*. Written by Brian Johnson, Angus Young and Malcolm Young, the catchy rocker is definitely among the stand-out tracks on one of the band's weakest records, managing to marry the rawness of 'DC's early days with the more modern melodic traits – something they didn't manage with so much accuracy on any other song on the album.

This is a simple tale of sexual prowess, with Johnson intoning lines like: 'We had the night, we had the time/She had the sugar I had the wine/Took my hand, shook me to the core/Told her not to touch but she was comin' back for more' with sleazy delight.

The song was the third single from *Fly On The Wall* and a success in the UK, reaching number 24 in January 1986, backed with 'Stand Up'. The 12" version also features a live version of 'Jailbreak' recorded in Dallas during 1985, on the *Fly On The Wall* world tour. The song also appears on the *Who Made Who* album and was one of the five tracks for which a promo video was shot, and came out on the *Fly On The Wall* VHS release.

SHEARMAN/BUZZ

Douglas 'Buzz' Shearman was the original singer with Canadian rockers Moxy, who at one point featured late-Deep Purple guitarist Tommy Bolin in their ranks. The band had built up a steady following in their native Canada, by 1977 had branched out into America itself and on 27 July of that year made the first of three headline appearances at the Armadillo World Headquarters in

Austin, Texas. The support band on all three nights was AC/DC.

Dogged by problems with his vocal chords, exacerbated by heavy drinking, Shearman left Moxy at the end of 1977, replaced by Mike Rynoski (ne Reno), who himself would later form AOR band Loverboy. Shearman returned to the Moxy ranks in 1979, and was one of the candidates allegedly under discussion for the role as singer in AC/DC when Bon Scott died in February 1980. However with his ongoing vocal problems affecting how long he could tour, Shearman was eventually passed over.

Shearman and the rest of Moxy would help out with Canadian rocker Lee Aaron's debut album, *The Lee Aaron Project*, but tragically Shearman himself was killed in a motorbike accident on 16 June, 1983. He was 33, the same age as Bon Scott when he died.

SHE'S GOT BALLS

Track number two on AC/DC's debut album *High Voltage* (it would move to track number eight on the international version), 'She's Got Balls' has long been one of the band's most popular songs.

Written by Bon Scott and Angus and Malcolm Young, the song relates to Bon's wife Irene Thornton, to whom the singer was married briefly. It transpires that Irene had complained to Scott that he'd never written a song about her, and he then came up with the lyric to 'She's Got Balls', paying testament to his lady in typical fashion: 'She's got style that woman/Makes me smile that woman/She got spunk that woman/Funk that woman'.

Although the track was recorded and released after Scott and Thornton had effectively separated (they eventually divorced in 1978), the pair remained on good terms until Scott's untimely death in 1980. 'She's Got Balls' was a staple part of the band's early shows whilst Brian Johnson told BBC Radio in 1981 the song was one of his personal favourites from the Bon era.

A live version of this tune, recorded at Bondi Lifesavers Club in 1977, appeared as the B-side to the 1986 re-issue of the 'You Shook Me All Night Long' single. This same version is included on the *Volts* CD in the *Bonfire* box set.

SHOCK TO THE SYSTEM

Shock To The System, by author Mark Putterford, is widely regarded as one of the best books yet written about AC/DC. Published by Omnibus in 1992, it takes a detailed look at the AC/DC story from the very early days up until the release of *The Razors Edge* in 1990 and the ensuing world tour. Putterford, a friend and colleague of the authors, has also penned similarly excellent works on Metallica (*A Visual Documentary* with Xavier Rus-

sell) and Phil Lynott (*The Rocker*). Putterford sadly died in 1994.

SHOOTIN' STAR

A song the band were rumoured to have recorded during the sessions for the *Powerage* album, yet was never released. The interesting thing is that nobody seems to have ever heard the track, it has never surfaced anywhere on bootlegs, and AC/DC themselves have never confirmed its existence. In fact, you'd have thought that should it actually exist, then the band would have included it in the *Bonfire* box set.

SHOOT TO THRILL

Second up on AC/DC's legendary *Back In Black* album, 'Shoot To Thrill' is another track from Brian Johnson, Angus Young and Malcolm Young that carries on the grand tradition of lewd lasciviousness left behind by the late great Bon Scott.

Eschewing any ideas that this might be about the literal joys of firing a gun, it is once more packed with the kind of sexual metaphors Scott used to have so much fun with, whilst making its somewhat libidinous point with more simple fare such as: 'All you women who want a man on the street/But you don't know which way you want to turn/Just keep a coming and put your hand out

to me/'Cause I'm the one who's gonna make you burn'.

The song, another in the highest range that Johnson has sung for AC/DC, has long been in the band's live set, and is also the second track on 1992's *Live*. Another live version cropped up on the B-side of the 1993 single 'Big Gun'.

SHOT DOWN IN FLAMES

Track number six from AC/DC's sixth studio album *Highway To Hell* is a simple tale of a man out on the pull, trying his luck, and crashing and burning.

Written by Bon Scott, Malcolm Young and Angus Young, as the lyric says, Scott is: 'Out on the town, looking for a woman/Gonna give me good love', but all too soon encounters such problems as: 'She was standing alone, over

by the jukebox/Like she'd something to sell/ I said Baby what's the going price/She told me to go to hell', or even later: 'Said baby, you're driving me crazy/Laid it out on the line/When this guy with a chip on his shoulder said/ Toss off buddy, she's mine'!

A live version of 'Shot Down In Flames' was released as the B-side to 'Touch Too Much' in 1979, and the song has featured in the band's live set during both the Scott and Johnson eras.

SHOT OF LOVE

The ninth track from AC/DC's 1990 album *The Razors Edge*. The song, written by Young brothers Angus and Malcolm, is typical of the more generic stories of misogynistic love which AC/DC have peddled since the death of Bon Scott, lacking the tongue-in-cheek warmth the late frontman brought to his own lurid tales.

SHOW BUSINESS

The eighth track on AC/DC's debut album *High Voltage*. Written by Bon Scott, Angus Young and Malcolm Young, the song displays the band's already somewhat world weary view of the entertainment business – poignantly one that still very much holds true to this day however – reflected in lines like: 'We smoke our buts/

They smoke cigars/We drown in debt/They drown in bars' which make it perfectly clear what the youthful AC/DC thought of record business types.

The song, very typical hard driving rock 'n' roll, is an ideal reflection of the early mix of glam rock and Chuck Berry-inspired music that helped forge AC/DC's sound and is one of the songs the band first performed on Australia's legendary music TV show *Countdown*.

The track evolved out of one called 'Sunset Strip', written by Malcolm Young and the band's original lead singer Dave Evans, which was revamped and given new lyrics when Bon Scott took over on vocals.

'Show Business' was eventually released outside of Australia on *'74 Jailbreak*.

SIN CITY

The sixth track on their fifth studio album *Powerage*, 'Sin City' is one of the few AC/DC tracks which obviously takes a deviation from the band's normal driving approach, in as much as it throws a bass solo into the mix – indeed the first bass solo for new boy Cliff Williams, who had joined the group prior to the recording process on the album starting.

Written by Bon Scott, Angus Young and Malcolm Young, the song deals, in lyrical terms, with the bright lights of Las Vegas, hit-

ting the town and enjoying the delights that it has to offer.

'Sin City' also features as the B-side to the 1978 single 'Rock 'N' Roll Damnation', a live version appeared as the B-side to the 1983 single 'Nervous Shakedown', and the song also features on the 1992 album *Live*.

SINK THE PINK

The fifth track from 1985's *Fly On The Wall*, and one of the better songs from the album, which showed that the ability to recreate the smutty heights of the earlier days was not beyond the band.

Written by Brian Johnson, Angus Young and Malcolm Young, the title of the track pretty much offers the only insight you need into what the song is about, yet in case that has escaped the reader, perhaps these lyrics will make things somewhat clearer: 'She gonna spit you out/Count your days/She says, choice is yours, casually/So why don't you do what comes naturally'.

The second single from *Fly On The Wall*, 'Sink The Pink' failed to chart, but the promo video for the song features on the *Fly On The Wall* VHS release, and subsequently on the *Family Jewels* DVD. Eagle-eyed readers might have noted that in said promo video, the lady clad in pink playing pool actually pots the number six ball twice in the same game.

The song is also included on 1986's *Who Made Who.*

SLADE/CHRIS

Chris Slade was the shaven-headed drummer who played with AC/DC from 1989 to 1994, appearing on *The Razors Edge* and *Live* albums; he was eventually replaced by returning drummer Phil Rudd.

Slade was born Christopher Rees on 30 October, 1946 in Pontypridd, South Wales, and his early musical career saw him working with artists as diverse as Tom Jones and Olivia Newton-John. Coming from the same area as Tom Jones, Slade actually drummed with Jones' backing band The Squires for eight years. He played on drums on Jones' massive 1965 hit single 'It's Not Unusual' and continued to tour with Jones up until 1969. He then quit to join a band by the name of Toomorrow, who featured a delectable young blonde Australian on vocals by the name of Olivia Newton-John. The group were the brain-child of Monkees creator Don Kirschner and appeared in a science fiction based musical film which starred Newton-John, and also cut one album, but things did not happen for the band and they'd disbanded by 1971.

Slade then worked with both Tom Paxton and Tony Hazzard before he made significant inroads into the world of rock music by being a founding member of the prog rock outfit Manfred Mann's Earth Band, who formed in 1972 out of the ashes of the '60s beat group Manfred Mann. Slade features on every Manfred Mann's Earth Band album from 1972's *Manfred Mann's Earth Band* to 1978's *Watch*, including such genre classics as 1973's *Solar Fire* and 1976's *The Roaring Silence* and performs on such classic hit tracks as 'Blinded By The Light', 'Joybringer', 'Davey's On The Road Again' and 'The Mighty Quinn'.

He then recorded with legendary Scots rocker Frankie Miller and also with Kai Olsen before joining Uriah Heep for two years, appearing on the 1980 album *Conquest*. On leaving Heep, Slade worked with Gary Numan before joining ex-Bad Company guitarist Mick Ralph's band. This group were then used by Pink Floyd guitarist Dave Gilmour as the backing band on his *About Face* world tour.

It didn't take long for Slade to then find himself alongside Jimmy Page, Paul Rodgers and bassist Tony Franklin in The Firm, with whom he recorded 1985's *The Firm* and 1986's *Mean Business*. In 1988 Simon Wright left AC/DC to join Dio, leaving the band short of a drummer as they built up to recording *The Razors Edge*. Legend has it that they were considering former

Guns 'n' Roses drummer Steven Adler for the position, until they discovered the extent of the drug abuse that had seen him thrown out of that band and instead turned to Slade. Malcolm Young had seen Slade playing for Gary Moore during the latter's *After The War* tour, where the drummer was temporarily filling in. Suitably impressed, Slade was not only remembered when it came to AC/DC mulling over potential drummers, he eventually got the nod from the band.

Initially Slade was supposed to be a temporary drummer working just on the album, but the Young brothers felt that the affable Welshman was fitting in so well that he was asked to join full-time. He toured with AC/DC on *The Razors Edge* world tour, appearing at their record breaking third headline appearance at Donington's Monsters Of Rock Festival in 1991, and on the subsequent 1992

album *Live*. However after the band had jammed with ex-drummer Phil Rudd, they decided to ask him back and Slade was shown the door, but not without the ringing endorsement of Angus Young who said at the time:

"Chris was probably the best musician in the band. We hate to lose him, but getting Phil back is worth asking him to leave."

Slade himself has nothing but fond memories of his time in AC/DC, telling the Classic Rock Revisited website:

"I was a huge fan of the band. I bought Highway To Hell as a fan. It was another case of not wanting to be intimidated but here you are standing next to Angus. I played it really straight with that band. People who were in successful bands at the time were calling them up and telling

them they wanted to audition for them. I pride myself, it's a professional pride, that I play with feel and feeling. I also have a laid back snare just as Phil Rudd does. I stole it from the drummer of the Average White Band.

"I often say it was the most fun I ever had with my clothes on. It was a pleasure and an honour

to play with those guys. Nothing ever went wrong with that band – never once was there a missed note or a missed cue. They are totally and absolutely professional."

Slade joined the noted UK prog rock act Asia upon leaving AC/DC, featuring on the albums *Aura* and *Silent Nation*, leaving the band when Asia's original 1982 line up decided to reform. He has since been concentrating on his own personalised drums and jewellery and can also currently be seen drumming in the band Damage Control alongside UFO bassist Pete Way, guitarist Robin George and Quireboys singer Spike.

SKYHOOKS

Skyhooks were an Australian glam rock band who were very

much the direct competition for AC/DC during their early years in Australia.

Like AC/DC, Skyhooks formed in 1973 in Melbourne and after the massive success of their debut album *Living In The Seventies* in their native country, were actually a bigger draw than the heavier AC/DC. 1975's *Ego Is Not A Dirty Word* continued the band's upwards momentum, as did 1976's *Straight In A Gay Gay World*. However Skyhooks remained very much an Australian phenomenon, whereas AC/DC ventured first to Europe and later to America throughout the

rest of the '70s, attracting worldwide acclaim.

By 1978's *Guilty 'Til Proven Insane* (which features the song 'Women In Uniform', later covered by Iron Maiden) Skyhooks had begun to splinter, and much-loved vocalist Graeme 'Shirley' Strachan quit before 1980's *Hot For The Orient*. The band reformed several times in the '80s and '90s to massive acclaim in Australia, but Strachan sadly died in a helicopter crash near Brisbane on 29 August, 2001.

The rivalry felt between both bands was revealed in letters Bon Scott had sent to his wife Irene Thornton, which went under the auctioneer's hammer in 2004.

SMITH/NEIL

Neil Smith (below, in motorcycle helmet) played bass for AC/DC from February to April

1974. He replaced original bassist Larry Van Kriedt and was in turn replaced by Rob Bailey. He had previously played in a band called Jasper, with drummer Noel Taylor, who also briefly joined 'DC. In recent times, Smith has played with a covers band called The Swinging Sixties.

SMITH/SILVER

Silver Smith was Bon Scott's one time girlfriend, whom he had first met in Adelaide whilst still a member of Fraternity. The pair remained friendly during his time in AC/DC, despite the fact that some in the AC/DC camp never warmed to her, on account of her allegedly introducing Scott to heroin. Her name drifts in and out of the Bon Scott story, cropping up one final time on the night of 18 February, 1980.

"In late 1978 I met Silver Smith with whom I moved into a flat in Kensington," Alistair Kinnear told *Classic Rock* magazine in 2005. *"She was a sometime girlfriend of Bon Scott. Bon came to stay with us for two weeks and he and I became friends. Silver returned to Australia for a year and I moved to Overhill Road in East Dulwich."*

Smith had returned to the UK and was once more living in London when she received a phone call from Kinnear on 18 February.

"I phoned Silver to see if she wanted to come along [to a gig],*"* Kinnear continued. *"She'd made other arrangements for the evening. However, she suggested that Bon might be interested, as he had phoned her earlier looking for something to do."*

Fatefully, Scott and Kinnear did meet up that night, which would end in the tragedy of Scott succumbing to acute alcohol poisoning in the back of Kinnear's car.

The fate of Silver Smith remains somewhat less clear.

SNAKE EYE

'Snake Eye' is a track recorded during the sessions for 1988's *Blow Up Your Video* which did not make it onto the final album. It did, however, crop up as the B-side to the single 'Heatseeker'. The song was written by Brian Johnson, Malcolm Young and Angus Young and deals with someone who is very much on the game; someone to be watching out for.

SNOWBALLED

The fifth track on 1981's *For Those About To Rock (We Salute You)* and written by Brian Johnson, Angus Young and Malcolm Young.

A fast paced rocker, the song deals with simply overdoing things in life and everything catching up with you, best typified by lyrics like: 'Howl of the wolf, snow in his eyes/Waiting to take you by surprise/Eye of the needle, head of the fight/Watch those teeth 'cause they're ready to bite'.

Rarely, if ever played live.

SO IT GOES

The first TV show on which AC/DC appeared in the UK. They might have been used to exposure in Australia of this sort, but here was a significant breakthrough. The show itself was screened by ITV in 1976 and became known for giving punk bands an opportunity to get on television. It was fronted by the late Anthony Wilson, who became a significant figure on the Manchester scene.

AC/DC appeared on the seventh show in the first series, which was broadcast on August 14, 1976 and were showcased in a slot called 'Opportunity Rocks', playing 'Jailbreak' live. Also on that programme were fellow Aussie Clive James, weirdly dressed up as portly Greek star Demis Roussos, A Band Called O (with whom 'DC would play a couple of weeks later at the Reading Festival), Patti Smith and rock 'n' roll legend Gene Vincent.

SOME SIN FOR NUTHIN'

The seventh track from AC/DC's 11th album, 1988's *Blow Up Your Video*, and written by the team of Johnson, Young and Young, 'Some Sin For Nothing' is as explanatory as its title. It basically hails the schemers of this world and that you have to make your own way, with lines like: 'But I ain't gonna be the fool/Who's gonna have to sin for nothing'!

SOUL STRIPPER

The fifth song on the Australian version of the band's debut album *High Voltage* and a rare example of an early AC/DC track penned solely by Angus and Malcolm Young. It was performed with original singer Dave Evans as well as Bon Scott, who of course sings the version on *High Voltage*.

The lyrics deal with falling prey to a woman who seems to have cast the ultimate spell on you, with lyrics like: 'Then she made me say things I didn't want to say/Then she made me play games I didn't want to play/She was a soul stripper, she took my heart/Soul stripper, tore me apart'.

Another notable feature of the song is the trade off guitar solo between Angus and Malcolm Young, one of the very rare times the two have done this in AC/DC.

SOUNDS MAGAZINE

The weekly British music publication that really championed AC/DC in their early days living in London. Not only did the paper constantly write about the band and their exploits, they also sponsored the successful 'Lock Up Your Daughters' tour in 1976.

The magazine was the first in Britain to put the band on their cover, with Angus appearing on the June 12, 1976 edition. An offshoot of *Sounds* called *Kerrang!* appeared in June 1981, and Angus was on the front of the first issue, captured live. The reason? 'Whole Lotta Rosie' had been voted the greatest hard rock song of all time.

SPEKTORS, THE

The Spektors were Bon Scott's very first band, who he helped to form in 1964. As well as Scott the group also featured John Collins (vocals), Brian Gannon (bass), Wyn Milson (guitar) and Murray Gracie (vocals/guitar). They were quite an attraction in the Perth area, and even won a local battle of the bands competition. The Spektors played the kind of beat music made popular at the time by the likes of the Rolling Stones, and as they developed then Scott would occasionally step up to the microphone with Collins taking over from him on drums. In 1966 both Milson and Scott chose to team up with members of fellow local band The Winstons to form The Valentines. The Spektors recorded little if no material, and what has turned up on compilations like *The Legendary Bon Scott With The Spektors And The Valentines* on the See For Miles label is taken from local television appearances.

SPELLBOUND

The tenth and final track on 1981's *For Those About To Rock (We Salute You)*, written by Brian Johnson, Angus Young and Malcolm Young, this is a nightmarish tale of finding yourself in a downward spiral and being unable to get out of it, exemplified by lines like: 'I can do nothing right/I never sleep at night/Can't even start a fight/My feet have left the ground/Spinning round and round'.

SQUEALER

Track number five on AC/DC's third album, *Dirty Deeds Done Dirt Cheap* – subsequently the ninth and final track on the international edition – and written by Bon Scott, Angus Young and Malcolm Young, this is a predatory tale of seduction, that, along with other early AC/DC songs like 'Can I Sit Next To Your Girl' and 'Little Lover', veer dubiously close to suggesting under-age sex.

In 'Squealer' we are dealt such lines as: 'She said she'd never been/Never been touched before/She said she'd never been/This far before', which are more suggestive than openly reprehensible.

STAND UP

Track seven from *Fly On The Wall*, this song, written by Brian Johnson, Angus Young and Malcolm Young, is one of the more forgettable on the album. It deals with sexual escapades in a manner almost as crude as the somewhat blatant title.

STARFIGHTERS

Starfighters were a British heavy rock band who featured Stevie Young, the nephew of Angus and Malcolm Young, on guitar – he is the son of their elder brother Alex. The band supported AC/DC on their *Back In Black* tour and Stevie Young stood in for Malcolm Young on the *Blow Up Your Video* tour when alcoholism forced the latter to take a break.

Starfighters formed in Birmingham in 1979 and signed to Jive Records, part of the Zomba group. They released *Starfighters* in 1981 and *In-Flight Movie* in 1983, both of which were produced by AC/DC engineer Tony Platt, but lost the interest of their label and soon split. They reformed in 1987 but could not get a record deal and quickly folded. There was a more recent reunion for a one-off charity show in Birmingham in November 2006.

STICK AROUND

The only track from the Australian version of *High Voltage* that's never been issued on any other record. The song, written by Bon Scott, Angus Young and Malcolm Young, deals with a man telling his woman not to leave him and that she'll have a better time with him, through lyrics such as: 'Then tonight you came home early/Packed a bag or two/It's been worrying me honey/ Just what you gonna do'.

The song can be unlocked on the remastered version of *'74 Jailbreak.*

STIFF UPPER LIP

Stiff Upper Lip, AC/DC's 14th studio album, was released in February 2000. It had been five years since *Ballbreaker* and a decade since *The Razors Edge*, and yet despite a less than hectic work schedule, the album was another success and has been certified Platinum in America (one million sales).

Veteran AC/DC producer George Young, older brother of Angus and Malcolm Young, returned to produce the album, for the first time in a solo capacity, having split with his old partner Harry Vanda. The word had been, stretching as far back as 1995's *Ballbreaker*, that the band were intending to return to the raw bluesy quality of *Powerage*, and whilst they did to a certain extent on *Ballbreaker*, the general consensus of opinion was that they'd certainly achieved this with *Stiff Upper Lip*.

From the grinding rock of the opening title track, through the likes of 'Meltdown', 'House Of Jazz' and 'Safe In New York

City', there's a swing and groove that had long been missing in AC/DC's music – though it surfaced occasionally on *Ballbreaker* – and which at last really did take long time fans back to what they deemed the band's golden age. And yet there's also a certain timeless quality to the sound which still attracted youngsters keen on discovering what all the fuss was about.

For the first time in aeons AC/DC sounded comfortable on record. Not safe, but comfortable with who they were, what they were doing and why they were doing it. No longer in a position where they needed to chase trends – not that AC/DC have ever truly been guilty of doing that – an older, more mature band slipped effortlessly into their groove and got down to the business in hand. Much of the credit goes to George Young, but then he, like no other producer, knows his brothers and their band inside out.

The groove was slightly slower, the tone a little lower and the mood a little darker, with Brian Johnson in particular, frequently singing in a lower register, and sounding better than he had done in ages. The beat from Phil Rudd and Cliff Williams is as metronomically rock steady as always, and the Young brothers continued to churn out riffs and solos with delightful ease. And to top it all, the songwriting seemed better than it had done for years.

Stiff Upper Lip reached number 12 in the UK, number seven in the United States and number three in

their native Australia. The album was re-issued as a special tour edition in January 2001 with bonus tracks, including the non-album track 'Cyberspace' (this had surfaced as the B-side to 'Safe In New York City'), some live material from a 1996 Madrid gig and the album's promo videos.

The ensuing tour was another huge success, and for a band written off many times, *Stiff Upper Lip* was the perfect response to the band's critics.

Full tracklisting: *Stiff Upper Lip/Meltdown/House Of Jazz/Hold Me Back/Safe In New York City/Can't Stand Still/Can't Stop Rock 'N' Roll/Satellite Blues/Damned/Come And Get It/All Screwed Up/Give It Up*

STIFF UPPER LIP
(Song)

The opening and title track of AC/DC's 2000 album was written by Angus and Malcolm Young, yet has very little to do with good old fashioned British reserve. With suggestive lines like: 'Well I'm out on the prowl/And I'll ball your thing/I got teeth that'll bite you/Can you feel my sting' the band's insatiable appetite for smut and innuendo remained unabated.

The song was the first single from the album, backed by live versions of 'Hard As A Rock' and 'Ballbreaker', and reached number 65 in the UK and number 115 in the US, where the band performed the song on the TV show *Saturday Night Live*. In the ensuing promo video, 'DC are driving along a road before getting out to play the track in the street. On exiting the car it can be clearly heard they've been listening to 'It's A Long Way To The Top (If You Wanna Rock 'N' Roll)'.

STIFF UPPER LIP
(DVD)

A live DVD released in 2001 from the Stiff Upper Lip tour and recorded at a show at Munich's Olympiastation on 14 June, 2001.
Full tracklisting: *Stiff Upper Lip/You Shook Me All Night Long/Problem Child/Thunderstruck/Hell Ain't A Bad Place To Be/Hard As A Rock/Shoot To Thrill/Rock And Roll Ain't Noise Pollution/What Do You Do For Money Honey/Bad Boy Boogie/Hells Bells/Up To My Neck In You/The Jack/Back In Black/Dirty Deeds Done Dirt Cheap/Highway To Hell/Whole Lotta Rosie/Let There Be Rock/T.N.T./For Those About To Rock (We Salute You)/Shot Down In Flames*

SUNSET STRIP

'Sunset Strip' is another rarity from AC/DC's very earliest days. Written by Malcolm Young and with lyrics from original singer Dave Evans, the song was performed at some early shows before it eventually developed into the track known as 'Show Business', which would feature on the band's Australian debut album, 1975's *High Voltage*. According to Evans, the song itself was made up during the band's first ever show – at Chequers Night Club, New Year's Eve, 1973 – with Malcolm starting up the tune and Evans inventing lyrics on the spot.

SYDNEY OLYMPICS

The Olympic Games came to Sydney in 2000 – time for a celebration not just of a sporting event that embraces the globe, but also of the best from Australian culture. Now, this is a country where rock music is massively successful and richly supported. So, presumably the best band to come out of Australia were going to be asked to participate? Well, that's what everyone believed. However, AC/DC were overlooked, much to the amazement and the annoyance of fans across that country, and indeed around the planet. Not that this snub really bothered the band themselves. When asked about it, Angus merely shrugged it off with the quip:

"It's not as if we wouldn't have passed their drugs tests!"

12 OF THE BEST

The 1978 AC/DC compilation album that never was. If that sounds a little mysterious, then it's easy to explain. That year Albert Productions, decided to release a 12-track compilation to try and augment their growing popularity, and to introduce newly acquired fans to their back catalogue. However, the idea was then scrapped, after objections from Atlantic Records, because there were concerns this might interfere with sales of the *Powerage* album.

Now, it's certain no copies of the record were ever pressed up. However, colour proofs of the proposed sleeve were printed,

and are said to be worth upwards of $1200. In addition, a handful of cassette tapes of the album are known to exist, and these are worth nearly $2000.

The full track listing would have been: *It's A Long Way To The Top (If You Wanna Rock 'N' Roll)/ High Voltage/Problem Child/ T.N.T./Whole Lotta Rosie/Let There Be Rock/Jailbreak/Dirty Deads Done Dirt Cheap/The Jack/Dog Eat Dog/She's Got Balls/Baby, Please Don't Go.*

TAMWORTH TOWN HALL

This became an infamous part of AC/DC history when, on December 16, 1976, the band played there as part of a triumphant return to Australia – except this was far from being a success! By the time the band returned home for this Aussie tour, which kicked off at the start of December, they had become the centre of an amazing controversy. They were actually denounced in the Australian parliament, for representing the sort of depravity and lewd behaviour which various esteemed members of this august body believed to be taking over polite society. The end was nigh for decency and morality – ahem! Where have we heard all of this before? Oh just about everywhere. In reality it probably wasn't AC/DC themselves who were being singled out, but they were chosen to represent just why everything was falling apart.

As a result, Angus was threatened with arrest on several nights for doing his famous moonie at the crowd, none of whom complained, it might be added. And TV documentary crews were trailing them everywhere, presumably hoping to get footage of the band engaged in drug-taking satanic orgies, not to mention raping, pillaging and boozing wherever they went. If that was the plan, then it failed, because AC/DC weren't about to give the media any ammunition.

But Tamworth (which is in New South Wales, and holds an annual country music festival)... now this was different. The mayor of the town, obviously believing that an anti rock 'n' roll stance would help with a re-election, banned the gig, with the full approval and backing of the local police. Worse was to follow, because by the time the show had been called off, AC/DC were already at the venue. One report claimed that they were locked in their dressing room, as a posse of angry and suitably tooled up citizens menacingly stalked outside the venue. Whether this is folklore or reality is open to question, but the fact is that AC/DC, by now the most famous international musical export Australia had at the time, were seen as scapegoats, and as a primary target.

However, despite the Tamworth set back, and also the fact that many supposedly religious radio stations, refused to play any of their records, the band carried on touring around the country, finishing up on January 30, 1977 in Sydney, with Aussie punks The Saints opening for them. And, overall it was a massively positive return. No other town followed Tamworth's example.

T.N.T.

The second AC/DC album, *T.N.T.* was released in December, 1975 and reached number two in the Australian charts, proving how swiftly they'd risen in popularity since their *High Voltage* debut.

The album was produced by George Young and Harry Vanda and features nine songs, including eight originals and a cover of Chuck Berry's 'School Days'. Amongst the songs are the likes of 'It's A Long Way To The Top (If You Wanna Rock 'N' Roll)', 'The Jack', 'Live Wire', 'High Voltage' and the title track; these have proven over the years to be some of the band's most enduring songs and have featured in many a live set.

Given that *T.N.T.* is but AC/DC's second album, one can only marvel at the quality of the songwriting on offer, as well as the fact that they'd already nailed the hard driving, blues-based hard rock sound that would become the band's staple.

T.N.T. was only released in Australia, and is also the only early AC/DC album for which there is no comparative International release, although seven of its nine tracks would feature on the international version of *High Voltage*, which was a compilation of tracks from the band's first two albums.

T.N.T. was also the first AC/DC record to feature long time drummer Phil Rudd.

Full track listing is: *It's A Long Way To The Top (If You Wanna Rock 'N' Roll)/Rock 'N' Roll Singer/The Jack/Live Wire/T.N.T./Rocker/Can I Sit Next To You Girl/High Voltage/School Days.*

T.N.T.
(Song)

The title track and fifth song on AC/DC's second album *T.N.T.* and the International release of *High Voltage*.

A frenetically paced rocker that plays on the band's sense of roguish charm and love of playing the outsider, it's typified by lines such as: 'See me ride out of the sunset/ On your colour TV screen/Out for all that I can get/If you know what I mean'.

Another AC/DC song that's proved popular with various US sports teams, it has also featured in the film *Talladega Nights: The Ballad Of Rocky Bobby* and was the soundtrack on a TV ad cam-

paign for *Napoleon Dynamite*. It has been covered by Sebastian Bach, Six Feet Under, Hayseed Dixie and Dynamite Boy.

'T.N.T. has long been a live favourite with the band and features on the 1992 album *Live*. Another live version from 1981 is on the B-side of the single 'Let's Get it Up'. Angus Young provides the intermittent chants of "oi" during the live shows.

TAYLORϟNOEL

Noel Taylor drummed with AC/DC between February and April 1974, having joined at the same time as bassist Neil Smith; both had previously been with Jasper. Taylor replaced Colin Burgess and was in return replaced by Pete Clack. Subsequently, Taylor featured in various bands, includ-

ing Bobby Dazzler, Boy Racer and, most notably, Speed Limit. These days, he plays in various '50s-style acts, most notably Legends Of OL55

THAT'S THE WAY I WANNA ROCK 'N' ROLL

The second track from AC/DC's 1988 album *Blow Up Your Video*. Written by Brian Johnson, Malcolm Young and Angus Young, the song is yet more unashamed homage to rock 'n' roll music, very much in a similar fashion to earlier Bon Scott era tracks like 'Rocker', with lines like: 'Party gonna happen at the union hall/Shaking to the rhythm 'till everybody fall/Picking up my woman in my Chevrolet/Glory hallelujah gonna rock the night away'.

The track, which featured in the live set on the *Blow Up Your Video* tour, was released as the second single from the album, reaching number 22 in the UK during April 1988. The 12" single version was backed with 'Kissin' Dynamite' and the previously unreleased 'Borrowed Time'. The 12" also came with a free patch.

THERE'S GONNA BE SOME ROCKIN'

The third track on the Australian release of *Dirty Deeds Done Dirt Cheap* – it was track number six on the International version of the album. Written by Bon Scott, Angus Young and Malcolm Young, the song is a simple ode to the joys of being in a band.

'Me and the boys/Are out to have some fun/Gonna put on a show/C'mon let's go' intones Scott in this short but effective blast of good time rock 'n' roll.

Rarely, if ever, performed live.

THIS HOUSE IS ON FIRE

Track number two from the 1983 album *Flick Of The Switch*, 'This House Is On Fire' was written by Brian Johnson, Angus Young and Malcolm Young. Chock full of trademark AC/DC innuendo, it warns of the effects a hot lady can have on you in lines like: 'Yonder she walks/Hittin' 103/A little tongue in cheek/Hot personality/She bring on the flames/And it's burning burning/My body's achin', tossin' and turnin'.

The song featured in the live set for the *Flick Of The Switch* tour, and a live version surfaced as the B-side of the single 'Nervous Shakedown'.

THIS MEANS WAR

The final track on the 12th studio album from AC/DC, *Blow Up Your Video*. Written by Brian Johnson and Malcolm and Angus Young, this furiously paced rocker is very much a call to arms, with lines like: 'When the flags are high, hear the battle cry/Treaty gone, see the bandit fly/Dig that trench, watch that blast/Shellshock come, coming fast'.

The song, one of the heaviest numbers ever recorded by AC/DC, was viewed very much at the time as the band's response to the burgeoning thrash metal movement, in an "anything you can do" manner.

THORNTON, IRENE

Bon Scott's first wife, Irene met the singer in 1971, following a gig he did with Fraternity at Largs Pier Hotel in Adelaide during 1971. She later recalled her initial impression of her future husband thus: "He had really tight jeans on so I said, 'What a well-packed lunch' And he said, 'Yes, two hard-boiled eggs and a sausage'. And we took off from there."

The pair got married on January 24, 1972, but were divorced six years later. On April 12, 2008, Irene sold off a collection of letters from her husband, plus their wedding and divorce certificates and private photos, in an auction at the Leonard Joel Art Auction House in SouthYarra, Sydney.

Her reasons?

"I didn't know where to take them. Last year, kind of spur-of-the-moment, I made photocopies of them and decided to do it. I would look at them from

time to time and they made me laugh. But now I feel that I can part with them. I was always worried about them whenever I moved: 'Where's that letter? Where's the record?'. But also I thought, 'I am on my own now, I'm not getting any younger, what's going to happen to them if something happens to me?'."

They were bought by rock fan James Young and, as this book went to press, he announced his intentions of displaying them publicly on the walls at the Cherry Bar in AC/DC Lane, Melbourne.

THUNDERSTRUCK
(Film)

Thunderstruck is a 2004 Australian film which tells the tale of four AC/DC fans who undertake a road trip to scatter a friend's ashes on Bon Scott's memorial plaque in Fremantle Cemetery, Perth. Directed by Darren Ashton, the film features the actors Ryan Johnson, Callan Mulvey, Stephen Curry and Damon Gameau.

The film's soundtrack did not feature AC/DC, but does include various AC/DC songs: 'It's A Long Way To The Top' and 'T.N.T.' covered by The Jack and Hayseed Dixie respectively, as well as the

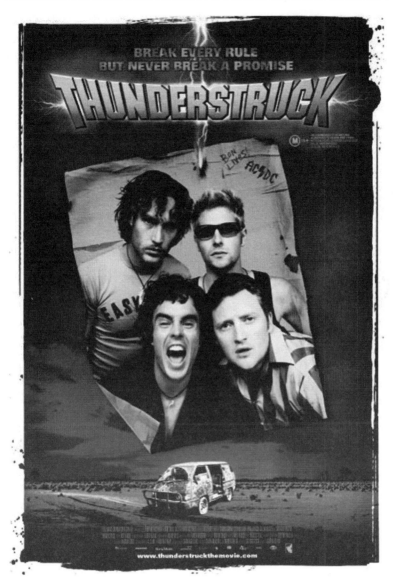

track 'Jupiter's Landscape' by Bon Scott and Fraternity; the last named was included on the compilation *The Complete Sessions 1971-72* (released in 1997).

The film was released in Australia on DVD.

THUNDERSTRUCK *(Song)*

The opening track from the 1990 album *The Razors Edge*, 'Thunderstruck' must rate as one of AC/DC's most popular and recognisable songs. Written by Angus and Malcolm Young, its intro builds slowly over a repeated refrain of 'Thunder' before Brian Johnson screams in with the vocal and the band build effectively into the song proper.

Although allegedly connected to an experience endured by Angus Young when he was in a plane that was struck by lightning, aside from the line 'You've been thunderstruck' in the lyrics, there seems little reference to this episode, which concentrates more on basically enjoying oneself.

The song was released as the first single from *The Razors Edge*, preceding the album, and reached number 13 during September 1990, the band's highest ever UK singles chart position. In the video for the song Angus Young can been seen using a one-handed tapping technique, although in the studio and on every live version that has surfaced he picks out every note, as can be seen on the DVDs *Live At Donington* and *Stiff Upper Lip*.

The song has proved immeasurably popular with sports teams, is used by a variety of different sporting franchises in the USA and an instrumental version is used by BBC radio for their Formula One motor racing coverage. It has featured in the films *Varsity Blues* and *The Longest Yard* and has been used by Australian car manufacturer Holden for TV commercials. 'Thunderstruck' has even inspired a students drinking game, in which a drink is to be had every time the word 'thunder' is used – a total of 33 in all.

TIGHTROPE

'Tightrope' is one of two songs, along with 'Out Of Bounds', recorded during the sessions for the *Flick Of The Switch* album, but allegedly stolen from the studio. Hence the reason they've never appeared in any form on an official AC/DC release.

TORONTO ROCKS (DVD)

A live DVD released in 2004 recorded at the 2003 Molson Toronto Rocks concert at Downsview Park to raise money for victims of SARS. The concert, in front of half a million people, featured AC/DC alongside the Rolling Stones, Rush, The Guess Who and Justin Timberlake.

The DVD features two songs from AC/DC's set, namely 'Back In Black' and 'Thunderstruck'.

TOTALLY BAKED

Totally Baked is a comedy film about marijuana that was released in 2007 – with Brian Johnson as its Executive Producer. The film also features three brand new Brian Johnson compositions, 'Chain Gang On The Road', 'Chase The Tail' and 'Who Phoned The Law', all gritty, blues based rockers that differ slightly from the normal AC/DC template but which will appeal to any AC/DC fan. All three songs were also performed live by Johnson and AC/DC bassist Cliff Williams as part of the Classic Rock Cares concerts.

TOUCH TOO MUCH

The fourth track from AC/DC's sixth studio album, their last with singer Bon Scott who would tragically die within a year of *Highway To Hell*'s release.

Written by Bon Scott and Angus and Malcolm Young, the songs is a tour de force of innuendo from lyricist Scott, and one of the most commercially minded tracks AC/DC had recorded up to that point. Lines like: 'She knew we were making love/I was so satisfied/Deep down inside/Like a hand in a velvet glove' got Scott's lurid point across with comparative ease.

'Touch Too Much' was released as the third single from *Highway To Hell* and reached number 29 in the UK charts on 2 February, 1980, just over a fortnight before Scott's untimely passing.

TRUST

Trust were a French heavy metal band, who toured with AC/DC and struck up a friendly relationship with the band.

Formed in 1977, Trust covered AC/DC's 'Ride On' on their debut album, 1979's *Trust 1* and both 'Problem Child' and 'Sin City' on 1980's *Repression*. Singer Bernard Bonvoisin's own style was often said to be similar to Bon Scott's, with whom he became good friends.

Trust are best known for the song 'Antisocial' from *Repression*, which was later covered by Anthrax, and for featuring drummer Nicko McBrain, who now plays for Iron Maiden.

Bon Scott was supposed to work with the band on the English lyrics for the *Repression* album – the group at that stage having only ever recorded their own songs in French. In fact the singer did begin the process, until his death completely scuppered these plans. Jimmy Pursey of Sham 69 took over from Scott in aiding Trust with their English. Most people believe that Bon would have actually done a better job, being more in tune with Trust's musical approach.

Interestingly, while working with Trust on English lyrics for *Repression* at Scorpio Sound Studio in London, Scott actually recorded a version of 'Ride

Trust with Bon Scott

On'. Check this out at www.trust.tm.fr/frameset_a.htm

TWO'S UP

Rather forgettable track from 1988's *Blow Up Your Video*, penned by Brian Johnson, Angus Young and Malcolm Young. With lines like: 'I love the way you slide and slip/Love the way you girls work out' it's not difficult to see what was on the band's minds when it came to writing the song.

Trust

UNRELEASED 1977 SESSIONS

According to several worthy AC/DC websites, the band entered Albert Studios in Sydney during July 1977 and recorded what amounts to almost an entire album's worth of material; most of the tracks either never saw the light of day or were re-worked into songs that would appear on later albums.

These sessions would almost certainly have been the very first recording experience for new bassist Cliff Williams, who joined

AC/DC in June 1977, and whose first duty as a band member was to sort out his visa with the Australian Embassy in London, a passage which did not run exactly smoothly (see Cliff Williams entry for further details), but once this had been duly overcome, Williams was on his way to Australia to begin working with his new colleagues.

Given this state of affairs, these initial recording sessions with Williams would have been somewhat exploratory, the band having decided they could work with Williams in his initial auditions held in London's Pimlico district, they would, nonetheless, also have needed to enter a recording studio to make sure the new bassist was equally at home with AC/DC within these new confines.

It is almost certain that the version of 'Touch Too Much' which features in the *Bonfire* box set, an early version of the song that would appear with different lyrics on 1979's *Highway To Hell* album, was recorded during these initial sessions. And given that the band's recording regime for 1978's *Powerage* album took place between February and March 1978, it's almost inevitable that early ideas for songs that appeared on *Powerage* would have been sketched out during these sessions.

Both 'Up To My Neck In You' and 'Kicked In The Teeth' were played on occasion in America during the band's *Let There Be Rock* tour, so one can assume that these tracks were also amongst those that were also recorded during these sessions.

UP TO MY NECK IN YOU

The seventh song on the European version of 1978's *Powerage* and the second to last on the so-called International version of the album. Written by the Young brothers and Bon Scott, 'Up To My Neck In You' is about as close to a love song as you were going get from AC/DC, and with lines like: 'Well I've been up to my neck in trouble/Up to my neck in strife/Up to my neck in misery/ For most of my life' one could be forgiven for thinking that Bon Scott was yet again unveiling another lurid chapter from his loveably sordid life. But he tempers this with the addition of: 'You came along when I needed you/And now I'm/I'm up to my neck in you'. A song of salvation that might be autobiographical, given Scott's love of writing from personal experience.

Although not played live on the band's original *Powerage* tour in 1978, the song received a new lease of life when AC/DC surprisingly featured it in their set for the string of outdoor dates they undertook in June and July 2001 in support of *Stiff Upper Lip*.

VALENTINES, THE

The Valentines were the second pop act to feature Bon Scott. They had evolved out of The Spektors, Scott's first band, for whom he drummed and occasionally sang, and another local Perth act The Winztons, and came together in 1966. Typical of the time, The Valentine's early sound can best be described as beat music, in a similar style to the Rolling Stones, Beatles and Australia's own Easybeats, the band that featured elder Young brother George and his future AC/DC production partner, Harry Vanda. Indeed several Valentines singles, notably 1967's 'She Said', 1968's 'Peculiar Hole In The Sky' and 1969's 'My Old Man's A Groovy Old Man' were penned by the Vanda/Young writing partnership.

Buoyed by their initial success, The Valentines moved to Melbourne in 1967 but soon suffered as a result of shifting musical tastes, and their particular brand of '60s pop became less popular. Scott shared lead vocal duties with Vince Lovegrove, who would later go on to manage The Divinyls, and the group moved

in a much more rock orientated direction.

An infamous drugs bust in September 1969 damaged the band's reputation and, despite still being popular back in Perth, The Valentines decided to call it a day in August 1970. Bon Scott then moved to join Australian progressive rock outfit Fraternity.

Although The Valentines were very much a singles band, Scott's subsequent success with AC/DC meant a resurgence of interest in them, and a 1987 compilation entitled *The Valentines* can now be found under the title *Bon Scott – The Early Years 1967-1972*.

VAN KRIEDT/LARRY

A talented musician in his own right, American born Larry Van Kriedt was AC/DC's very first bass player, and one of the few members who've been accorded the honour of returning to the band's line-up.

Born in San Francisco in 1954, the son of renowned jazz musician David Van Kriedt, his family moved to Sydney in 1969, where

the young Van Kriedt began to indulge his own passion for music.

He joined AC/DC in November 1973 and remained with them until February 1974, when he was replaced as bassist by Neil Smith. Van Kriedt did return for a further stint on the bass for the band in early 1975 after Rob Bailey had been fired, but he was once more ousted as George Young took over until a suitable permanent bassist could be found.

Since leaving AC/DC Van Kriedt has gone on to make something of a name for himself in the jazz world, indulging his passion for playing saxophone.

VANDA/HARRY

Born Johannes Hendricus Jacob Vandenberg in Holland on 22 March 1946, Harry Vanda has long been the musical partner of elder Young brother George, producing no less than seven AC/DC albums.

Vanda's family emigrated from their native Holland to Sydney

Larry, second from left

in 1963, and within a year the 18-year old Vanda had secured himself a place as lead guitarist in Australia's most popular band at the time, The Easybeats. By 1966 Vanda had struck up a successful writing partnership with Easybeats rhythm guitarist George Young, and the duo were responsible for penning all The Easybeats material from then on in, including their most popular hit, 'Friday On My Mind'.

The Easybeats eventually ground to a halt in England in 1969, but Vanda and Young remained in the country working under such names as Paintbox, Band Of Hope and Marcus Hook Roll Band – who would, at one point, also feature both Angus and Malcolm Young. By 1973 however, the pair had returned to Australia and secured a position as in-house producers at Albert Productions, where they would write and produce the massive 1978 John Paul Young hit 'Love Is In The Air' and also work with such acts as Rose Tattoo, Cheetah and the Angels.

It was during this time that Vanda and Young made a name for themselves as producers of AC/DC, helping guide the band through the early stages of their

Harry Vanda, centred, with Easybits

career and setting in stone the classic AC/DC sound to be found on such early triumphs as *Let There Be Rock* and *Powerage*. They would return to work with the band in 1988 for *Blow Up Your Video*, which saw a resurgence in the band's popularity.

In the late '70s Vanda and Young formed the studio only project known as Flash And The Pan, a new-wave sounding project whose 1983 song 'Waiting For A Train' was a huge international hit. The pair returned to producing in the '80s, working with Jimmy Barnes and INXS on the smash hit 'Good Times' (from *The Lost Boys* film soundtrack), Meat Loaf and also writing for the *Australian Idol* TV show.

Vanda has recently split with Young and Alberts to set up his own record label and recording studio, Flashpoint Music, with his son Daniel.

UANILLA ICE

The rapper was sued in 1992 for using a sample from the AC/DC track 'Highway To Hell' on his own song 'Road To My Riches' from his album *Extremely Live*. The oddity of sampling a song for a live recording aside, this happened when the white rapper's career was going into freefall. Vanilla Ice has also been known to cover AC/DC's song 'Big Balls', a live version of which can be heard on www.youtube.com.

UELUET UNDERCROUND, THE

Not to be confused with the pioneers of alternative rock, New York's Velvet Underground, Australia's The Velvet Underground were the first band proper that Malcolm Young ever played with. Young joined in 1971, at which time they were known for performing covers of bands like The Doors and Jefferson Airplane. The arrival of the 18-year old Young, as well as Australian vocalist Andy Imlah, meant the band extended their repertoire to include covers of songs by Young's then hero, Marc Bolan. The group became a popular live attraction on the Sydney dance-club circuit, but by the end of 1972 Malcolm had grown increasingly frustrated with their limited repertoire, and harbouring dreams of forming his own band, he quit.

This was the location for AC/DC's first show on the European mainland. It took place on July 16, 1976, at a club called Cortina, when the band supported Swedish act The Jigs. Vinberg has a population of some 2000 people, and is around 100 kilometres from Gothenburg.

VINBERG

VINEYARD STUDIOS

AC/DC spent time in Vineyard Studios, located in Bridgwater, Somerset, during the summer of 1976 working on songs for a planned EP, and recorded four

The Velvet Underground

tracks: 'Love At First Feel', 'Carry Me Home', 'Cold Hearted Man' and 'Dirty Eyes'. Although in the end the idea for this release was scrapped, all of these songs have subsequently been released in one form or another. It's not thought that any copies of the EP were ever pressed up.

VOLTS

Volts is the name given to the compilation disc of material included in the 1997 four CD box set *Bonfire*, which contains a mixture of rarities and some previously released material from the Bon Scott era. A full track breakdown is:

1) 'Dirty Eyes' – a work-in-progress, a very early version of what would turn out to be 'Whole Lotta Rosie'.

2) 'Touch Too Much' – a version of the song that appears on *Highway To Hell*, with different lyrics and riff structure.

3) 'If You Want Blood (You've Got It)' – The same track as features on *Highway To Hell* but with different lyrics.

4) 'Back Seat Confidential' – an early version of what would turn out to be 'Beating Around The Bush', which features on *Highway To Hell*.

5) 'Get It Hot' – as found on *Highway To Hell*, but again with different lyrics and riffs.

6) 'Sin City' – a live version of the song, recorded on *Midnight Special*.

7) 'Walk All Over You' – a live version taken from the *Let There Be Rock: The Movie* soundtrack.

8) 'T.N.T.' – live version, also culled from the *Let There Be Rock: The Movie* soundtrack.

9) 'She's Got Balls' – a live version recorded at Bondi Lifesavers in 1977 and also found as the B-side to the single 'You Shook Me All Night Long'.

10) 'School Days' – the version to be found on the Australian only edition of *T.N.T.*

11) 'It's A Long Way To The Top (If You Wanna Rock'n'Roll)' – the same version that can be found on *T.N.T.* and the International release of *High Voltage*.

12) 'Ride On' – the same version that appears on *Dirty Deeds Done Dirt Cheap*, but with some hidden interviews to be found following the track itself.

WALK ALL OVER YOU

The third track from *Highway To Hell* is an unashamed ode to the kind of love in which Bon Scott used to clearly enjoy indulging. Written by Scott and Angus and Malcolm Young, the bouncy rocker boasts such delectable lines as: 'Oh baby I ain't got much/Resistance to your touch/Take off the high heels and let down your hair/Paradise ain't far from here'.

'Walk All Over You' was one of four tracks from *Highway To Hell* to have a promotional clip filmed for it, which features on the DVD *Family Jewels*.

WALKER/CLINTON

Clinton Walker is an Australian author and historian, best known for his biography on the late AC/DC singer Bon Scott, *Highway To Hell: The Life And Times Of AC/DC Legend Bon Scott*.

Written in 1994, a revised and expanded version of the book was released in 2005. It is, without a doubt, the finest written work on the late Scott that currently exists.

Walker Clinton

WAREHOUSE STUDIOS
Vancouver

Warehouse Studios in Vancouver is a studio complex owned by the Canadian rocker Bryan Adams. This is where AC/DC recorded 1990's *The Razors Edge*, 2000's *Stiff Upper Lip* and 2008's *Black Ice* album. It is apparently the oldest brick building in Vancouver.

WEMBLEY STADIUM

One of the great venues on the planet, Wembley has long been associated with the best sporting and musical events, ever since it first opened in 1923. The list is so long it might take another book to actually chronicle exactly what has happened at the famous old landmark. But among the shows to be held there, one that particularly interests us took place on August 18, 1979. That's when The Who headlined, with special guests The Stranglers, plus AC/DC and Nils Lofgren. It was an eclectic bill that was dubbed 'The Who And Friends Roar In'

This was the first major gig in Britain for the re-formed Who, now featuring Kenny Jones on drums, taking over from the late Keith Moon. The show was sold out, although Who guitarist Pete Townshend felt that it was too expensive to stage, and that Wembley itself wasn't really suited to major rock gigs such as this. Incidentally, tickets were an astonishing £8! Shows how times have changed.

Lofgren was the first act on, and his set in the heat of the day was well received, especially when he did his trademark somersaults on a prepared trampoline at the back of the stage.

AC/DC followed, getting some 45 minutes to show their worth, which they did – to a massive response. Of all the bands on the bill it was this lot who were probably closest in style to what Who fans enjoyed – lots of energy and attitude. It didn't even seem to matter when the PA system cut out during the final song, 'Whole Lotta Rosie'. The band just kept playing until the sound was restored, and then came back for a demanded encore, playing out with 'Rocker'. Whether this was planned remains open to question. While 'DC might not have expected to perform an encore, nonetheless it's also unlikely they'd have been allowed to stretch their set out.

Whatever, the fact is the crowd were very keen for more from

Bon Scott et al, and they were arguably the best band of the day. The Stranglers didn't get a strong response from a generally indifferent audience, while The Who were patchy and there were those who felt that Moon's absence was a crucial factor. However, to claim that the headliners were below par is not to suggest they weren't still impressive and rapturously received.

It is known that there is a DVD bootleg of this show around, which includes footage of all the bands, including AC/DC. For those wishing to track it down, this is called *The Who And Friends Roar In.*

245

AC/DC's set list that day was: *Live Wire/Shot Down In Flames/ Walk All Over You/Bad Boy Boogie/The Jack/Highway To Hell/Whole Lotta Rosie/Rocker*

WHAT DO YOU DO FOR MONEY, HONEY

The third track on 1980's *Back In Black* album. Written by Brian Johnson, Angus Young and Malcolm Young, the song's somewhat self-explanatory title leaves the listener in no doubt what the song might be about. Neither do lines like: 'You're loving on the take/ Always on the make/Squeezing all the blood out of men/They're all standing in queue/Just to spend the night with you/It's business as usual again'.

WHAT'S NEXT TO THE MOON

The sixth track from AC/DC's 1978 album *Powerage*, 'What's Next To The Moon' was written by Bon Scott, Angus Young and Malcolm Young, and features quite an aggressive, if somewhat ambiguous, lyric from Scott, seemingly telling the tale of a man taking retribution against his woman, before getting his collar felt and confessing all.

'All right officer I confess/Everything's coming back/I didn't mean to hurt that woman of mine/

It was a heart attack', are the kind of lines that would land the band in all sorts of hot water in these enlightened times.

AC/DC have only performed the song three times live, all during their *Stiff Upper Lip* tour. On early Australian pressings of *Powerage* the song was referred to as just 'Next To The Moon'.

WHISKEY ON THE ROCKS

The tenth track from AC/DC's 13th studio album *Ballbreaker*. Written by Angus and Malcolm Young, the song seems to hark back to the style and content of 'Have A Drink On Me' from *Back In Black*, with lines like 'You were drinking Mai Tais, Singapore Sling/Beam me up Jim, it's time to come in/I'll have one more afore ye close up the door/It's on the house mac, it's whiskey galore'.

Interestingly, despite the apparent unabashed love of alcohol promoted in the lyric, Angus Young is teetotal, whilst Malcolm Young endured problems with alcohol, forcing him to withdraw from part of the band's *Blow Up Your Video* tour.

WHISTLE BLOWER

Much like 'Let It Go', 'The Cock Crows" and 'Rave On', 'Whistle Blower' is a track known to have been recorded between July and October 1999 at Vancouver's Warehouse Studios during sessions for what would become *Stiff Upper Lip*. And much like the aforementioned tracks, it did not make the final running order of the album and has so far remained unreleased.

WHO MADE WHO

1986's *Who Made Who* is, in fact, the soundtrack to the Stephen King film *Maximum Overdrive*, and the closest thing AC/DC have ever come to releasing a greatest hits compilation.

The soundtrack features a mixture of classic AC/DC songs and some lesser known album tracks, along with three new compositions written especially for the film, these being 'Who Made Who', 'D.T.' and 'Chase The Ace'. The latter two songs mentioned here are 'mere' instrumentals, with 'Who Made Who' itself becoming a big hit single for the band. Five other instrumentals were written and recorded during the sessions for *Who Made Who*, but they didn't make it onto the soundtrack. These were: 'Scared', 'Death City', 'Human's Here', 'Bad Boy' and 'Contre Attack'.

The album reached number 11 in the UK charts and 33 in America.

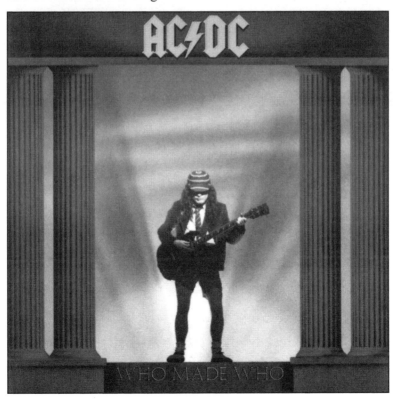

Full tracklisting: *Who Made Who/You Shook Me All Night Long/D.T./Sink The Pink/Ride On/Hells Bells/Shake Your Foundations/Chase The Ace/ For Those About To Rock (We Salute You)*

WHO MADE WHO
(Song)

The title track of AC/DC's 1986 album, the soundtrack to Stephen King's film *Maximum Overdrive*. The song, which was released as a single from the album, was written by Brian Johnson, Angus Young and Malcolm Young and deals with a futuristic world, somewhat in keeping with the film's rather risible plot, which revolves around machines developing a life of their own and attacking humans.

The popular single, which reached number 16 in May 1986 on the UK charts, had an accompanying video, directed by David Mallett, the centrepiece of which sees AC/DC fans dressed as Angus, all playing red guitars and marching along in time to the tune.

WHO MADE WHO
(VHS)

A VHS that was released in 1986, in conjunction with the *Who Made Who* album. The VHS features promo video clips

for some of the tracks from the album. Although it has not been released on DVD, most of the tracks have since appeared on the *Family Jewels* DVD.

Full tracklisting: *Who Made Who/You Shook Me All Night Long/Shake Your Foundations/ Hells Bells/For Those About To Rock (We Salute You)*

WHOLE LOTTA ROSIE

What is quite probably AC/ DC's most popular tune, 'Whole Lotta Rosie' is to be found on the band's fifth studio album *Let There Be Rock*.

The song features such delightful lines as: 'She ain't exactly pretty, ain't exactly small/Forty two, thirty nine, fifty six/You could say she got it all', and it doesn't take a rocket scientist to work out what Bon Scott, who wrote the song with Angus and Malcolm Young, is singing about.

The track tells the tale of a night of passion Scott once spent with the titular Rosie, a groupie from Tasmania who would turn up to the band's shows. On AC/DC's appearance for the BBC's *Rock Goes To College*, Scott announces that the song is about, "The biggest, fattest woman who ever fornicated", whilst on *Live At Atlantic Studios* he introduces it as being about, "a Tasmanian devil, weighs 305 pounds".

Scott also told American radio:

"Rosie was this lady who used to live opposite the hotel we used to stay in Tasmania. She'd be able to see which bands would be staying there, and she'd invite you over to party at hers. I went over there, and she's a big lady, you know, and she just kind of got her body on mine the minute I'd got through the door. There wasn't really much I could do, I kind of had to just go with it. I wish I hadn't, you know, boy do I wish I hadn't, but hey, it happened. She'd come to our shows too, and she'd be in the front row. She was like 6ft 2" and weighed about 300 pounds. She was like a mountain!"

The definitive version of the song appears on the 1978 live album *If You Want Blood*, with the double-call from the crowd of "Angus, Angus" during the song's staggered intro. It also features

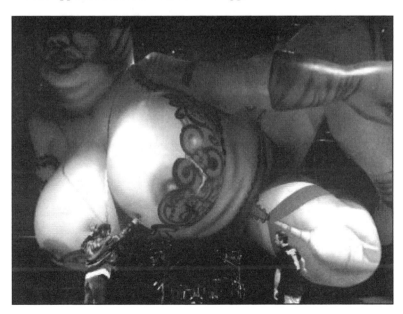

on the 1992 album *Live*, as well as *Let There Be Rock: The Movie* and the *Stiff Upper Lip* DVD.

The song, which has always featured in AC/DC's live set since it was written, was once covered by Guns N'Roses. In recent years, the live performance of 'Whole Lotta Rosie' has been accompanied by a huge inflatable Rosie stage prop.

WILLIAMS, CLIFF

Cliff Williams has been AC/DC's bassist since he replaced Mark Evans in June 1977, following the release of *Let There Be Rock*. A much needed rhythmic rock, the very fact that British born Williams has remained

in the band's line-up for so long, given the plethora of bassists who came and went in the band's early days, is a good indication that his solid and reliable performances are just what a band like AC/DC requires, rather than technical flash and wizardry.

Williams was born in Romford, Essex on 14 December, 1949, although his family had moved to Liverpool by the time he was nine years old. Williams' musical career began following a two-year stint as an engineer, when he joined progressive rock band Home, who also featured future Wishbone Ash guitarist Laurie Wisefield. Home were signed to Epic Records, who also now have AC/DC on their roster, and released their debut album, *Pause For A Horse* in 1971. Their real big break came when the band supported Led Zeppelin at the Wembley Empire Pool in London

(now known as the Wembley Arena) on their Electric Magic shows in November 1971. Home released two more albums, the self-titled *Home* in 1972 and *The Alchemist* in 1973, but by 1974,

after what seemed like such a promising start, they appeared to have morphed into the backing band for folk rocker Al Stewart, something which clearly did not sit well with some members of the band.

Williams quit Home to form a new group, Bandit, along with vocalist Jim Diamond and future Roger Waters drummer Graham Broad. Bandit released the album *Bandit* in 1977, and the same year recorded with the legendary British blues legend Alexis Korner on what would eventually be released as *The Lost Album* in 1995. By this time however, Williams had seen an advert in the classified section of *Sounds* magazine, seeking a new bassist for AC/DC.

"I had an audition in Pimlico, in a tiny room," Williams recalled in 1996. *"The first tracks I*

played with them were 'Live Wire', 'Problem Child' and, if I remember, some blues. The manager (Michael Browning) told me afterwards I had the job. The idea was that I left London to go to Australia to start record-

ing Powerage, but Australian immigration service wasn't good with me. In fact, the guy who had my folder told me, 'I don't know why an English musician got the job. An Australian one would have done it fine'. I told him he could have cost me my job!"

Williams eventually made it out to Australia and has been a member of AC/DC ever since, appearing on all 18 studio, compilation and live albums the band have released since then and every tour, bar a few dates in 1991

when he was replaced by one Paul Gregg (for reasons never fully explained).

Williams is always to be found stage left of Phil Rudd's drum riser, back towards the walls of amplifiers that form AC/DC's back line, supplying the relentless beat that drives the AC/DC machine ever onwards, only ever venturing towards the front of the stage with metronomic precision, to supply backing vocals along with Malcolm Young, before, without a glance backwards, retreating back to his normal

position and thudding away on his huge bass.

During Williams' early years with AC/DC he would frequently use a Precision bass, although on some live performances he can be seen using a Fender Jazz bass. However by the time of 1980's *Back In Black*, it is widely believed that he was using a non-reverse Gibson Thunderbird bass.

This was, in turn, replaced by a P bass for 1981's *For Those About To Rock (We Salute You)* and a Steinberger for 1983's *Flick Of The Switch*. He returned to his

trusted P bass for much of the '80s, diversifying to a Gibson SG re-issue for 1985's *Fly On The Wall* album. The Jazz bass had returned for 1990's *The Razors Edge* and for 1995's *Ballbreaker* onwards, a Music Man StingRay strung with Addario flatwound bass strings has been his instrument of choice.

Williams is also known to play live with a bass strap on his arm and often with his fingers taped up. When quizzed on this by French AC/DC website Are You Ready in 1995, Williams responded:

"It's because I'm a poser, ha ha. I protect my right hand because the guitar hurts my fingers – my index finger jumps all the time. As for the bandage on my arm, it's down to some scarring I've had since I was a child. My skin is fragile there and the bass strap prevents it from getting hurt."

Since joining AC/DC Williams has worked infrequently with a handful of people, appearing on the track 'I Want My Heavy Metal' from Adam Bomb's 1985 album *Fatal Attraction*, and more recently in 2002 with the Bosnian group Emir And Frozen Camels on their album *San*.

He currently lives with his wife and children in Florida, as does band mate Brian Johnson, with whom he recently performed and recorded under the banner Classic Rock Cares during AC/DC downtime.

WILSON/B.J.

Barrie James Wilson is an ex-Procol Harum drummer who has also worked with Frankie Miller and Joe Cocker and drummed on the soundtrack to *The Rocky Horror Picture Show*.

He was called up by AC/DC after they fired Phil Rudd during the recording of *Flick Of The Switch* in 1983 and helped out drumming on several sessions for the album before Simon Wright joined the band on a full time basis. Apparently no sessions on which Wilson played were used on the album.

WILSON-SLESSER/TERRY

Terry Wilson-Slesser was the vocalist for the band Back Street

Crawler, whom AC/DC supported on their first visit to England in 1976. He was allegedly considered for the role of singer for AC/DC after Bon Scott died, but fellow Geordie Brian Johnson got the job and Wilson-Slesser set out on a solo career which still continues to this day, also touring occasionally with Free drummer Simon Kirke in Freeway (Wilson-Slesser had been in Back Street Crawler with the late Free guitarist Paul Kossoff).

WIMBLEDON THEATRE

The location where AC/DC were filmed for their appearance on the *Rollin' Bolan* TV show – their British TV debut. The band were shot on July 13 1976, with the programme being aired on August 28. This show was put together by veteran British TV executive Mike Mansfield, who had extensive experience in the pop field. It was primarily intended as a showcase for one-time glam god Marc Bolan, hence the title, and he played five songs in all.

Two of the tracks AC/DC performed, 'Live Wire; and 'Can I Sit Next To You Girl' are included on the *Plug Me In* DVD.

WINDMILL ROAD STUDIOS

This is where the band went for pre-production on what was to be *The Razors Edge* album. Located in Ireland, the intention was to bed down new drummer Chris Slade, and get ready to go into the recording studio with Harry Vanda and George Young. Except that things suddenly changed, and the decision was made to go with another producer, Bruce Fairbairn, and his own studio, Little Mountain in Vancouver.

Whether Vanda and Young were actually involved with the Windmill Road sessions is a moot point.

WRIGHT, SIMON

Short, stocky and powerful, Simon Wright drummed for AC/DC between 1983 and 1989, appearing on the albums *Fly On The Wall*, *Who Made Who* and *Blow Up Your Video*, and playing on the subsequent world tours. Being a powerful drummer he was ideally suited to the task when a friend of his spotted an advert stating "Heavy rock drummer wanted. If you don't hit hard, don't apply!"

Born in Alden near Manchester on 19 June, 1963, Wright's first musical endeavours came as an 18-yuear old, drumming for the band Tora Tora, who managed to finance their own single 'Red Sun Setting' which they released on the Mancunian Metal label. He next moved on to another Manchester band AIIZ, who were making something of a name for themselves in the burgeoning New Wave Of British Heavy Metal scene and had recorded a live album *The Witch Of Berkley* with original drummer Karl Reti, as well as supporting the likes of Girlschool and Black Sabbath.

Says Wright on joining AIIZ:

"I started work in the construction industry and enjoyed some of the work, but I could hear the

drums along the motorway calling me in the distance, ha! So off I went, left the job and joined a Manchester band called AIIZ."

Wright recorded one single with AIIZ, 'I'm The One Who Loves You', which saw the band heading in a more commercial direction than their early sound, but having failed to make the desired impact

the group floundered and soon disbanded.

Wright and AIIZ guitarist Gary Owens would surface next in Tytan, a band that originally featured the ex-Angle Witch rhythm section of Kevin Riddles and Dave Dufort and who also included future Lion frontman Kal Swann. However Dufort departed as the band, who had already released a promising 12" single 'Blind Men And Fools', were readying their debut album *Rough Justice*. Ex-Judas Priest drummer Les Binks had helped out prior to Wright's arrival. Simon Wright played on three tracks on the aforementioned album but the band's label, Kamikaze, had run into financial difficulties, and by 1983 Tytan were no more.

Unbeknownst to Wright as he pondered what looked like a rather bleak future, problems within the AC/DC camp between Malcolm Young and drummer Phil Rudd were also coming to a head, eventually boiling over as the band worked on their 1983 album *Flick Of The Switch*, which resulted in the departure of Rudd. AC/

DC initially drafted in ex-Procol Harum drummer B.J. Wilson to help complete the sessions for the album, but this was always a temporary move, and they were soon on the look out for a more permanent member. Wright applied for the vacant position, not knowing who the band involved was. Indeed as with many things throughout their career, AC/DC conducted their business away from the spotlight and with a minimum of fuss. Wright had two auditions for AC/DC; the first drumming along to various songs without any knowledge as to who it was he was trying out for, and the second one playing with AC/DC themselves, before sitting down to discuss touring plans with his new band mates.

"I answered an ad in Sounds magazine," recalls Wright on his big break with AC/DC. *"It's always worth looking in the classified section of your local music paper under 'Musicians Wanted'"*

Wright's first job was to feature in the promo videos for the potential singles from Flick Of The Switch. *As Rudd had drummed on the album – no sessions featuring B.J. Wilson were eventually used – and his name had appeared on the album credits, many AC/DC fans were largely unaware that a change of personnel had even occurred. Wright would go on to feature on 1985's Fly* On The Wall, *1986's* Who Made Who *and 1988's* Blow Up Your Video *albums as well as the subsequent world tours before leaving the band in 1989 to take up an offer from Ronnie James Dio to join his group, Dio.*

"Lots of good memories with AC/DC," Wright says of his time

with the band. "Brian is the funniest bloke I have ever met. Ten jokes a minute. He would have you crying with laughter. As for the shows, well there were some massive shows that would make your hair stand up. All great memories, I'm proud to have been a part of it."

Wright features on Dio's 1990 album *Lock Up The Wolves* before Ronnie himself returned to the Black Sabbath fold to record *Dehumanizer*. During the break from Dio, Wright joined AC/DC sound-a-likes Rhino Bucket, with whom he recorded 1994's *Pain* album before moving on to work with UFO. Wright would fea-

ture on their 1999 album *Werewolves In London* and also work with main UFO protagonists Phil Mogg and Pete Way on their 1999 Mogg/Way album *Chocolate Box* before returning to the Dio fold, with whom he remains to this day. He has since appeared on the following Dio albums: *Magica* (2000), *Killing The Dragon* (2002), *Evil Or Divine* (2003) and *Master Of The Moon* (2004).

Wright has also appeared on albums by the Michael Schenker Group and Europe's John Norum as well as on the 1998 AC/DC tribute album *Thunderbolt* and a 2005 Iron Maiden tribute album to boot.

X - AS IN X-MEMBERS OF THE BAND

The following have all featured in AC/DC at one time or another, many for a very brief period, and one or two, surprisingly, called back for a second shot:

Rob Bailey
bass
Apr 1974 – Nov 1974

Colin Burgess
drums
Nov 1973 – Feb 1974,
Sept 1975 – Oct 1975

Ron Carpenter
drums
Feb 1974

Peter Clack
drums
Apr 1974 – Nov 1974,
Nov 1975 – Jan 1975

Russell Coleman
drums
Feb 1974

Tony Currenti
drums
Nov 1974

Dave Evans
vocals
Nov 1973 – Sept 1974

Mark Evans
bass
Mar 1975 – Jun 1977

Paul Gregg
bass
1991

Bruce Howe
bass
Mar, 1975

Paul Matters
bass
Mar 1975

Neil Smith
bass
Feb 1974 – Apr 1974

John Proud
drums
Nov 1974

Chris Slade
drums
Nov 1989 – Jun 1994

Noel Taylor
drums
Feb 1974 – Apr 1974

Larry Van Kreidt
drums
Nov 1973 – Feb 1974, Jan 1975

B. J. Wilson
drums
May 1983

Simon Wright
drums
May 1983 – Nov 1989

Alex Young
bass
Sept 1975

George Young
bass
Nov 1974, Jan 1975
– Mar 1975

Stevie Young
rhythm guitar
May – Nov 1988

YOU AIN'T GOT A HOLD ON ME

The sixth track on AC/DC's Australian debut album *High Voltage*. Written by Bon Scott, Angus Young and Malcolm Young, the song is a simple telling of how one man refuses to let his woman wrap him around her little finger.

'But don't count on me givin it/ All back to you/Just because I'm hooked on livin'/Doesn't mean I'm hooked on you', sings Scott on the song, which also appeared on *'74 Jailbreak*.

YOU SHOOK ME ALL NIGHT LONG

One of AC/DC's best known and most popular songs, 'You Shook Me All Night Long' is track seven on 1980's *Back In Black*.

The simple tale of a night with a beautiful woman, written by Brian Johnson, Angus Young and Malcolm Young, the lyric, which shows how well the trio had gelled so soon after Johnson's appointment, features such innuendo-laden fare as: 'She was

a fast machine/She kept her motor clean/She was the best damn woman I had ever seen/She had the sightless eyes/Tellin' me no lies/Knocking me out with those American thighs'.

The track was released as the first single from *Back In Black* and reached number 38 in the UK charts during September 1980. The single was backed with 'Have A Drink On Me'. The song was released a second time in 1986 after it had featured on *Who Made Who*, but could only reach number 46 in Britain, being backed this time with live versions of 'She's Got Balls' (from a 1977 Bondi Lifesavers gig) and a 1983 live version of 'You Shook Me All Night Long'.

Two different videos exist for the track. The first release was accompanied by a live style promo video in the same manner as all those shot for *Back In Black* and can be found on the Dual Disc version of that album. For the second issue, David Mallett filmed a promo video featuring Brian Johnson, in trademark flat cap, stomping around his home town of Newcastle, with Angus and Malcolm Young trailing him in schoolboy outfits. This is the most frequently seen version and culminates in an explosion of suggestion and flesh, and gyrating scantily clad models.

The song also appears on 1992's *Live* and a different live version can be found on the soundtrack to the Howard Stern film *Private Parts*, in which the band also appear.

The track has been covered by many artists, but recently the version by divas Celine Dion and Anastacia at a VH1 Divas concert in Las Vegas was voted the worst cover version of all time in *Total Guitar* magazine. Other artists whose cover versions have fared somewhat better include Kid Rock, Phish, Hayseed Dixie, Shania Twain, Tori Amos, Big & Rich, Kelly Clarkson, Melissa Etheridge and Harem Scarem.

YOUNG/ALEX

Born Alexander Young in Glasgow on 28 December, 1938, Alex Young is the older brother of Angus and Malcolm and the father of Stevie Young.

When, in 1963, the Young family emigrated to Australia, bassist Alex decided to remain in

Scotland to pursue his own musical interests, which in 1967 led to him forming a psychedelic band called Grapefruit. They came to the attention of John Lennon, who introduced the band to the press and even invited Grapefruit's singer John Perry to sing on The Beatles' 'Hey Jude'.

Grapefruit called it a day in 1969, at which time Alex hooked up once more with brother George and his Easybeats partner Harry Vanda, working with them in London on post-Easybeats projects Paintbox, Tramp and the Marcus Hook Roll Band, who would also feature the youthful Angus and Malcolm Young.

Alex continued as a session musician, and in 1976 AC/DC recorded a track he wrote by the name of 'I'm A Rebel'. Produced by George Young and Harry Vanda, allegedly during sessions in September 1976 outside of Alberts and with a drunk Bon Scott on vocals, the track has never been released.

It was, however, recorded by German metal band Accept for their 1980 album *I'm A Rebel*.

Young now lives in Germany and works for Albert Productions.

YOUNG/ANGUS

Angus Young is perhaps the most identifiable guitarist in rock 'n' roll, clad in his school boy outfit and headbanging across the stage whilst tearing off another guitar solo from the cherry red Gibson SG guitar. And alongside his elder brother Malcolm and fellow band members, he has fired AC/DC to being one of the most popular and best loved hard rock bands the world has ever known.

Born Angus McKinnon Young in Glasgow on 31 March, 1955, Angus was just eight years old when the Young family took advantage of the £10 fare to Australia to seek a better life for parents William and Margaret and their eight children. But not before the young Angus had already had his first taste of music as enter-

Art has remained an interest to Angus ever since.

Little wonder then, when elder brother George became, at 19, a major pop star in The Easybeats, that music loomed even larger in the younger brothers' lives.

"One day George was a 16-year-old sitting on his bed playing guitar, the next day he was worshipped by the whole country,"

Angus recalls, noting an occasion he came home from school to discover 100 excited girls trying

tainment when his elder sister Margaret took him to see jazz musician Louis Armstrong, to this day one of Angus' heroes.

Arriving in the new land, Angus and elder brother Malcolm had to make their way in a whole new life – including a new school system.

"It was so military," Young has recalled of his school days. *"I was an unhappy schoolboy. Always played truant. I was a bad pupil and really only liked art because you could do what you want."*

to get a glimpse of George Young, pop star.

The elder Young's pop notoriety didn't make for a smooth path for Angus, who was pilloried at school and whose parents, as a result, made strenuous efforts to keep the younger siblings away from a musical career.

"Dad was still asking George when he was going to get a proper job,"

said Angus. However, with elder brothers Alex and George

already bitten by the music bug, it was almost inevitable that their younger brothers would follow suit. Already having an incredibly close relationship with Malcolm, his older brother by two years, Angus was inspired by watching Malcolm perform with The Velvet Underground. Whilst still at school he played with a band called Kentuckee, with whom he would rehearse straight after school, and still in uniform. They even demoed a song, 'Evie', made famous by former Easybeats singer Stevie Wright, on the advice of brother George. Kentuckee became Tantrum, by which time Angus had left school (at the earliest possible age of 14 years and nine months) and was biding his time by working as a janitor and also gaining employment in a typesetter's.

"I started playing on banjos and re-strung them up with six strings," Angus recalled in 1983 of his first guitars. *"[But] an acoustic guitar, an old bang up little ten-dollar job that was probably the first thing I started playing on. Me brother Malcolm got a Hofner off of one of me other brothers and he got a Gretsch and passed the Hofner on to me after much squabbling. It was semi-acoustic and had all been packed with cotton.*

But I never used to really take it as a serious thing; I just used to fool around with it. When I was about 14 was when I really started playing it seriously. I got an amplifier for about sixty bucks that used to distort all the time. It was a Phi-Sonic."

When Malcolm Young, who had decided he'd had enough of playing other people's songs and was going to form his own band, decided that instead of a piano player he wanted another guitarist, the young Angus leapt at the opportunity.

"You and Malcolm playing together will last two weeks,"growled father William.

Malcolm and Angus formed AC/DC in November 1973 when Angus was 18 years old and played their debut gig at Chequers on New Years Eve 1973. By this time Angus had already adapted, at his sister Margaret's suggestion, his Ashfield Boys High School outfit into stage gear, although at various times he would also dress as Spider-Man, Zorro, Super Ang and even as a gorilla. But equally eye-catching was his stage manner, which included frantic headbanging and his spasms, during which he'd throw himself to the floor and cavort in circles whilst soloing like a madman. This allegedly occurred originally when Angus tripped on his guitar cable at one gig, and attempted to carry on as if nothing had happened. It would later prove a handy habit for dodging anything thrown on stage at gigs on Australia's notorious pub circuit.

"The club owners always used to say 'Who's the little guy?'" Angus stated. *"We'd always have to lie and say 'Oh he's a dwarf'. That got me in."*

AC/DC's rise to the top of Australian music was swift. With the arrival of Bon Scott, something of a father figure to the diminutive guitarist, the band became ever more popular with each album, before, with Angus aged 21 (although the record company would say he was just 16 at the time) the young hopefuls set out across the world as their plans for domination fell into place.

Cavorting around the stages of the world, Angus' act developed tenfold, his metronomic head-banging, duckwalking like hero Chuck Berry, spasmodic soloing and strip-teasing and arse bearing wowing fans the world over. For sure, the youngest Young in AC/DC was loving every minute of seeing each new album outsell the last.

Speaking of his on stage dynamics in 1983, Angus told a reporter:

"I don't get headaches. When you first start you're going to get sore bones. But I've never had any real headaches from it. I've had headaches from travelling. Sitting around for 12 hours will give you a headache, because you're not doing anything. I don't think about anything on stage either. It's like two different people. Sort of split. To me the whole show is over and done within five minutes. It's like watching a movie.

"In certain countries they told me I couldn't do the striptease when I first went there – Japan, Spain. But somehow I did and got away with it. It just depends. But then again, the people from the authority come and laugh. I remember when we first toured

through Britain there was a big campaign to stop us playing everywhere. They used to send along the vice squad, and they were embarrassed about it all, too. They couldn't see there was any wrong in anything I did."

But tragedy was just around the corner, when singer Bon Scott lost his life to acute alcohol poisoning, aged just 33. Angus was 25 years old.

"Bon was like a father to us all," Angus would tell *Sounds* magazine in the weeks following Scott's death. *"He was about ten years older than I was and had all the experience and knowledge. If we had a personal problem, Bon was the one we went to. He was a special person. One of a kind."*

Angus and brother Malcolm threw themselves back into work with AC/DC, with the blessing of Bon's parents, adding Brian Johnson to the band's line-up and hitting even further heights with *Back In Black*. From there the remainder of the '80s and '90s must have seemed like a rocket ride, attaining the rewards and riches that Angus Young could once have only dreamed of.

And yet, like many in AC/DC, Angus Young is an intensely private person, despite the fact that he is easily the most recognisable member of the band. He married his Dutch wife Ellen just prior to Bon Scott's death, and lives in both Holland and Sydney in Australia. Even when away from the glare of the spotlight, Angus is most likely to be found noodling away in the studio, either coming up with riffs on his own or jamming with his brother Malcolm.

"Mal will call me up and say 'I'm bored, what you got?'" he says of his writing relationship with his brother. *"And I'll tell him I'm done. He'll say 'Gimme two weeks' and then we'll meet up and off we go.*

"He'll get something and I'll play along. It's a natural thing. I suppose it's just something we do well together. He seems to have a great command of rhythm and he likes doing that. That to me is more important

because if we're playing live and something goes wrong with my gear and my guitar drops out, you can still hear him and it's not empty. He's probably got the best right hand in the world. I've never heard anyone do it like that. Even Keith Richards or any of those people. As soon as the other guitar drops out, it's empty. But with Malcolm it's so full. Besides, Malcolm always said that playing lead interfered with his drinkin' and so he said I should do it."

As for Angus' often incendiary and trademark guitar solos, the player himself adds:

"Soloing was pretty easy for me because it was the first thing I'd ever done. I just used to make up leads. I never even used to know the names of any chords until Malcolm told me and then I picked it up from there. I don't regard myself as a soloist; it's a colour, I put it in for excitement. It's not a great loss if a solo has to go. We've recorded songs without solos."

Young recently hit the headlines (a rarity in itself) over the new house he is having built in the quiet Dutch town of Aalten. *The Sunday Telegraph* newspaper reported that locals are up in

arms over the size of the three storey mansion, which is reported to have a basement studio and a lot of bedrooms.

"It's a big house in a little town," one local was reported as saying. *"It stands out. Look at it and you see it doesn't fit. Angus doesn't want to stand out, he is shy and no one really knows him. Why build something like that."*

The newspaper went on to report that it had observed Mrs. Young, who has apparently helped design the house, checking on the building progress, but when questioned she merely replied: "I don't want to talk to you about it. My husband is very private and this has nothing to do with you."

A local politician who approved plans for the building amusingly

stated: "On the drawings it didn't look that big."

Not everyone is at odds with their famous neighbours however. One resident was happy to report:

"They are good neighbours. I don't see him much but she is friendly with my children."

YOUNG/GEORGE

"George doesn't let anything go when you're working with him," says Angus Young. *"He doesn't come in and say, 'Hey, that's shit,' but he comes in and gives you an honest answer. He still gets you to think that there is more than one way to skin a cat.*

And that's how he's always been good like that. I love watching him do it sometimes. Just the way he sits there and listens to what you've got. Then he might grab something like a bass or a piano and just hammer away with you. He's a very creative guy."

George Young is the elder brother of Angus and Malcolm Young and the one family member, aside from the two guitarists themselves, who has probably exerted more influence on AC/DC.

Born George Redburn Young in Glasgow on 6 November, 1947 and one of eight children who emigrated to Australia in 1963. And it was the 16 year old George who was the first to make something of a name for himself in the music scene when he was a founding member of The Easybeats, who would become one of the first Australian bands to have an international hit with 'Friday On My Mind' in 1966. The Easybeats were by far and away the most successful Aus-

tralian band of the '60s, but by 1969 they had called it a day, and Young and fellow guitarist Harry Vanda, who'd written most of the band's songs, remained in the UK to work on further projects. These included Paintbox, Grapefruit and the Marcus Hook Roll Band (the latter two with elder brother Alex).

Young returned to Australia with Vanda, where the two became in-house producers for Alberts, and would end up writing hits for other Aussie artists, including John Paul Young's 'Love Is In The Air'. They also wrote for the likes of the Bay City Rollers, INXS and Jimmy Barnes and would later work with hard rocking Australians Rose Tattoo, Cheetah and The Angels.

However it was their work with AC/DC that helped propel the band to superstardom and George Young's early patronage of his younger brothers was invaluable.

"He'd take our meanest song and try it out on keyboards with arrangements like 10cc and Mantovani," Angus explained. *"If it was passed, the structure was proven, then we took it away and dirtied it up."*

Young (along with Vanda) would produce every AC/DC album from 1976's *High Voltage* to 1978's live *If You Want Blood*, and George actually played bass with the band in the early years, even appearing on some of their early recordings. However, after *Powerage* the group's label, Atlantic Records, stepped in, suggesting a new producer might lend a more polished sheen in the studio that would be more palatable to American audiences, and 'Mutt' Lange was brought in to work on what would be some of the band's biggest recordings.

Young then turned his attention to working with Vanda in the studio only project Flash And The Pan, who had a massive hit in the UK with 1983's 'Waiting For A Train'. However, Young

and Vanda returned to work with AC/DC on 1988's *Blow Up Your Video* and Young alone would helm 2000's *Stiff Upper Lip*.

Speaking of the band's relationship with the elder Young brother, Brian Johnson was quoted as saying:

"George? I love George. George Young, the boys' [Angus' and Malcolm's] brother. He's lovely. He's just great, he gets the best out of us."

YOUNG, JAMES

Another nephew of Angus and Malcolm, James Young is the drummer with The Poor who are managed by Def Leppard guitarist Phil Collen.

YOUNG, MALCOLM

"We just try hard to please ourselves really. You gotta do what you do best. You get lots of people saying, 'Oh, when are they gonna change?' and plenty say, 'Don't change'. We couldn't change 'cause we only know the stuff we like – straight ahead rock 'n' roll, no frills, and good performances. The music really is the important thing, that's the bottom line, personally that's all I'm interested in, I'm not even much up for the rest of the thrills of it. Even the press – I'm not a big mover and shaker in those areas and never wanted to be. If I were out of a job, I'd be back at the factory, I think. We were all fitters and turners. That's what they called 'em back then in the metal trade, steel work. It was like apprenticeships, four of the guys were fitters and turners and Angus worked with lead."

His 5ft 5" frame almost dwarfed by his enormous white Gretsch guitar, stoically positioned just to the right of Phil Rudd's drum

riser, Malcolm Young remains the driving force of AC/DC's music. Despite the rock steady beat laid down by the rhythm section of Cliff Williams and Phil Rudd, despite the cavorting around the stage of singer Brian Johnson, or the more manic approach of brother Angus Young on lead guitar, it is Malcolm who relentlessly drives AC/DC onwards.

Born in Glasgow on 6 January, 1953, Malcolm Mitchell Young was ten years old when the family emigrated to Australia, settling in the West Sydney suburb of Burwood. And much like his younger brother Angus, he didn't bother too much with his education,

drifting out of school and into a job in a bra factory, whilst working hard at following his elder brother George into the music world, much to the displeasure of his parents. "We didn't get much encouragement," Malcolm recalled.

However that didn't stop him joining up with local covers band The Velvet Underground in 1971, aged 18, a move which finally allowed him to give up his day job as nights were spent trawling around Sydney's night club circuit. Yet within two years, Malcolm's own intense drive and distaste for playing cover versions had led him to quit The

Velvet Underground with plans to form his own band. He'd also noted with equal distaste, the use of overdubs when recording for brother George's Marcus Hook Roll Band, and decided any venture he undertook would provide a more instant, electrifying brand of rock 'n' roll.

AC/DC was that band, with Malcolm joined by younger brother Angus and initially guided by the experienced hand of older brother George. Malcolm is very much the leader of AC/DC, some have suggested with an iron hand, and one only has to look at the plethora of musicians who filtered through the early line-ups to note the cut-throat determination to find what

he believed to be the ideal AC/DC line-up.

And AC/DC do very little, if anything, without Malcolm Young's say so and never have done. His disparaging view of AC/DC's competitors giving an insight into the single-mindedness with which he drives his band onwards.

"Time is the ultimate test," he told *Classic Rock* in 2005. *"I haven't seen anything with a good act – like we've got with Angus and Brian, and we used to have with Bon. The problem is there's a lack of showmanship. You need a good tight act, with a star out at the front."*

That has always formed the basis of AC/DC's act. With Malcolm happy to remain the driving force from the back of the stage, Angus Young's manic stage persona and the laddishness of first Bon Scott and later Brian Johnson acting out the starring roles.

Behind the scenes, it is Malcolm, along with brother Angus, who remains the major cog in the musical engine, coming up with the relentless riffs, musical motifs and increasingly these days, lyrical ideas for AC/DC's albums. It's that drive which built the band up to the verge of superstardom when Bon Scott was cruelly taken from them. At the time rumours circulated that his position in the group was being considered, which, given the success of *Highway To Hell*, seems unthinkable. Malcolm naturally dealt with such rumours as he always had and always would in future. He said nothing, but just got on with the job in hand.

"I just called up Angus and said 'Do you wanna come back and rehearse?'"

he offered, in the wake of Scott's death, when he found himself sat at home moping. And with the blessing of Scott's parents, AC/DC were back up and running

with new singer Brian Johnson at the helm and even greater success awaited them.

It was quite clearly the toughest decision the then 27-year-old guitarist and band leader would ever have to make, and surely the one which went a long way to creating the man who has led AC/DC ever onwards since. Explaining his and the other members' decision to carry on with the band, Malcolm would later explain:

"Should you carry on with the name? All sorts of thoughts went through our minds. We were just sittin' around not doing anything because of respect too, you know, and not knowing and not caring. We just got a hold of each other one day and just said, 'Look, we've come up with lots of music before Bon died, so why don't we just get together and sit down and at least... at least we can do something, we can play guitar.' So we did that and a lot of good music came from that period because something kicked in there. We didn't have to do it, but inside there was stuff coming out that probably wouldn't have ever appeared. It made us grow up really quick I think."

Malcolm had to take his own problems in hand, however, in 1988, when forced to sit out part of the band's *Blow Up Your Video* tour as he fought severe alcohol problems, although at the time the AC/DC machine simply claimed he was tending to his own sick son (Young lives in England with his wife and two children, returning to Sydney every Christmas). Yet the elder Young brother came back to the helm, revitalised.

"We're not going to fall into the trap of old age," he told *Classic Rock. "We can't get up there and play things like 'Highway To Hell' and 'For Those About To Rock' and 'The Jack' quietly. You gotta stay young. We want to look tough and fit. We have been around for over 30 years and we want to stay around for a lot longer.*

"I'll be gettin' a gold watch soon, huh? I don't think there is any retirement in the music industry. I don't really know anyone that's retired. If they have it means nobody wanted them anyway. With most musi-

cians it's like the Titanic, they go down with the ship. You feel a part of that responsibility, even with the kids. But you do feel a responsibility that if the kids keep wantin' it, and I'm talkin' kids now that are 40, 45, we'll keep doin' it for them. As long as we believe that we've got the right thing to put out, and that's what we always strive towards – the great song. We're still lookin' for it, like everyone is. We would love to get something somewhere near what the guys in the 1950s were doing. Not sound-wise, but the quality of the rock 'n' roll. You know back then they had it all, the swing and all that stuff that gets kids up these days. AC/DC play basically what was going on with Chuck Berry, Little Richard, Jerry Lee Lewis – trying to create the excitement and get the mood. We want to keep the flag flyin'. I think we're the only guys, with the exception of the Rolling Stones. They're about ten years, 15 years older than us guys so we've still got a long way to go and we like to learn from their mistakes. Once you move you're confusing the kids – they'd say, 'These guys have gone off rock 'n' roll.' We want to keep that around for another millennium."

Malcolm is as famous for playing his white Gretsch guitar as Angus is for his trademark cherry red Gibson SG. His instrument of choice is a '63 Gretsch Jet Fire Bird, given to him by AC/DC producer Harry Vanda, although he has also been known to play what appears to be a semi-hollow bodied 1959 White Falcon, which was used on the *Back In Black* and *For Those About To Rock (We Salute You)* tours, until, according to Malcolm, someone "fixed it", losing his desired sound, and it was subsequently sold at auction. The '63 Gretsch was, in typical Malcolm Young style, modified by Young himself many years ago, apparently adjusting the neck pick up, tone and volume. Like most guitarists, there is indeed a Malcolm Young Signature Model, the G6131SMY, which is a customised 1962 Reissue Jet model with a single Filtertron pick up, which will set back budding guitarists a cool £900. Like Angus, Malcolm prefers Marshall amplification but has also been known to use custom made Wizard amps on tour as well.

If Young has been the guiding force behind AC/DC's relentless rise to success, then looking at AC/DC's career one can only judge his stewardship an enormous success. Not bad going for the supposedly shy, quiet member of the band.

"I don't think any bastard knows who I am anyway," laughs Young.

We think they probably do.

YOUNG/MARGARET

Margaret Young is the sister of Angus and Malcolm Young. She was the eldest of the Young children who emigrated with the family to Australia from Glasgow. Although she has never worked in the music industry, Margaret Young's influence on AC/DC has been immeasurable.

It was Margaret who took the young Angus to see his hero Louis Armstrong in Scotland, when he was aged six or seven. She was also responsible for suggesting that Angus, who was already wearing his school uniform in some pre-AC/DC bands when he'd turn up straight from school to play, should begin wearing the outfit for AC/DC. Margaret is also credited with coming up with the band's name, after she allegedly saw the lettering on her sewing machine.

Margaret Young would marry Easybeats tour manager Sam Horsburgh, and their son, Sam Horsburgh Jr. is employed at Albert Productions as an engineer, where he's worked with Flash And The Pan and engineered the live version of 'She's Got Balls', the one featured on the *Volts* collection in the *Bonfire* box set.

YOUNG/STEVIE

Stevie Young is the son of Alex Young, and nephew of Angus and Malcolm. Originally the guitarist for Stabber, he made a name for himself in Starfighters, who supported AC/DC on their *Back In Black* tour and would also tour with Ozzy Osbourne and Judas Priest. Stevie would later fill in for uncle Malcolm on AC/DC's *Blow Up Your Video* tour when the latter was overcoming alcohol related problems.

Following his stint touring with AC/DC, he formed Little Big Horn, who were managed by his brother Fraser (who has also worked with Guns 'n' Roses and Iron Maiden) and for whom Malcolm produced the original demos. But, despite some good press and a lot of hard work, they failed to make the grade.

Young had more recently been working with the band The Up Rising, but they have since split up and little has been heard of him since.

ZOMBA

Zomba is the music company which at one time managed AC/DC producer 'Mutt' Lange, as well as owning Jive, the successful record label.

Formed in South Africa by musicians Simon Calder and Ralph Simon in 1971, its original remit was to release records, promote concerts and publish music. In 1975 the pair relocated to London and renamed the company Zomba, after the capital of Malawi, whose tribes allegedly have superior hearing. By 1978, Zomba's tentacles had spread to New York, and soon it had hits with acts as diverse as Billy Ocean and Def Leppard, as well as handling the publishing rights for the likes of Elvis Costello and the Boomtown Rats. They developed a relationship with 'Mutt' Lange' after he had produced the *Highway To Hell* album. Lange's stock would rise even further after he helmed the 42 million-plus-selling *Back In Black* record.

Tony Platt, who engineered both *Highway To Hell* and *Back In Black* alongside Lange, and would later engineer *Flick Of The Switch*, was also an in-house producer for Zomba throughout the '80s, and Angus and Malcolm's nephew Stevie Young's band Starfighters were signed to Jive for two albums in the early '80s.

Zomba would become increasingly powerful within the music industry throughout the the'80s and '90s, and became involved with a wide range of artists, such as the Stone Roses, John Lee Hooker, Backstreet Boys, N-Sync, Tupac Shakur and Britney Spears.

The company is currently a quarter owned by the major label group BMG; Simon sold his stake in the firm to Calder and subsequently set up a new company, Scintilla, in San Francisco. Calder remains CEO of the Zomba Group.

AC/DC DVDs from Chrome Dreams

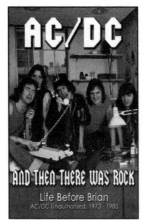

AC/DC - And Then There Was Rock
DVD Documentary
Cat: CVIS379
Charting the band's early years, up to the tragic death of Bon Scott in 1980. Includes interviews with original singer Dave Evans, original drummer Colin Burgess, school friends of Bon, Angus and Malcolm, Bon's lifelong friend Vincent Lovegrove, and biographers Malcolm Dome and Clinton Walker among others. A fitting tribute to the memory of Bon Scott, containing rare footage and music of him in his earlier bands, previously unseen photographs and much more!

AC/DC - Back In Black
A Classic Album Under Review
DVD Documentary
Cat: CVIS379
'Back In Black: A Classic Album Under Review' is a documentary film which revisits and reassesses this astonishing work. With the entire album dissected track by track by engineer and assistant producer Tony Platt, and with rare footage, band interviews and live performances all under the gaze of our panel of esteemed experts, this is an enlightening, informative and downright entertaining film about an extraordinary record.

AC/DC - Highway To Hell
A Classic Album Under Review
DVD Documentary
Cat: CVIS379
With the help of those who worked on the record, friends of Bon Scott, AC/ DC biographers and others, this film goes behind the scenes to tell the story of this remarkable album.
Featuring rare footage of the group, interviews with Bon Scott and Angus Young, exclusive contributions from friends, colleagues, journalists and biographers, every track from the album reviewed and reappraised by a panel of esteemed experts and plenty more besides.

Available from all good record stores, Amazon and from
www.chromedreams.co.uk

AC/DC Books from Chrome Dreams

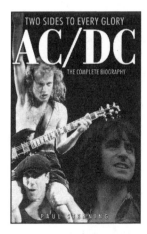

ISBN
1 84240 308 7

AC/DC - Two Sides To Every Glory
by Paul Stennings

The band's complete story under one cover. Author Paul Stenning, a major fan of this extraordinary group, has left no stone unturned in his quest to find the truth about AC/DC, spending months in Australia, speaking to more than 50 friends, colleagues, confidantes and witnesses to what really happened.

ISBN
1 84240 088 6

Maximum AC/DC
The Unauthorised Biography of AC/DC
Cat: ABCD054

A 60-minute spoken word biography of AC/DC featuring interview clips throughout and covering all eras of their extraordinary career. Newly revised and updated edition now available.

ISBN
1 84240 305 2

AC/DC X-Posed
Unpublished and Rare Interviews Set
Cat: CTCD7038

'AC/DC X-Posed' provides huge insight into the group with a series of interviews covering the two distinct eras of the band's history – those featuring Bon Scott and Brian Johnson as vocalist.

Available from all good record stores, Amazon and from
www.chromedreams.co.uk

THIS BOOK IS DEDICATED TO THE MEMORY OF
BON SCOTT
1946/1980